SOCIAL LEGISLATION IN INDIA

Volume Two

Prof. K.D. Gangrade (*b.* 1926), Former Vice-Chairman of Gandhi Smriti and Darshan Samiti, New Delhi, has been a former Pro-Vice-Chancellor, Dean, Faculty of Social Sciences, and Head, Department of Social Work, University of Delhi. He has also taught at the University of Manchester, U.K. and Tata Institute of Social Sciences, Mumbai. He has served the United Nations as well in various capacities. Prof. Gangrade has 12 books to his credit. He is recipient of Samaj Gaurav (1988) from the Bhartiya Sangthan, Rashtra Ratna (1998) from Viswa Jagriti Mission, and Radha Raman Award (2000) for outstanding contribution to education.

SOCIAL LEGISLATION IN INDIA

Volume Two

K.D. GANGRADE

CONCEPT PUBLISHING COMPANY (P) LTD.,
NEW DELHI-110 059

ISBN 13: 978-81-8069-807-1 (P.B. Set)
ISBN 13: 978-81-8069-808-8 (P.B. Vol. I)
ISBN 13: 978-81-8069-809-5 (P.B. Vol. II)

Reprinted 2011
First Published 1978

Published and Printed by

Concept
Since 1974

Concept Publishing Company Pvt. Ltd.
Regd. Office:
A/15-16, Commercial Block, Mohan Garden
New Delhi-110059 (India)
Phones : 25351460, 25351794, *Fax* : 091-11-25357109
Email : publishing@conceptpub.com,
Website: www.conceptpub.com

Editorial Office:
H-13, Bali Nagar, New Delhi-110 015, India.

Contributors

Justice S. Rangarajan, LL.M. (Madras).

Dr. Tahir Mahmood, Reader in Law, University of Delhi.

Mr. Baldev Kohli, M.A. (Econ) Panjab University, LL.B. Delhi University, LL.M. London University. Reader in Law, Delhi University.

Prof. S. Venkataraman, B.A. B.L., M.L. Editor, Madras Law Journal & The Supreme Court Journal.

Dr. S.A. Ali, Indian Institute of Islamic Studies, New Delhi.

Dr. B. Shivaramayya, B.Sc. (Andhra University), B.L. M.L., Yale LL.M., Mc. Gill, D.C.L. Reader in Law, Delhi University.

Dr. Jyotsana, Shah B.A. (Hons) Bombay University, Dip. S.S.A. Tata Institute of Social Sciences, Bombay, Ph.D., Sociology, Charles University, Prague, Czechoslovakia. Director, Social Defence Department, Government of Gujarat.

Dr. M.P. Singh, B.A., LL.B. (Agra): LL.M. (Lucknow), LL.M. (Columbia) LL.D. (Lucknow) Reader in Law University of Delhi.

Mr. S.D. Gokhale, B.A. (B.U.), Diploma in S.S.A. Tata Institute of Social Sciences, Bombay. Asstt. Secretary-General International Council on Social Welfare, Regional Office for Asia and Western Pacific.

Dr. A.S. Bedi, B.A., LL.B. (Delhi), LL.M., S.J.D. (Michigan U.S.A.), Reader in Law, Delhi University.

Dr. B.C. Ghosal, M.B.B.S. (Nag) & D.P.H. (Calcutta), Assistant Director General (Health Administration) Directorate General of Health Services, New Delhi.

Prof. G.B. Krishna Rao, B.E. (Hons), Dip T.C.P., Dip. T. P. (London), LL.B. Professor of Planning in School of Planning & Architecture, New Delhi.

Dr. V.A. Seyid Muhammad, M.A., LL.B. Ph.D. (University of London).

Dr. S.N. Dubey, Dip. S. S. A. (1962) Tata Institute of Social Sciences, Bombay, M.S.W. (1966) University of Hawaii, U.S.A. Doctor of Social Welfare (1969), Professor, Department of Social Welfare Administration, Tata Institute of Social Sciences, Bombay.

Mr. S.P. Joshi, B.A. (Hons.) Econ. (Bombay University; Dip. S.S.A. Tata Institute of Social Sciences, Bombay. Depty Labour Commissioner.

Dr. S.D. Balsara, B.A. (B.U.), LL.M. (B.U.), LL.M. (Stanford). Principal, Government Law College, Bombay.

Preface

The second volume on Social Legislation in India is a collection of critical articles written by experts. I am extremely grateful to the writers for their valuable cooperation and contributions. My thanks are also due to Professor K.B. Rohatgi Director, South Campus, University of Delhi for collaborating with me in writing the introduction to the volume. The research team consisting of Dr. Usha Banerjee, Mr. R.K. Srivastava and Mrs. Rajkumari Chandrashekharan deserve a word of thanks for their assistance in the work. Dr. Usha Banerjee's timely help has enabled this volume to be completed in time.

I am also thankful to the Department of Social Welfare, Government of India for financial assistance to take up this project.

Delhi School of Social Work; **K.D. Gangrade**
January 7, 1978

Contents

K.B. Rohatgi and K.D. Gangrade

Introduction

A pioneer study of social legislation in India—its role and social welfare—was published by the Planning Commission in 1956. Much change has taken place since. The present comprehensive study in two volumes should be welcome in that it updates the earlier study.

In a society ridden by caste prejudices, illiteracy and narrow sectarian outlook, social legislation can be introduced only in stages. Century-old customs, traditions and beliefs, howsoever primitive they may look to the modern eye, cannot be thrown out overnight. To mould the Indian society consisting of several religions, faiths, linguistics and ethnic groups, and sub-cultures into one compact unit is a herculean task by any standard.

One can reform society either through welfare measures, which must be provided in abundance, or through persuasion by creating a strong public opinion against age-old prejudices, and, lastly, by legislation. The first two of these measures failed to make any appreciable impact; they failed to touch the downtrodden millions who needed it most. Social workers, Sarvodya workers and others engaged in persuasive methods could reach out only to a small segment of our vast and variegated population. Besides, persuasion had only a temporary effect. To illustrate the point, Mahatma Gandhi carried on a crusade against untouchability and for the uplift of Harijans, but did not succeed in either in his lifetime.

Even the constitutional provision abolishing untouchability and various other legislative measures—such as the Untouchability Act—could not root out the evil. This was so because, although the government of the day, with its majority in Parliament, may pass a social measure, its implementation requires the support of strong public opinion. To take another example, the dowry system prevalent in our society is a curse which has ruined, or even ended, millions of innocent lives. The government tried to curb this evil by passing a legislation against dowry as far back as 1956. Yet, in the absence of a strong public opinion, which could not be built up, the Anti-Dowry Act just could not be enforced. Similarly, although the Child Marriage Restraint Act was enacted in 1929 it failed to completely stop child marriages, and one can still find its occurrence in one form or another in our society, particularly in villages.

Enlightened public opinion may, indeed, not only prepare the ground for a piece of social legislation, but even force the government to enact it. But, in our country, enlightened public opinion means the opinion of the elite which constitutes a microscopic minority. The mass media, particularly radio and television, will, one hopes, be more effective in forming mass public opinion in favour of social uplift through legislation.

The two volumes here presented are complementary. The first volume contains the factual statement of the various social legislations at present on the statute book. The emphasis is necessarily on legislation dealing with personal matters like marriage, divorce, inheritance and the like. The second volume is the work of specialists, who have discussed at length the various enactments dealing with specific problems. They have pointed out the extent to which laws have tried to bring about social change or the new possibilities that legislation can open up. The first volume has been written by the active association of a study team consisting of Prof. S.N. Ranade, Dr. K.D. Gangrade, Mr. Harish Chandra, Mr. Baldev Kohli, Dr. Jaffar Hussain, Dr. M.P. Singh, Mr. S.S. Pandey and Miss Veena Bakshi. The Committee was assisted by a research team comprising Mr. R.K. Srivastava, Dr. Usha Banerjee and Mrs. Rajkumari Chandrashekhran.

Chapter I of the first volume deals primarily with Fundamental Rights and Directive Principles of State Policy as enshrined in our Constitution. Certain fundamental and basic rights have been guaranteed to all citizens by the Constitution. Article 14 guarantees equality before law and equal protection of law. Article 15 lays down that the State shall not discriminate against any citizen in respect of employment solely on the ground of religion, caste, race, sex, or place of birth. Article 16 provides for equality of opportunity for all citizens in matters relating to employment or appointment to any office under the State and prohibits discrimination on grounds of religion, race, caste, sex, place of birth or residence. Article 17 reiterates the declared policy of Government to abolish untouchability and its practice in any form is forbidden and makes any disability arising out of untouchability a punishable offence.

Article 23 has a direct bearing on social welfare legislation; prohibits traffic in human beings and beggars and other similar forms of forced labour and declares contraventions of these provisions to be punishable in accordance with law. Article 24 provides that no child below the age of 14 shall be employed in any factory or mine or engaged in any hazardous employment.

The Constitution also provides for freedom of conscience and the right to profess, practise and propagate any religion.

The Directive Principles of State Policy contain principles and guidelines on which future legislation is to be based. The authors have focussed attention on the ultimate goals, so that all the future legislation may be directed towards achieving these.

The second chapter refers to Marriage and Divorce. Section A of the chapter deals with Child Marriage Restraint Act, 1929, popularly known as the Sharda Act. Many people may not be aware that the Act is applicable to all communities and to all persons living in India. This legislation, along with the disintegration of the joint family system and economic compulsions, has helped raise the age of marriage and has curbed the practice of child marriage. The author has listed the penalties for child marriage in contravention of the law. This will greatly help social workers active in this field.

Section A of Chapter III deals with marriage and divorce in Hindu Law. Prior to 1956, Hindu marriage was considered to be a sacrament, a tie which could not be dissolved by any human agency. While the husband was free to have as many wives as he liked, the law insisted that a Hindu wife could have only one husband, whether he treated her well or not. The wife, economically totally dependent on the husband, had no protection against ill or even inhuman treatment.

The Hindu Marriage Act for the first time granted right to the spouses to ask for judicial separation and divorce on certain grounds. Thus the marriage tie, considered sacred for thousands of years, can now be legally dissolved. But the legislation has rightly avoided easy divorces and is a happy compromise between the needs of the society and tradition.

Section B of the same chapter deals with the Mohammedan law concerning marriage and divorce. The Mohammedan law is mostly Koranic law, applicable to all Muslims. No legislation has touched this law to any appreciable extent. A Muslim male can have four wives at a time and can, at his own sweet will, divorce any or all without assigning any reason. The wife could not ask for divorce except in very rare cases. It was only Muslim Marriage Dissolution Act, 1930, that came to the rescue of the Muslim wife, enabling her to ask for dissolution of marriage on certain grounds.

Section C deals with Christian law of marriage and divorce. There is a sizeable population of Christians in India. Many of them, living in the South, were governed by customary laws, and there was a great variety of customs prevalent among newly converted Christians. Some of them had married according to their older customs even after conversion. The law enacted in 1972 has introduced certainty and uniformity in this field. This legislation is in a way precurser of many other legislations in the field of Family Law. The Indian Divorce Act, 1869 also deals with divorce among Christians. The Act contains several provisions regarding judicial separation, nullity of marriage. divorce and maintenance.

Section D deals with Parsee law of marriage and divorce, enacted in the year 1936. Prior to this there were no law dealing with Parsee marriages, and they were governed by customary law. The Parsee Marriage and Divorce Act, 1936, stipulates the requisites of a valid marriage and various matrimonial reliefs.

Section E deals with Special Marriage Act, 1954. It enables the persons belonging to different religions or castes to contract a civil marriage through the court. It also regulates judicial separation, divorce and maintenance, etc.

Chapter III deals with Law of Inheritance and Succession.

Section A discusses at length the Hindu Succession Act, 1956. From time immemorial, Hindus have been governed by two sets of laws, Mitakshara and Dayabhaga, both based on commentaries of learned jurists. The traditional Hindu law had relegated women to a lower position in matters of inheritance and succession. The daughter was not entitled to any share in her father's property. The wife, on the death of her husband, was not entitled to a share because the property of a deceased male Hindu devolved on surviving male coparceners. The Hindu Women's Right to Property Act, 1937 tried to give some protection to woman by granting her a limited right to property. She could hold property of her husband after his death as a limited owner during the lifetime but she had no power to alienate the property, and after her death the property devolved on the heirs of her husband. Under the Hindu Succession Act, 1956, daughter is now entitled to hold a share in the property of her father. She is also entitled to succeed to the estate of the deceased husband as absolute owner.

Section B deals with the Mohammedan Law of Inheritance. The author has discussed at length the various principles and rules relating to inheritance among Muslims. This is one area where so far legislation has not interfered, though there is a demand from enlightened Muslims to rationalise the principles of inheritance and Succession.

Section C deals with Indian Succession Act, 1925. There was no law in India dealing with succession and inheritance among communities other than Hindus and Muslims. The first attempt was made with this Act. The legislation has put everything beyond doubt regarding inheritance and succession among non-Hindus and non-Muslims.

Chapter IV of the volume deals with the law of adoption. The traditional law authorised a sonless Hindu father to adopt a male child. Once a person was adopted, there was a severing of his connection from the family of his birth, and he was transplanted in the adopted family. The traditional Hindu Law did not permit a widow to adopt a son unless specially authorised by the deceased husband. The Hindu Adoption Act removed many of the lacunae of the traditional law and gave right both to the male as well as female to adopt a child of any sex. The law of adoption is applicable only to Hindus. As for Muslims, though there is no Koranic law to that effect, adoption is regulated by custom. Recently a demand has been made by educated Muslims for enactment of a law authorising adoption among Muslims.

Chapter V deals with the laws relating to minority and guardianship, viz. Indian Majority Act, 1875 and Guardians and Wards Act, 1890. The other sections of the Chapter deal with natural guardians, testamentary guardians, *de facto* guardians and guardians appointed and declared by the court. The next section deals with Muslim Law of Religious and Charitable Endowments, mostly in the area of wakf. The law of wakf has been amended by the Act of 1913 and the Act of 1930. The two Acts have removed much of the confusion in this area. The Wakf Act, 1954 is a progressive piece of legislation. The Indian Trusts Act, 1882, to which reference has been made, was enacted to regulate private trusts and trustees.

Chapter VI of the first volume deals with various other religious and charitable trusts. Reference has been made to the prevalent legislation in the field, for example, Charitable Endowment Act, 1890, and Charitable and Religious Endowment Act, 1920. These two Acts deal with effective control over the management and administration of religious endowments belonging to both Muslims and Hindus.

Chapter VII discusses at length the law relating to destitutes and handicapped. The Bombay Prevention of Beggary Act, 1959 has been adopted as a model by many States. It is designed to prohibit begging and to authorise the arrest of persons who practise it. The Act also provides for rehabilitation of beggars. The Code of Criminal Procedure, 1973, tackles the problem of adult vagrancy by providing various preventive measures. The Children Act, 1960, on the other hand, deals with juvenile delinquency. The Lepers Act, 1898 provides for segregation and medical treatment of lepers.

Chapter VIII deals with the law relating to correctional administration. While the traditional theory was to punish the criminal, as deterrence to others, the modern theory, instead of punishing the criminal, lays great emphasis on reforming him because, after all, a criminal is the product of social environment and so an effort should be made to rehabilitate him. Both the Indian Penal Code and the Criminal Procedure Code deal with the various corrective measures. The Prevention of Offenders Act, 1958, the Prison Act, 1900, and Transfer of Prisoners Act, 1950, and various jail manuals deal with persons who are sent to prison. The Children Act and Borstal Schools Act deal with juvenile delinquents and outlines various correctional measures for their rehabilitation.

Chapter IX highlights the relation between law and morals particularly in the realm obscenity. The Indian Penal Code forbids publication of any matter of obscene nature. The Cinematograph Act, 1952 contains a wide variety of measures that are designed to regulate and restrict motion pictures in social interest. The Act refers to two kinds of certificates 'U' and 'A'. A picture is meant for general public exhibition if it is granted 'U' certificate, while the screening of a picture is restricted to adults only in case it is granted 'A' certificate. The Dramatic Performance Act, 1876 prohibits performance in a public place of any drama of scandalous, defamatory, depraved or of corrupt nature. The Indian Penal Code, again, defines various offences such as homosexuality, unnatural sexual offences, adultery, etc. The basic Indian law relating to prostitution is contained in the Immoral Traffic in Women and Girls Act, 1950, applicable to whole of India. With the strict enforcement of the Act, most of the brothels and houses of prostitution have been effectively controlled.

Chapter X deals with untouchability. Article 17 of the Constitution specifically abolishes untouchability and prohibits its practice. In the year 1955, the Parliament passed the Untouchability (Offence) Act. In 1976, the Act was renamed as Protection of Civil Rights Act. Even though the legislation has been on the statute book for over 22 years, hundreds of instances of cruelty to Harijans and persons belonging to lower or scheduled castes have occurred and keep occurring, mostly in remote villages. Restrictions in admission to places of worship and in access to public wells and other places of public interest are common. There is a great deal of scope for social workers in this field because legislation alone cannot abolish untouchability.

The next section deals with the Medical Termination of Pregnancy Act, 1971. This piece of legislation has come as a result of the pioneering efforts of those who believe in controlling population. The Indian Penal Code earlier held termination of pregnancy to be an offence. The permissible methods of controlling population being contraceptives, loops, family planning, education, sterilization, etc. This Act now authorises a registered medical practitioner to terminate unwanted pregnancy on medical and moral grounds. This enactment has been hailed by all right thinking people.

The last chapter of the First Volume deals with legal aid. While in theory equality before law and equal protection of laws are ensured in practice those who can afford it are more equal than the others. Cases are decided by courts on the basis of arguments advanced by the adversary parties. A party that can engage best legal brains on enormous fees has naturally an edge over the other party that cannot afford any legal assistance. Attempts have been made recently to provide free legal aid to indigent litigants. There is a proposal for a central Act for dealing with legal aid to the poor. A committee has been appointed under the chairmanship of Mr. Justice Bhagwati of the Supreme Court to recommend measures to be adopted by the Central and State Governments for giving legal aid to the poor.

The Second Volume dealing with legislation and social change begins with the chapter written by Mr. Justice S. Rangarajan discussing Hindu family law. Justice Rangarajan has emphasized the dual social character of law, i.e., the whole body of law of a given society and the network of internal relationships intimately linked with law-making, law applying and law enforcing institutions and processes. He makes the point that our courts have not supplied leadership as regards the role of law as an instrument of social change but have left it to the legislatures. Measures like Hindu Marriage Act, Hindu Succession Act, Adoption Act, which have revolutionised the whole concept of Hindu law, were all acts of legislatures.

Chapter II, written by Dr. Tahir Mahmood advocates reform of Mohammedan law to bring it in tune with the current thinking. Most Muslim personal laws were enacted prior to independence, the most important of which was the Muslim Marriages Dissolution Act, 1939. The Shariat Act, 1937 was the culmination of a long-drawn struggle by Muslims to fulfil their cherished desire that customary law should not prevail over customary law—in the matters of marriage, divorce, intestate succession and all other aspects of family relations. Dr. Tahir Mahmood regrets that Dowry Prohibition Act was not made applicable to Muslims, though he concedes that the custom of excessive *Jahez* prevalent among Muslims is prohibited. He strongly recommends that the Muslim law should provide for monogamy as has been done in other Muslim countries including Pakistan, which is a theocratic State.

Chapter III deals with intestate and testamentary succession amongst Hindus—very ably written by Mr. Baldev Kohli. Mr. Baldev Kohli has traced the rules of inheritance and succession in a historical perspective starting with the Caste Disabilities Removal Act, 1850, Special Marriage Act, 1872, The Hindu Inheritance Act, 1929, The Hindu Women's Right to Property Act, 1937, and culminating in the Hindu Succession Act, 1956, which does away with the age-old distinction between Hindus governed by Mitakshara and Dayabhaga schools. Shri Kohli has pointed out certain lacunae in the Act which have created some problems. While Hindu Succession Act has made the position of a Hindu woman much better than in any other system, many women are ignorant of their rights or are persuaded to forego them. For example, while a Hindu daughter is entitled to a share in the property left by her deceased parents, in practice most of them are made to surrender their rights in favour of their brothers and other relations. There is a great deal of scope for social workers to take up their cause.

Chapter IV also deals with intestate and testamentary succession amongst Hindus. It is a detailed discussion of some of the theoretical aspects of the points earlier discussed by Mr. Kohli. The author, Shri S. Venkataraman, has highlighted certain lacunae which need to be plugged: for example, Scheduled Castes, and Scheduled Tribes stay outside the Act till the Central Government by notification otherwise provides. The Act also does not cover succession of Hindus who marry under the provisions of the Special Marriage Act. Similarly, devolution of agency rights in agriculture is not effected by the Act. The coparcenery system has made serious inroads in the share of a daughter. While the son on his birth gets a share in the joint family, the daughter gets a share only on partition or death. The father can also deprive the daughter of her right by willing away the entire property to the son.

Chapter V deals with inheritance among Muslims and has been written by Shri S.A. Ali. He sets forth with clarity the shares of four classes of heirs under Muslim law, namely, sharers, residuaries, distant kindreds and unrelated successors. He pleads for legal facility of adoption being made available to Muslims, citing the examples of other Muslim countries where adoption has been legally recognized.

Chapter VI, written by Dr. B. Shivarammyya, is on the Indian Succession Act, 1925, applicable to Europeans, Anglo-Indians, Jews, Armenians and Parsis. One very glaring lacuna pointed out by him is that when two Hindus marry under the Special Marriage Act, 1954, they are entitled to adopt under the Hindu Adoptions and Maintenance Act, 1956, but the adopted child is not entitled to succeed to their property on intestacy under the Indian Succession Act, 1925.

In the next Chapter dealing with the welfare of children under Indian laws, Mrs. Jyotsna Shah has touched on all aspects of such laws, beginning with the Directive Principles of State Policy and the Fundamental Rights in the Constitution. She has also discussed the national policy on children outlined in the resolution of 1974. She has referred two aspects of Hindu Marriage Act and Adoption Act which deal with the welfare of children and to various labour laws, prohibiting employment of children under certain age in factories and mines. Juvenile delinquency and rehabilitation of delinquent and neglected children are dealt with at length. Mrs. Shah feels that much more needs to be done for the welfare of children, and suggests finally that a high level commission be set up to examine various civil and criminal laws and procedures affecting children to see that they are in conformity with the Directive Principles of State Policy and the National Policy on child welfare.

Dr. M.P. Singh has discussed the legal framework of adoption amongst Hindus in Chapter VIII of the Second Volume. The Act is applicable to Hindus only and deals with matters such as the persons who can adopt, persons who can be adopted, the conditions for adoption and the rights of adopted child. Dr. Singh has strongly recommended speedy enactment of the Adoption of Children Bill, 1972 still pending in Parliament. It will go a long way in the direction of a uniform civil code envisaged by Article 44 of the Constitution, because it will apply equally to all Indians irrespective of one's religion.

Chapter IX dealing with guardianship of minors under the Hindu law has been authored by Shri S.D. Gokhale. He has traced the concept of guardianship through the ages *vis-a-vis* the Guardians and Wards Act, 1890.

Dr. A.S. Bedi has dealt with a very complex issue, namely juristic framework for protection of morals in India in Chapter X of the Second Volume. He has listed various offences in the Indian Penal Code dealing with the problems of obscenity. He has referred to the Young Persons (Harmful Publications) Act, 1956, which was intended to prevent publication of material harmful to young persons. He has advocated organization of moral councils for protection of public morals in India.

Dealing with Public Health Legislation in India, Dr. B.C. Ghosal has referred to various Acts, such as Vaccination Act, 1880, Epidemic Diseases Act, 1897, Prevention of Food Adulteration Act, 1954, Registration of Births and Deaths Act, 1969, and Medical Termination of Pregnancy, Act, 1971 as also the Medical Act, 1886, the Dentist Act, 1948, The Nursing Council Act, 1947, the Indian Red Cross Society Act, 1920, and the Indian Medical Council Act, 1956. Shri Ghosal has strongly advocated that due consideration must be given to the report of the Public Health Committee and a Central legislation on the lines suggested by the Committee be taken in hand. He has referred to various labour legislations dealing with the health of workers such as Workmen Compensation Act, 1923, Maternity Benefit Act, 1961, Employees State Insurance Act, 1948, and Employees Provident Funds Act, 1952 etc.

Prof. G.B. Krishna Rao in Chapter XII deals with Urban Land Ceiling and Regulations Act, 1976 and its implications for urban development. The idea behind ceiling is to prevent concentration of wealth in a few hands and to ensure more equitable distribution of natural resources of the country. The enactment is of far-reaching consequences but the author has pointed out certain ambiguities and inconsistencies in it.

Chapter XIII dealing with Wakf law and administration of

wakfs in India has been written by Shri V.A. Seyid Muhammad. He has traced the origin of wakfs in India and elsewhere. He refers to various Acts which have a bearing on wakfs, beginning with the Religious Endowment Act, 1863, and going to Qazi Act, 1864, and Religious Charitable Trust Act, 1890, Wakf Validating Act, 1913 and 1930, and Mussalman Wakf Act, 1923, the Wakf Act, 1954 and the Public Wakfs Act, 1959. The vast potential income from wakfs and the social and economic problems facing the Muslim community have transformed the institution of wakfs from a strictly religious place to great social significance. According to the author, the successful channelling of the resources of the wakfs into socially useful and purposeful avenues will be of great service to the Muslim community and to the country as a whole.

In Chapter XIV on Social Welfare and Panchayati Raj Institutions, Professor S.N. Dubey has traced the history of the development of Panchayati Raj since independence. He has referred to Article 40 of the Constitution which lays down that the State shall take steps to organize village panchayats and endow them with such powers and authorities as may be necessary to enable them to function as units of self-government. In pursuance of this directive, measures have been taken to develop village panchayats at village level, the Panchayat Samiti at the block level, and the Zilla Parishad at the district level. This introduces democracy at the grass-roots level. Most of the social welfare work has been transferred to Panchayati Raj institutions. At the end of the chapter, the author has listed eight suggestions for ensuring effective implementation of social welfare programmes by the Panchayats. He has also advocated active association of voluntary organisations with social welfare services.

Shri S.P. Joshi has discussed Social Security Legislation in India in Chapter XV of this Volume. His main thrust is on social security measures provided by the Employees State Insurance Act and various benefits in sickness, maternity, disablement etc. He has advocated strict compliance with penal provisions of the Act, and imposition of enhanced and deterrent penalties for defaulters.

The last chapter of the volume dealing with the legal aspects of untouchability has been written by Prof. S.D. Balsara. He has traced the historical background dealing with untouchability and culminating in the enactment of the Untouchability Offences Act, 1955. He has also discussed at length the various measures taken by the Government to improve the conditions of persons belonging to Scheduled Castes and Scheduled Tribes, referring to special reservations and privileges assured to them. He has pleaded for the continuance of all these privileges. The Untouchability Act has been renamed Protection of Civil Rights Act, and there is a proposal to appoint a Commissioner for Civil Rights.

To run through the whole gamut of social legislation, to analyse each one, to pinpoint the lacunae, and to suggest corrective action is by no means an easy task, but one well worth attempting. It is in this belief that the two volumes were planned. If we have to translate the Directive Principles of State Policy into action, we might have more and more social legislations in years to come, and these two volumes may soon become out of date. It is hoped they will. It is therefore suggested that this kind of exercise should be done periodically, preferably once in five years to serve as a helpful hand-book for social workers as well as lay voluntary workers who go out in the countryside to make people aware of their rights. Written in layman's language and in a lucid style, the two volumes, it is hoped, will be of great help to them.

S. Rangarajan

CHAPTER I

Legislation and Social Change: Hindu Family Law

Legislation to bring about social change can be either direct or indirect. The historical school, led by Savigny, who applying to law parts of Hegel's philosophy regarded law as an organic growth indigenous to every society, was opposed to legislation, especially legislation adopting foreign institutions and laws. But there has been a considerable body of opinion in support of the possibility and even desirability, of using law to bring about social change. Today Soviet jurists[1] recognize this possibility; in fact Soviet law is used extensively to bring about and regulate social change.[2]

Yehezkel Dror[3] says:

> The two basic concepts of our investigation are social change and law. Society is always undergoing processes of change; human generations follow one another and different persons fulfil various social roles. The concept 'social change' does not refer to this constant change in the population of every society, but refers to changes in the society

1. In particular, Kechekayan, Professor of Law at the Moscow Institute.
2. Hazard (1953) and Berman (1950) discuss the use of parental law as an instrument for changing society through education by law.
3. Excerpts from his article in Tulane Law Review, Vol. 33. have been published in Penguin's *Modern Sociology Readings: Sociology of Law*, edited by Vilheim Aubert, pp. 90-99. The pages from the said article have been wrongly numbered pp. 749-801; the corrrect page numbers are 787-802. But some other passages, not extracted in the above, from the said article appear to have special relevance and they are quoted.

as such, including the various social institutions, roles and status definitions, accepted ideologies, value patterns, pattern variables and value-profiles. In other words, the concept of social change refers to changes in social structure or in culture.

Social change can be initiated by various factors, including changes in the physical environment of the society; changes in the genetic constitution of the population; contact with other societies; internal social change, such as general social movements and new technological or social inventions.[4] One of the characteristics of all contemporary cultures is a high rate of social change. In modern Western societies a high rate of social change, associated especially with changes in technology, has become accepted as a permanent feature of social life, while the various so-called under-developed societies, still relatively static, aim at achieving an even higher rate of social change, so as to enable them rapidly to reach the level of technical development characteristic of Western societies. Contemporary sociology devotes much attention to the study of social change, but as yet its basic pre-conditions and processes are little understood, and very little is known of basic problems, such as whether human societies are able to exist in a state of permanent high rate of social change, and for how long, and how high-rate social change influences the mental stability of the individual.

Society consists of a large number of social institutions and components; social change in most cases begins in some of these institutions or elements, which in turn influences other institutions and elements until the whole of society changes. This raises the problem of the extent to which certain components of society and culture can change without bringing about changes in other aspects of society, and the extent to which some components of society and culture can remain static despite changes in other aspects.

This problem is closely related to the more general one, i.e. to what extent the various aspects of society form an interacting system, every change in one part of which must bring about corresponding changes in all other parts. The more

4. Barnett, *Innovation: The Basis of Cultural Change* (1953); also Parsons, *The Social System*, 480 (1951).

autonomous a certain area is, the more it can be studied in isolation from the other institutions of its society and the easier it is to compare it with parallel areas in other societies. On the other hand, if a certain area of culture or social activity is very closely interwoven with other aspects of the same society, it becomes difficult to study it in isolation and nearly impossible to compare it by itself and outside its social context with parallel areas in other societies.

The application of these concepts to our field of inquiry becomes clear when we take into account the character of law, which from the point of view of the social sciences constitutes a part of the culture of every society.

However we may define law, it must be regarded for our purpose as a part of the culture of every society. Applying our previous analysis of social change to the relationship of social change and law the questions arise as to how far is it independent of other parts of culture and society. How far do changes in law follow changes in other aspects of society? How far do changes in law bring about changes in other aspects of society?

In other words, we can define the problem as one of the relative autonomy of law *vis-a-vis* other components of society. Its central concerns are the processes creating a lag (the concept of 'lag' as referring to the differential rate of development of various social institutions and the resultant maladjustment between them was mainly developed by W. P. Ogburn,[5] especially in his book, *Social Change* (1922). For a modern discussion of this concept see Wallis[6] The Concept of Lag, 29; *Sociology and Social Research*, 403 between law and other components of society and culture and the processes adjusting law to society and society to law.

The relationship between law and social change is further complicated by the dual social character of law. The whole of the law of a given society forms a system consistent within itself and with a whole network of internal relationships, which constitutes a sub-system of that society's total culture and is intimately linked with its law-making, law-applying and law-

5. Ogburn W.P., *Social Change*, 1922.
6. Wallis, "The Concept of Lag", *Sociology and Social Reseach*, 403.

enforcing institutions and processes. Furthermore, law is a pervasive element of every social institution and plays an important role in all of them. Thus, family law forms a part of the whole of law and cannot be understood in isolation from the legal system as a whole; but family law is also an internal and essential part of the family institution, and cannot be fully understood without consideration of it.

The dual social character of law—the whole of the law of a given society forming a system consistent within itself and with a whole network of internal relationships, thus constituting a sub-system of that society's total culture and being intimately linked with its law-making, law-applying and law-enforcing institutions and processes—makes it obligatory to understand the entire "cultural-whole" (especially family law as an internal and essential part of the family institution), but not in isolation. There are some interesting examples of this, to which Dror himself refers, including those of the operation of the various law-associated processes in primitive societies. Speaking of a "sub-system" in sociological terms one has to think of possible conflicts generating between the main and the sub-systems.

Discussion is herein confined to the impact of legislation on social change because it has been felt (in my submission rightly) that our courts have not supplied the leadership is this area but have left it to the legislature.[7] There are, however, wider questions, which arise, for instance, as the family in society which raise both sociological and legal questions (more predominantly the former) to which reference is not possible in the course of this brief article.[8]

The literature pertaining to social change is exponentially explosive. After Roscoe Pound articulated the concept of social engineering through the law at the turn of this century, we have works[9] arguing for the application of engineering principles to

7. Caplow, Theodre, *Towards Social Hope*, Basic Books, 1975.
8. For a lively discussion of these aspects and a new look at these problems see Robert Thamm, *Beyond Marriage and the Nuclear Family*, 1975.
9. I have been able to read only the first (1970) but not the second (1975) edition by Robecca McCulloch Smith featuring an emphatic approach as a framework and making generalizations about relationships aided by specific case studies.

projects for social change and offering hope for success if the principles set down are rigorously observed. There is much greater concern than ever, of a very realistic nature, about the limiting and neurotic qualities characterizing many contemporary living situations and extending the enquiry should go beyond discussion of marriage and family living into such relevant and often ignored topics as love; emotions and need-gratification within inter-personal relations and family forms; the roles of men and women within marriage, and how society and the institution of marriage create and influence these roles.[10] The insights which are necessary to discuss the institution of marriage, the family setting etc. in today's context could be had from a vast amount of literature that already exists concerning the life-styles in several parts of the globe. Klemer's *Marriage and Family Relations*[11] focuses attention on trial marriages, changing definitions of normal sexual behaviour and thorough examination of behavioural situations. The setting is that men and women have learnt to live 'efficiently', though not 'effectively', as single adults; nonetheless, marriage and family are continuing 'goods' in a changing society. Posing the question "what is happening to marriage and the family?"[12] Klemer suggests that relationships can be understood when they are examined in the context of social history and the predisposing cultural experiences of the individuals concerned. Levis Strauss has suggested that the cultural myths have a way of thinking themselves through the minds of those concerned.

But what changes take place and are identified by those who are believed to be overtaken by them itself becomes one of acute difficulty. Klemer refers to William Ogburn and Meyer Nimkoff asking in the middle of this century 18 of the best known family experts to list the most significant changes in the American family during their professional life-times brought out replies widely variant. Among the 63 changes that were listed, only one, namely, the increasing divorce rate, was mentioned by all. It would be interesting to notice the eight changes which were

10. Chapter 3, First Edition.
11. Klemer, *Marriage and Family Relations.*
12. *Ibid*, pp. 21, 22.

mentioned by at least half of them: (1) increasing divorce rate; (2) wider diffusion of birth control and/or decline in family size; (3) decline in authority of husbands and fathers; (4) increased sexual intercourse apart from marriage; (5) increase in the number of working wives; (6) increasing individualism and freedom of family members; (7) increasing transfer of protective functions of the family to the state; (8) decline of religious behaviour in marriage and family. Incidentally, this is a typical example of the "applied sampling" technique which is much less expensive, but quite comparable to, the most precise methods now in use. This technique represents a significant departure from many others which demand sophisticated statistical knowledge and extensive resources and involve much higher expenditures. Such a technique is still to be exploited in many areas of socio-legal concern. It is not every lawyer on the rolls who may have to be consulted. Carefully selected lawyers who have practical experience in this and related fields could be asked questions so framed as to bring out information which may be helpful in identifying or even measuring changes in specified fields.

Many erudite books have already been written on modern marriage, family life etc. Carl C. Zimmerman[13] has traced the life-cycle of family systems throughout the history of Western civilization. He described it as a movement from the 'Trustee Family' (individual rights are subordinated to the welfare of the family group) to the "Domestic Family" (weakened family control) and then to the "Atomistic Family" (familism replaced by individualism); from the atomistic there is a predictable movement to the domestic.[14] Talcott Parsons[15] suggested that the changes were functional adaptations to the increasing specialization of other social institutions; i.e., the modern family was doing the only thing it could to meet the requirements of a changing society. What is significant according to Klemer is the two aspects: (1) the change in determination to stay married; (2) the loss of satisfaction in marriage because of unrealistic marriage expectations—a feature more common in a society like

13. Zimmerman, Carl C., *Social Structure of the Family*, 1959.
14. *Newsweek* (13-2-1967) quoted by Klemer, p. 23.
15. Barrington Moore, *Political Power and Social Theory*, 1959.

ours which has suddenly become ascription-oriented and women have now the tacit threatening power that men have always had. The failure in marriages is ascribed today not so much to "new frictions" as to a "new unwillingness to tolerate old frictions".[16] There seems to be no greater factor contributing to the stability of marriage than a determination that it should persist. Such an attitude predisposes an individual to think or act in one way or another; values, however, are different—they are the enduring criteria which the individual uses to make judgments.

There is, however, an extreme view[17] for which there are fortunately only few supporters. It holds (a) that the family is no longer functionally necessary and that it is probably dysfunctional in a modern industrial society, (b) that there is no need to give affection, and kinship itself is obsolete. But there seems to be no adequate substitute for the biologically and culturally conditioned affectionate function; there still is need for some one who will "bandage at the end of each day bruised egos", for some one, comparable to the old grand-mother, as a house-holder. The insecure individual, too long looking at his own tender self has need to improve his relatability to other individuals. It is not frustration born of failure to dominate as one would like to suppose at the close of the Women's International Year, because in not a few cases, there is disappointment, and even frustration when there is no male dominance. One tires of a state of "guilty tolerance" and longs to escape into "peaceful co-existence". There is greater longing by both partners—aggrieved and errant—for helping each other, through communication, to understand their emotional involvements and psychological needs.[18]

The question, however, is how far social attitudes (which are changing), social institutions and legal instrumentalities do not hold, or even hinder, this kind of longing to find its natural fruition. Leonard S. Cotrell[19] observes that differing role expectations account for most difficulties; people try to recreate

16. Klemer, *Marriage and Family Relations*, p. 260.
17. Roles and Marital Adjustments, 1933.
18. Klemer, *Marriage and Family Relations*, p. 40.
19. Role, Theory and Marriage Counselling, *Social Forces*, 35 (March, 1957), p. 206.

relational systems or situations which were obtaining in their own earlier family groups. Closely related to this role theory of marital adjustment is the sociologic conceptual framework of *symbolic interactionism*, though some writers use these concepts interchangeably.

Klemer[20] postulates, in general, that the greater the congruence of the perception that each partner has of himself and his marriage roles with the perception of his mate, the more satisfactory the marriage. Testing these concepts, A.R. Mangus[21] "hypothesized that marriage problems resulted from the presence or absence" of "harmony, consistency, and congruity among the role expectations of those participating in marriage"; "the most pressing, inter-personal problems in marriage arise out of the disparities among the role concepts and self concepts that are pertinent to the marriage situation". Robert Williamson perspicaciously identified the cause of divorce as "breakdown in the image of the other person and his or her ability to personify the role desired. "These are often supplemented by marriage counsellors by reference to concepts of personality development emerging from clinical psychology. After several years of marriage counselling, Klemer believed[22] "the only genuine happiness in marriage comes from anticipating the pleasure your partner will get from what you have to give, both physically and emotionally. It is that simple, yet that difficult".

It would indeed appear naive to believe that the solution of such a difficult and complicated problem is that easy or simple. But there is much to ponder over in what Klemer says for those who want a solution to this vexed problem.

Some of the features which one may regard as basic may be easy to list and, hopefully, without much controversy. A relationship of man and woman, generating happiness in the sense explained above, of caring and striving for the happiness of each other, is for the bulk of us a far better state than that of remaining single. Difficulties may be felt in the matter of attaining or establishing such a relationship—a different question. This relationship, or even one less ideal than this, could be supported by a determination to stay together. To put

20. Klemer, *Marriage and Family Relations*, 1966, p. 535.
21. *Ibid.*
22. *Ibid.*

it at least negatively it seems that not having such a determination may induce a breakdown more easily than when there is such determination. Genuine cases where people cannot stay together do necessitate the putting an end to that relationship. The conventional methods by which such separation has been attempted provide a range of attitudes from making it very easy or altogether difficult. Judicial processes at work in this delicate area have not been able to find the delicate tool that is needed to sever the tie only when in each case it has been found that efforts to sustain it are nearly exhausted. In whatever way the laws are made the way in which they are worked out would be of the utmost importance. In other words, rules for detailed application in each case may not be possible to draft; a human agency has to work within a great framework of the law.

On almost every aspect of matrimonial relief divergent views have been expressed. There is, for instance, diversity of opinion concerning the granting of restitution of conjugal rights. Prof. Raj Kumari Agarwal has not only treated this subject in her book[23] but has also made a plea for the abolition of this remedy in an article. She has indicated a kind of counselling procedure as a substitute with the wise caution that failure of such conciliation should be considered a ground of divorce. As it is working out in practice, it is only a legal strategy to be employed by the quarrelling spouses, and it often becomes a battle of wits; the remedy of restitution, therefore, could usefully become one of reconciliation. Nonetheless, even the recent report of the Law Commission has not recommended its abolition. It is respectfully submitted that this is one instance which would indicate the need for a comprehensive revision of marriage and family laws, provided they can be implemented by family courts but not by the present court system relying on the adversary procedure.

Even concerning the grounds of matrimonial relief, such as impotency, nullity, cruelty, adultery, desertion etc., there is room for considerable difference of opinion as to what would constitute each of these grounds; they are easily gathered from any text book of Hindu law, more easily from Prof. Raj Kumari Agarwal's book since it discussed fully under their

23. Agarwal, Raj Kumari, *Matrimonial Relief Under Hindu Law*, pp. 8-36.

respective heads. There is no need, therefore, to refer to these aspects here. These were codified by the Hindu Marriage Act, 1955; the Hindu Adoptions and Maintenance Act, 1956 was also placed later on the statute book. Recently the Law Commission has reviewed the Act of 1955 without being able to free it from the constraints of the earlier statutory framework. A measure of social reform may have to be reviewed at least every two decades when the earlier flush of enthusiasm has abated in the light of global sociological insights. There is a conceptual confusion in treating the Hindu marriage both as a sacrament and as a contract. Marriage has of necessity to be treated as a contract if and when it is to be dissolved, but treating it at the same time as a sacrament makes it exceedingly difficult to define collusion and to decide whether collusion between husband and wife may be permitted. The most classic case of confusion is the Special Marriage Act, which provides for divorce by consent for persons who are married under that Act and yet makes a reference to "collusion". It would be best to have a clearer idea of the court's role in this matter: Is it or is it not to give relief to the spouses on being satisfied that the marriage does and cannot work. Or will the court find convenient shelter in a mass of legal technicalities even where it is so satisfied? In the matter of negotiating so many delicate matters that could sustain a marriage or lead to its breakdown the adversary procedure seems most ill-suited. Are not, persons suffering from matrimonial bruises bruised still more by going through this adversary procedure? Is there any reasonable hope of even the best of attempted reforms[24] healing such wounds? Is not the family court the only feasible alternative for resolving such disputes? Of course, it must be ensured that it is manned by properly trained persons, with a legal background certainly, but free from the trammels of the adversary procedure so that they have greater leeway in treating matrimonial tensions more realistically and delicately and finding the satisfactory solutions?

The writer had occasion recently[25] to advocate, for certain petty disputes, a Small Claims Court which the parties them-

24. Report No. 59 of Law Commission.
25. Seminar on Legal Aid held at Delhi inaugurated by the Prime Minister.

selves could approach directly and which the trained judges, with the help of others, would either settle quickly or resolve on merits. If this suggestion is accepted it would pave the way for family courts more suited to the requirements of our people. The writer has also pointed out on many occasions that no realistic legal reform is possible without uncovering the bewildering variety of legal problems inevitable in such a wide sub-continent as ours and further compounded by the fact that most problems do not come to light because of a large proportion of the population being effectively outside the legal framework owing to poverty and absence of legal aid. This applies to matrimonial matters as well. But a caution seems called for here. Large masses of our population live in rural areas and are illiterate. Under misguided urge to extend the benefit of sophisticated laws to them, it may not be wise to deprive them of the benefit of divorce according to custom.[26] If most of them are happy with customary divorce, it would be cruel to drive them to courts with their grievances, when even those who seek the aid of courts fail to adequate or quick relief. It would be folly to throw such additional load on the adversary procedure when the existing backlogs are crushingly heavy. It was a very perceptive critic who said that in such an eventuality "adversary would become adversity".

The family court seems an obvious requirement, not only to give relief to the heavily congested courts but also to save those who feel compelled to go to them for the resolution of their matrimonial and family disputes from frustration. With a properly constituted and staffed family court it may be possible to save several marriages which are now foundering on the rock of adversary system. The existing work load on judges at almost every level is incredibly high.[27] Alongside measures

26. As a young person I sat and watched the panchayats among Kallars, formerly described as a criminal tribe, in the South. The settlement of financial matters appeared to be the first concern. There was the custom of paying the bride price. This and other related financial matters had to be settled for effecting a dissolution. Dissolutions were fairly easy and very rarely was any practical difficulty encountered either in the matter of remarrying or of custody of children.

27. Recently a Brazilian Judge wanted to know the kind of work load on judges at the High Court level; when I merely described to him what I was doing without even referring to what was done on the

for a speedy and satisfactory settlement of marriage disputes, there must be an earnest attempt to settle all disputes, including claims to property, consequent on, or as a prelude to disoslution of marriage, if the whole exercise is to be prevented from becoming unrealistic and farcical. These native instrumentalities lost their effectiveness largely because of the imposition of a formal court system, which enabled the person who lost at the panchayat to take the matter to the British Indian Court where he could twit not only his adversary but also those who had decided against him.[28] Some of the deficiencies in the substantial law could be made up, but we must first recognize that the Achilles heel of the present system is the exposure of those with grievances in the family law area to the adversary procedure of courts. In spite of all the skill which highly competent judges can bring to bear on them, even under the adversary procedure, these disputes are eminently unsuitable for such treatment. A system of family courts is therefore the best way out.

Some difficulties have been raised from the constitutional angle. It should be possible to overcome them by resort to a constitutional amendment. But even within the existing framework, family courts could at least function in the manner of administrative courts, though with a different procedure calculated to serve the desired ends which would leave the door open for judicial review, as in any other dispute decided by administrative courts or tribunals. In this connection it may be well to consider whether there should not be separate appellate courts to hear appeals against the decisions of administrative courts, on the model obtaining in West Germany. We hear much less of the German administrative court system

---

average by others, he expressed his astonishment by saying: "if a third of this were attempted by the Brazilian Judge he would swoon under the weight of it."

28. A study of this kind sponsored by the writer a few years ago did not come to fruition. A few zealous workers who volunteered to carry such a study were not supported by funds or by any organization. It seemed to the writer, on such slender material as was being made available in the course of such studies, that the true causes of disputes were not being placed before the courts; if anything, there was purposeful distortion and the blame for this had to be laid primarily at the door of the present adversary procedure.

(functioning almost as a separate court system under the Supreme Administrative Court)[29] than about the French Administrative Law. This is not the place to discuss this rather important subject, but a reference to German Administrative Court system may not be amiss in the context of the need for providing for Family courts and for appeals against the decisions of such courts. The West German Administrative Courts have a history of more than a century, not taking into account the breaks during authoritarian regimes. It seems to the author that we can learn much from the West German experience—which promises to be useful to us, especially in view of the proliferation of administrative tribunals and courts in our country in probably the same *ad hoc* manner as in England. We do not even seem to have a complete list of these; their structure and composition have not been systematically studied. It is time we had a White Paper on the functioning of such administrative tribunals; this may provide an occasion to consider the creation of family courts as well.

The point sought to be made here is that there is not much sense in trying to reform, by legislation, marriage and family laws unless and until we decide to dispense with the adversary procedure for resolving such disputes. This is an obvious area where substantive legislation cannot by itself bring about the desired social change or cope with the change that is believed to be under way or to have already taken place in society. Legislation may change or help change and is considered probably the cheapest instrument by which change can be directly brought about, but it will remain absolutely ineffective without support not only from all instrumentalities of the law but also from other sources. The adversary procedure, on which exclusive reliance has been made by legislation in this field, seems to be the least suited vehicle for bringing about the desired change. It has proved to be a medium in which such disputes get distorted by having to suit the needs of that procedure. A case study of decided cases in the Delhi area alone, employing the interview technique, could provide valuable material to check the correctness of this statement.[30]

29. Ernst K. Pakerscher, Administrative Law in Germany: *Citizen* v. *State*, American Journal of Comparative Law, 16, 1968, p. 309.
30. *Op. cit.*, pp. 797-801.

If one may make guess, those who come to our courts with such problems feel, by and large, frustrated. It is humbly submitted this is not good for the health and tone of the adversary system even in areas where it has proved effective.

Legislation, if it is completely against social mores, is hardly effective. One has to think more of the enforcement of such legislation, much more than of its educational value. But more for educative purposes, much greater and more intensive efforts will be necessary, and even then quick results will not be achieved. It is well known that any social change that relies purely on education will skip at least one generation. Habits and traditions die hard. If social evil, such as dowry, is to be eradicated some drastic steps would be required. Such steps may include raids on premises where marriages take place, thorough searches, and insistent examination of all those concerned. Social reforms require a determined political will and, of course, a social consciousness of the evil. The best way of nursing the evil is to tinker with it.

In many significant areas legislation can bring about social change indirectly. As Dror points out, such action calls for reliance on legal means as aids to conscious attempts at bringing about the desired social change. Law can, for instance, create public bodies and invest them with power to make a direct assault on social evils. Or law can create new legal duties which enable direct action to come into play; here education is an important ally.

Referring to the case of Turkey, a society which became westernized remarkably under Mustapha Kamal Pasha, Dror says that the reception of Western law in Turkey showed that it had a significant influence on some aspects of social life, while certain other aspects were but little influenced by the new laws meant to regulate them. But in Israel, the attempt to change family habits of certain immigrant groups through legal norms failed. Basic institutions rooted in traditions and values, such as the family, seem to be extremely resistant to changes imposed by law.

But further comparative studies are necessary to make assertions of any specific kind. The experiences of Japan, Communist China and of some of the developing countries can provide relevant and useful material. Dr. Dror sums up:

"Social changes and changes in the law are constant and interacting processes, present to a considerable extent in all contemporary societies . . . By examining and defining the conditions under which law can induce social change and by emphasizing the limits upon the use of law to induce social change, a significant contribution can be made to the development of law-making as a main object of policy studies."

To hazard a guess, it appears that any attempt at direct social change has to be commensurate with the problem to be solved. and the law, both substantive and procedural (e.g. the change from the adversary procedure to more informal ones) must be realistically tailored to meet the challenge in all its immensity, intensity and extent.

Tahir Mahmood

CHAPTER II

Indian Legislation on Muslim Marriage and Divorce

All marriage legislation relating to Muslims, now in force in India, had been promulgated before Independence. After 1947, neither Parliament nor any state legislature has enacted any matrimonial law specifically or exclusively applicable to Muslims, although both are empowered by the Constitution to make laws on marriage and divorce for any as well as all communities. The Directive Principles require the State to "endeavour to secure a uniform civil code which includes laws relating marriage and divorce throughout the territory of India". However, the only step hitherto taken in this direction is represented by the Special Marriage Act, 1954, available as an alternative choice to religion-based marriage laws. A sizable number of Muslims have indeed exercised this choice, made use of its provisions. But generally speaking, marriages and divorces among Muslims still take place in accordance with Islamic personal law as modified by legislation in the pre-Independence era. We shall, therefore, begin with an account of the modifying laws enforced before 1947.

The British rulers, while establishing their juridical authority in the subcontinent, had accepted local custom as well as locally prevailing personal laws as "rules of decision" for the adjudication of family law cases among all native communities including Muslims. They did not, however, exclude "rules of decision" from the purview of their general untrammelled legislative power. They exercised this power in two different ways: (i) by enacting several general laws expressly or impliedly superseding the contrary rules of all the personal laws of whatever community and (ii) by enforcing legislative measures concerning, and applying to, particular religious communities. An illustration of the first, in the field of family law, was the Child Marriage Restraint Act, 1929, which governed all Indians alike. Examples of the second were the Shari-'at Act, 1937 and the Dissolution of Muslim Marriages Act, 1939. We must have occasion to refer also to the regional dower laws enacted in the erstwhile princely states of Oudh and Kashmir (now both parts of the Indian Union), and to the marriage-divorce registration laws enforced in some eastern regions of British India.

MUSLIM LAW IN BRITISH INDIA

The Muslim Personal Law (*Shari-'at*) Application Act, 1937, has been the principal authority for the application of Muslim law in the sub-continent. Behind it is the legal history of the battle for supremacy between unwritten custom and written personal law, which this sub-continent has witnessed since time immemorial. At the advent of British rule, this "battle" was raging not only in the Hindu community, but also among the convert Muslims in several parts of the country. The latter had, in many regions, retained their pre-conversion customs relating to succession, inheritance and family relations, while their adopted religion, represented by the *'ulama*, required their total submission not only to the religious tenets of Islam but also to its matrimonial and succession laws. The Hindus, of course, had the sanction of religion in allowing local custom and usage to prevail over and supersede religious legal texts. Guided by the practice of the majority, the legislature as well as the judiciary in British India accepted and began enforcing the supremacy of custom over personal law in respect of all the communities, including Muslims. Laws to that effect were enacted in all parts of the country[1] and where the law was silent or ambiguous, the courts still placed custom above personal law.[2] At the turn

1. See Bombay Regulation IV of 1827, Section 26; Punjab Laws Act, 1872, Section 5; Madras Civil Courts Act, 1873, Section 16; C. P. Laws Act, 1875, Section 5; Oudh Laws Act, 1876, Section 3; Ajmer-Mewar Regulation III of 1877, Section 4; NWFP Law and Justice Regulation, 1901, Section 27.
2. See Bengal, Agra and Assam Civil Courts Act, 1887, Section 37 as

of the century, Muslim religious leaders of various groups and in various places launched movements against adherence to un-Islamic customs under legislative sanction and judicial patronage.

Women had their own reasons for supporting these movements under the customary law, women had no right to property and no competence to interfere in their own matrimonial matters. Even a Muslim woman in whose family customary law was prevalent could not thus seek divorce in any circumstances whatsoever, nor get a share in the property left by her deceased relations, although Islamic law did confer on women significant rights in both these matters (though not as extensive as those enjoyed by men). Several organizations of enlightened Muslim women in India demanded enforcement of Islamic law in order to obtain at least that legal status which their religion allowed.

The efforts made by the religious leaders and by the spokesmen of women led to the enactment of first sectarian, then provincial and, finally, central laws, all providing that Muslims would be governed in all family matters by the law of Islam, notwithstanding any custom or usage to the contrary. The sectarian laws enacted for this purpose were the Mapilla Succession and Wills Acts, 1918-1928, and the Cutchi Memon Acts, 1920-1938. At the provincial level, a Shari-'at Application Act was enforced in 1935 in the erstwhile N.W.F.P. Enacted on the basis of a bill drafted by the local unit of the *Jami-'at al-'Ulama Hind*, the Act became the forerunner of the central Shari-'at Application Act, 1937.

The (central) Muslim Personal Law (*Shari-'at*) Application Act, 1937, had three purposes in view. First, to avoid "Labour in the shape of research which is the chief feature of customary law",[3] since Islamic religion was a "veritable code too well known to admit any doubt". Secondly, to fulfil "the cherished desire of the Muslims in India that customary law should in no case take place of Islamic law".[4] Lastly, to raise the status of women, since under customary law the status of Muslim women

interpreted by the Privy Council in *Mohd. Ismail* v. *Lala Sheomukh*, 18 I. C. 571 (P.C.).

3. See the Statement of Objects and Reasons, *Gazette of India*, Part V (1935).
4. *Ibid.*

was "simply disgraceful".[5] In two separate sections the Act of 1937 specified (i) those subjects in regard to which all Muslims of India would be compulsorily governed by Islamic law, and (ii) those in respect of which a Muslim would have the option to adopt Muslim law (in preference to a contrary custom, if any) for himself, his minor children and their descendants.[6] The latter category included only adoption, wills and legacies,[7] while marriage and divorce were placed in the first category along with intestate succession and all other aspects of family relations.[8] By making Islamic law applicable in matrimonial matters and inheritance, regardless of any contrary usage, the Act of 1937 indirectly enabled Muslim women to enjoy fully their rights relating to property and divorce, etc. as sanctioned by Islamic law. The Act specifically referred to Islamic legal institutions of dissolution of marriage (*tansikh*), *khul* ' (divorce by husband at the instance of wife on mutually agreed terms), dower (*mahr*), maintenance (*nafaqa*), and women's property.[9] It also empowered district judges to dissolve the marriage of a Muslim woman in accordance with Islamic law.[10]

Thus, though no substantive legal provision was included in it, the *Shari-'at* Application Act of 1937 may be regarded as an important place of social legislation which had the effect of restoring to Muslim women all those rights which their religion conferred on them but which the society denied them.

MATRIMONIAL LEGISLATION OF THE BRITISH PERIOD

Registration Laws: Long before the enforcement of the *Shari-'at* Application Act, 1937, a local law providing facilities for voluntary registration of marriage and divorce by Muslims was enacted in Bengal. Known as the Bengal Muhammadan

5. *Ibid.*
6. The distinction between the two categories was made at the insistence of the then Muslim League party in the legislature and was meant to safeguard the interests of the Muslim zamindars who wished to stick to their customary powers of adoption and bequest.
7. Section 3.
8. Section 2.
9. *Ibid.*
10. Section 6, deleted after the enactment of the Dissolution of Muslim Marriages Act, 1939 (infra).

Marriage and Divorces Registration Act, 1876, it still exists in the states of West Bengal and Bihar. Assam and Orissa adopted the same law in 1935 and 1949 respectively. None of these laws, however, made registration of either marriage or divorce obligatory. The legislature's hope that the Muslims would come forward to avail themselves of the benefit of these laws, was never fulfilled in any substantial degree; they still remain infructuous.

Dissolution of Muslim Marriages Act, 1939: The most important enactment relating to Muslims is the Dissolution of Muslim Marriages Act, 1939. It occupies a prominent place in the history of Indian social legislation. Many of the former princely states passed laws substantially on the same lines. But only in Kashmir does the law still survive; in all other states the regional laws have been gradually replaced by the central Act. It is worthwhile to study this important legislative measure in its historical perspective.

We have noted earlier that the *Shari-'at* Application Act of 1937 not only made dissolution of marriage one of the subjects in regard to which Islamic law, as contradistinguished from customary law, would be applied; it also empowered district judges to entertain divorce petitions by Muslim women in accordance with that law. But there were no such petitions, because an overwhelming majority of Indian Muslims belonged to the *Hanafi* school of Islamic law[11] which did not permit judicial dissolution of marriage. Religious leaders and prominent Muslim lawyers had been debating the problem even before the enactment of the *Shari-'at* Application Act, 1937. The debate required a topicality when cases of apostasy by Muslim women began to be reported from different parts of the country. Many Muslim women, desiring to get rid of their

11. It may be noted here that Islamic law is divided into many schools and sub-schools out of which four prevail in India. These are: *Hanafi*, *Shafi'i*, *Ithna 'Ashari* and *Isma'ili* schools. Sunni Muslims of India belong to the *Hanafi* school except in the southern states where *Shafi'i* school, too, has prevailed. The Shi'as in India belong to *Ithna 'Ashari*, while Khojas and Bohras of Western India belong to the *Isma'ili* school. The Shari'at Application Act of 1937 makes no reference to these various schools, but the judicial practice in India has been to apply the law of the school to which the parties in a particular case may belong.

husbands, abandoned their religion since, under the traditional law as applied in India, apostasy by a Muslim woman automatically dissolved her marriage with the Muslim husband. The absence of a clear law specifying the grounds on which an Indian court could grant divorce to a Muslim wife, thus, had serious repercussions. Religious leaders and jurists, therefore, decided to act quickly. In 1931, the Muslim ruler of Bhopal enforced a law, derived from the *Maliki* school of Islamic law, empowering local courts to dissolve the marriage of a Muslim woman on certain specified grounds. Religious leadership in British India, too, began thinking on the same lines. The *Jami-'at al-'Ulama Hind* made strenuous efforts in this regard. Its leaders prepared a draft bill which, after considerable revision and modification, was introduced in the central legislature in 1936 and became law in 1939. Its provisions, originally derived by the *'ulama* from the *Maliki* school of Islamic law but later adapted to Indian conditions by the British Indian legislators and known as the Dissolution of Muslim Marriages Act, 1939, now govern the divorce rights of Muslim women almost in the entire country, except the Jammu and Kashmir State where a local law passed by the ruler of Kashmir in 1942 has been retained.

The one part of the Act of 1939 enumerates the grounds on which all those circumstances in which a court may issue a decree for the dissolution of a Muslim marriage at the request of the wife. The other part relates to the effect of conversion and reconversion. The two parts together, however, do not make an exhaustive or complete law. According to the High Court of Nagpur it has only "crystallised a portion of Islamic law" and should therefore be applied "in conjunction with" the general provisions of Islamic family law.[12] And in some cases the courts have described the Act as a piece of "declaratory legislation". It cannot be denied, though, that the law, even as it was, did ameliorate the lot of Muslim women by enlarging their rights, which, under their traditional law as then applicable in India, were extremely limited.

Section 2 of the Dissolution of Muslim Marriages Act, 1939 specifies eight grounds on which a Muslim wife may seek dissolution of marriage:

12. *Jamila Khatoon* v. *Qasim Ali*, A.I.R. 1951 Nag. 375.

(i) disappearance of the husband for four years or more;
(ii) the husband's failure to provide maintenance for two years or more;
(iii) his imprisonment for seven years or more;
(iv) his failure to perform marital obligations for three years or more;
(v) his impotency since marriage;
(vi) his insanity lasting for two years or more, or leprosy or a virulent venereal disease; and
(vii) his cruel treatment of the wife.

The eighth ground on which a marriage may be dissolved is based on the Islamic principle of "option of puberty" (*khiyar al-bulugh*), which, along with other rules, ensures free consent of parties in every marriage contract.

As regards disappearance of the husband without leaving any information as to his whereabouts, while the classical Shi-'a law permitted dissolution of marriage after four years, the traditional *Hanafi* law practically denied to his wife any opportunity to marry another man.[13] In recent years, the four-year waiting rule has received the sanction of law in many non-Shi'a countries, e.g., Egypt, Sudan, Jordan, and Syria.[14] The Act of 1939 had adopted it much but with the proviso that when a suit is instituted by a wife, uncles, brothers and all legal heirs of the husband shall invariably be made parties thereto.[15]

Failure by the husband to provide maintenance to the wife for a period of two years cannot be made a ground for dissolution of marriage if the wife has lost her right by her own conduct that would be a "fraud" on the Act of 1939.[16] Thus, a wife who has herself deserted the husband cannot seek dissolution of marriage under this Act.

Imprisonment for seven years or more can be made a ground for dissolution of marriage as soon as the final order of conviction is made by the appropriate court. The wife is not required to wait till he has actually served a portion of the sentence, as

13. The traditional rule requires the wife to wait till all other family members of about her husband's age have died.
14. For details see T. Mahmood, *Family Law in the Muslim World* (1972).
15. See 2.
16. *Khatija* v. *Abdullah*, A.I.R. 1943 Sind 65.

under the laws in some West Asian countries.[17]

Desertion lasting for at least three years (which is described in the Act as failure to perform marital obligations) is another ground on which the aggrieved wife can seek relief. It is an established principle that constructive desertion is as bad as actual desertion. Therefore, a wife who is sent by her husband to her parents and is not called back for the next three years, while social custom does not allow her to return unless sent for, the man may be regarded as guilty of desertion in the eyes of law.[18]

Of the four diseases—viz., impotency, insanity, leprosy and virulent venereal disease—impotency must be proved to have been existent since the time of marriage, and insanity to have lasted for at least two years. The remaining two can be grounds for divorce irrespective of their origin and duration. Parallel provisions are to be found in modern divorce laws of many Muslim countries.[19]

Cruelty on the part of the husband includes habitual assault, leading an immoral life or forcing the wife to do so, interference with her property, obstruction in the observance of religion, and failure to treat co-wives equitably (in case of a polygamous husband). While the first of these amounts to physical cruelty, the rest answer the description of what is known in law as mental cruelty. Obstruction in the observance of religious practices is regarded as cruelty in the context of intermarriage between that while Sunnis and Shi'as, whose religious practices greatly differ. Moreover, if a Muslim wife abandons Islam, her marriage remains intact so long as her husband himself does not choose to divorce her. If the husband does not divorce her but instead interferes with her observance of the new religion, she can move the court for dissolution of marriage.

Where a Muslim has two wives (which is rarr) or more (which is nearly non-existent) and denies equitable treatment to one of them in violation of the specific Qur'anic directions in the matter,[20] the aggrieved wife can seek dissolution of her

17. Supra f.n. 15.
18. *Fakhruddin* v. *Hamidan*, A.I.R. 1953 All. 57 (D.B.).
19. Supra f.n. 15.
20. *The Qur'an*, IV:3

marriage with such a man. Statutory enforcement of the Qur'anic direction was the most the State could do in the conditions prevailing in India in 1930s. Now, realizing the radical change that has taken place since then, the courts have begun wondering if a second marriage by a Muslim does not in itself amount to cruelty under the Act of 1939, particularly since the first wife cannot reasonably expect any respect or peace in the home.[21]

The only ground for dissolution of marriage not involving the conduct of the husband is "option of puberty". Here the conduct of the girl's guardian who gave her in marriage before she attained puberty is involved. In Muslim law a girl under the age of puberty may be given in marriage by her guardian (though in India this is an offence under the Child Marriage Restraint Act, 1929)[22]. However, if a girl below the age of puberty has been given in marriage by a guardian other than her father or father's father, she may, after attaining puberty, repudiate the marriage instead of allowing its consummation. This legal principle of Islam has been adopted in the Act of 1939 with two significant modifications. First, while Islam left the fact of "puberty" (which it deemed a physical phenomenon) to be ascertained by evidence, the Indian law has fixed it at the completion of fifteen years, even if physical maturity may have been attained earlier. Secondly, under the Indian law the relief is available to the girl even if the marriage was arranged by her father or grandfather. Only in Jammu and Kashmir the traditional law on this point has been retained (Dissolution of Muslim Marriages Act, 1942). It is notable that a girl who wishes to avail herself of the Indianized form of "option of puberty" has to obtain a decree from the court; she cannot (unlike the position under the classical law) herself dissolve the marriage on that score. In this respect the law in India conforms to the law of Iran which is the only country in West Asia where "option of puberty" has now been subjected to judicial confirmation.[23] An Indian girl can, however, invoke this

21. *Itwari* v. *Asghari*, A.I.R. 1960 Alld. 684.
22. Under this Act, marriage of a male child below the age of eighteen and that of a female child below the age of fifteen years is punishable (though not invalid), irrespective of their religion or personal law.
23. See the Family Protection Law, 1967 (Iran), art. 10.

legal provision also as a defence to a suit for restitution of conjugal rights brought by her husband.[24]

The list of grounds for dissolution of a marriage, as specified in the Act of 1939, is illustrative and not exhaustive. This is clear from the addition of a residuary clause in the Act saying that the court can grant a decree on any other ground "recognized as valid for the dissolution of marriage under Muslim law".[25] In a recent case,[26] the Kerala High Court has read into this clause the "breakdown theory" of divorce which in its opinion is the basis of the entire Islamic law of divorce. In this case "incompatibility to a repellant degree" was accepted as a ground for divorce. In an earlier case,[27] the same High Court had held that failure to provide maintenance, mentioned in the Act as one of the grounds for divorce, stood in the nature of a pointer indicating breakdown of marriage. The judicial opinion, thus, seems to be that any circumstance which reasonably indicates an irretrievable breakdown of marriage could be taken notice of while entertaining a suit under the Act of 1939. Justice Krishna Iyer (now of the Supreme Court), who decided both the aforementioned Kerala cases, has in a recent article asserted that "the only system of marital law in India which accepts the ultra-modern but responsibility realistic ground of 'breakdown' as against 'fault' is Islam."[28]

Khul' and *mubara'a*, which are the two forms of divorce at the wife's initiative, as well as *talaq tafwid* (delegated divorce) are mentioned specifically in the *Shari'at* Application Act of 1937 along with other subjects in regard to which the law of Islam is enforceable in India. In the first two cases the wife may, offering to forego in part or in full her post-divorce financial rights (to be more specific, her deferred dower), ask the husband to divorce her. Under the law, as traditionally interpreted, it is upto the husband to accept or reject the offer. In Pakistan (as also in Bangla Desh), however, the wife can claim a *khul'* as of right.[29] In India, the court may dissolve a

24. *Nizamuddin* v. *Hussaini*, A.I.R. 1960 M.P. 212.
25. Section 2 (ix).
26. *Abubacker Haji* v. *Mamu Koya*, 1971 K.L.T. 663.
27. *Yusuf Rowthan* v. *Sworamma*, 1970 K.L.T. 477.
28. V.R. Krishna Iyer, 'Reform of the Muslim Personal Law' in T. Mahmood (ed.), *Islamic Law in Modern India*, 30 (1972).
29. See *Khurshid Bibi* v. *Muhammad Amin*, P.L.D. 1967 S.C. 97.

marriage under the Act of 1939 on the basis of an agreement of *khul*'; but whether a wife can ask for a *khul*', even against the wishes of the husband is yet uncertain. Of course, "incompatability to a repellant degree" has been accepted as a ground for proceedings under the Act of 1939.[30] *Talaq tafwid* (delegated divorce) stands, in India, for an authority vested in the wife by virtue of the marriage-deed to pronounce a divorce on behalf of the husband in certain situations (e.g., if the husband contracts a second marriage). The High Court of Kerala in a recent case did not pronounce on whether such an authority can be exercised by a wife without initiating proceedings under the Act of 1939.[31]

The Act of 1939 controverted the belief that abandonment of Islams by a Muslim wife would *ipso facto* dissolve her marriage with the Muslim husband.[32] The exception is a non-Muslim woman who adopts Islam, marries a Muslim, and then returns to her earlier faith after the marriage; re-conversion would automatically dissolve the marriage.[33] The husband may divorce the reconverted wife whenever he likes. The Act of 1939 does hot impose on him any obligation to retain the marriage tie with a convert wife nor in any way affects his power to pronounce an extra-judicial divorce.

In India, while the right of Muslim women to divorce are well confined by the Muslim Marriages Act, 1939, men continue to enjoy the right of dissolving marriage unilaterally and without reference to any court. Their only obligation is to pay the dower and the cost of the wife's maintenance during the period of *idda* (nearly three months). Amendments in the Act of 1939 so as to extend the law of divorce to men as well would not be repugnant to the spirit of Islamic law.[34]

Regional dower Laws: The Dissolution of Muslim Marriages Act, 1939, does not empower the court to go into the question whether the dower payable under a marriage contract is inadequate for the wife or excessive for the husband. Only in two particular regions of the country, namely, Oudh and Kashmir (now both parts of the Indian Union), local laws

30. *Supra* note 28
31. *K.C. Moyin* v. *Nafeesa and others*, A.I.R. 1973 Ker. 76.
32. Section 4.
33. *Ibid.*
34. Supra f.n. 32.

entitle the court entertaining a dower claims to decrease the amount "with reference to means of the husband and status of the wife.[35] But the court has no corresponding power to enhance the amount of dower. It is doubtful if the two regional laws can stand the constitutional test of equal protection of law.

FAMILY LEGISLATION AND THE MUSLIMS AFTER INDEPENDENCE

The Muslim personal law, along with all the modifications upto 26 January 1950, were implicitly recognized by the Constitution, subject to the legislature's power to alter, amend and repeal all laws in force on that date.[36] Unconditional powers to embark upon family legislation were conferred on Parliament and State legislatures, and the State was directed to secure for the citizens a uniform civil code. These powers have not, however, been so far exercised in regard to the personal law of Muslims. No aspect of the triditional Muslim law has, after 1950, been modified in this country. Indeed some of them have been protected by legislative action.

On two occasions, Parliament took care not to touch certain classical legal principles of Islam, on the demand of the Muslim community, while promulgating family welfare legislation otherwise applicable to all Indians alike. The first was when the Dowry Prohibition Act, 1961—which declared all dowry transactions to be offences punishable by law—specifically excluded from its purview the Muslim law of dower (mahr).[37] This was done on the ground that the Islamic concept of *mahr* is entirely different from dowry in that it is in the nature of a post-divorce relief. The Act does, however, invalidate the custom of excessive *jahez* prevalent among the Muslims, since *jahez* cannot be distinguished from dowry, specially when demanded by the male party to an intended marriage.

The second occasion Parliament chose to subvert a progressive measure to traditional law on the demand of Muslims. It arose at the time of the revision of the old Criminal

35. T. Mahmood, 'Divorce in Muslim Law', *Hindustan Times*, Delhi, 18-2-73 reproduced in the author's book *Islamic Law and the Future Civil Code of India* (1972).
36. See Oudh Act, 1876, section 5; and J & K State Muslim Dower Act, 1920, Section 2.
37. See art. 372 (1).

Procedure Code, 1898. Section 488(3) of the old code had empowered the courts to pass maintenance orders in favour of wives whose husbands neglected them, without, however, foreclosing other remedies, if any, available under different personal laws. The courts entertained petitions from all aggrieved wives regardless of the communities to which they belong. In a case[38] the Kerala High Court stressed that "it would be improper for an Indian court to exclude any section or community born and bred up on Indian soil from the benefit of that law". In the new Criminal Procedure Code of 1973, the corresponding provision empowers the courts to make an order for payment of maintenance also in favour of a divorced wife.[39] But the demand of a section of Muslims, a rider was added: that while applying this provision the court shall give due consideration to whether the divorced wife has received from the husband her full entitlement under the personal law of the parties.[40] The objection of the Muslims was based on their belief that under Islamic law a husband cannot be compelled to provide maintenance to his divorced wife beyond the period of *'idda*, which extends to about three months. (As a matter of fact under Islamic law the husband cannot stop the maintenance allowance before the expiry of *'idda*, but there is nothing in the texts to show that he cannot continue to provide it even after that). It remains to be seen how the courts interpret the words "shall give due consideration".

In 1954 Parliament put on the statute book a secular law of marriage and divorce but made it applicable only to those parties to a marriage which voluntarily chose to be governed by it. Under this Special Marriage Act, 1954, any two Indians, whether or not professing the same religion, can marry; also, an existing marriage solemnized under any of the prevailing personal laws can be turned into a secular marriage by registration under the Act. The Act enforces strict monogamy. permits only judicial divorce on the grounds specified in the Act, does not prescribe any ceremonies, and provides several remedies and reliefs. Thus, if two Muslims choose to contract a marriage under this Act, their personal law ceases to apply.

38. See the preamble of the Act.

39. *Shahulameedu* v. *Subaida Beevi*, 1970, K.L.T. 4.

40. Criminal Procedure Code, 1973, Section 125.

The same effect will follow if a Muslim couple married in accordance with Islamic law registers the marriage under the Act. Moreover, a Muslim—man or woman—can under this Act, freely marry any non-Muslim, notwithstanding the restrictions on inter-religious marriages in Islamic law.[41] By contracting or registering his or her marriage under the Special Marriage Act, 1954, a Muslim does not cease to be a Muslim. As explained by Fyzee, "it is a doctrine clearly received by the law in India that a Muslim who, in obedience to the law of the land, deviates in some aspects only from the law as laid down in the *Qur'an* does not necessarily abjure Islam."[42] This author has found an investigation that the "conflicts" between the Indian law of 1954 and the Qur'anic matrimonial law are without any substance.[43] It is, however, a fact that the Act of 1954 is becoming increasingly popular at least among progressive Muslims.

41. Under Islamic law, a woman can marry none but a Muslim man, but a man is allowed to marry a *kitabiya*, i.e. Christian and Jewish women.
42. A.A.A. Fyzee, *Outlines of Muhammedan Law*, 357 (1964).
43. T. Mahmood, *Marriage and Divorce in Secular Legislation*, a research monograph to be published under the auspices of the Indian Law Institute, New Delhi.

Baldev Kohli

CHAPTER III

Intestate and Testamentary Succession amongst Hindus

The origin of Hindu law can be traced back to Srutis. Over ages it was elaborated upon by Smrities and commentaries, and made more complex by customs. The Muslim rulers took its existing shape though not interfered with the personal law of Hindus. But the present form was given to Hindu law by judicial interpretations and legislative enactments both during the British regime and since independence. The following Acts deserve special mention:

1. Caste Disabilities Removal Act, 1850, which removed the rule of forfeiture of right to property on change of religion or loss of caste.
2. Special Marriage Act, 1872, which provided for succession to the property of any Hindu marrying under this Act, and of the offspring(s) of such marriage, to be regulated by the Indian Succession Act, 1865, instead of the Hindu law.
3. The Hindu Inheritance (Removal of Disabilities) Act, 1928, which removed all bars to inheritance and right to joint family property on grounds of disease, deformity or physical or mental defect except congenital lunacy or idiocy.
4. The Hindu Law of Inheritance (Amendment) Act, 1929, which introduced sister(s) son's daughter(s), and daughter's daughter(s) as heirs and ranked them, in

the order of succession, below father's father but above father's brother(s).

5. The Hindu Women's Right to Property Act, 1937, which enhanced the rights of widows of coparceners (who were entitled only to maintenance) in that it gave them the place of their deceased husbands, though not labelling them coparceners.

Even before independence, enlightened Hindus had pressed for substantial reforms in Hindu law. The response was the appointment in 1941, of the Hindu Law Committee to look into the need for change and to suggest reforms in the Hindu law. After a checkered history of a quarter century, the report of the committee fructified in Acts: (i) Hindu Marriage Act, 1955; (ii) Hindu Succession Act, 1956; (iii) Hindu Minority and Guardianship Act, 1956; and (iv) Hindu Adoption and Maintenance Act, 1956. These Acts abrogated the rules previously applicable, whether by virtue of any text or rule of Hindu law or any custom or usage having the force of law, in respect of matters dealt with in these Acts. They also superseded all legislation, Central as well as State, inconsistent with the provisions of these Acts.

Some important areas of Hindu law, however, have remained untouched to a great extent by the process of amendment and codification. Obvious examples are the Hindu Mitakshara joint family, and property and partition in such a joint family. Hindus have been generally governed by two main schools of law—Mitakshara and Dayabhaga.[1] Mitakshara law applies to Hindus all over India except the Bengali speaking population of Bengal and Assam to whom Dayabhaga law is applicable. In relation to succession, there are two main differences between the two systems: (i) While Mitakshara endows son(s) grandson(s) and great-grandson(s) with an interest equal to the father's in the ancestral property, Dayabhaga does not do so. (ii) While, on the death of a coparcener,[2] Mitakshara applies

1. Schools named after the two commentaries—Mitakshara and Dayabhaga. Former is a commentary on Yajnavalkaya Samriti, written in 11th century by Vijnaneswara and latter is a digest of many codes, written in 12th century by Jimutavahana.
2. A male member of the joint family who is within four degrees of male descent from the head of the family.

the principle of survivorship, Dayabhaga applies the principle of succession.

With the passing of the Hindu Succession Act, 1956, it is this Act that regulates testate and intestate succession to the property of any Hindu dying on or after 17th June, 1956. The Act extends to the whole of India except the State of Jammu and Kashmir (which adopted the provisions of this Act in 1956 in the form of Jammu and Kashmir Hindu Succession Act). The Act was extended to the Union Territories of Dadra and Nagar Haveli by Regulation 6 of 1963 and to Pondichery by Regulation 7 of 1963. Although Goa, Daman and Diu became part of India on 20th December 1961, the Act is not yet applicable to these areas.

The Hindu Succession Act, 1956 lays down a uniform and comprehensive law of succession and applies alike to persons governed by the Mitakshara and Dayabhaga Schools. It applies also to those in certain parts of South India who were previously governed by Marumakkatayam, Allyasantana and Nambudri systems of Hindu law.[3] The Act defines 'Hindu' in such a manner as to include all persons domiciled in India who are not Muslim, Christian, Jew and Parsi. The Act applies to Scheduled Castes but not to Scheduled Tribes.[4]

DEVOLUTION OF INTEREST IN MITAKSHARA COPARCENARY PROPERTY

A male Hindu governed by Mitakshara law, dying intestate, may leave behind two different categories of property (i) his interest in the ancestral property,[5] and (ii) his self-acquired or separate property. In the ancestral property, in the hands of a

3. Provisions in the Act relating these three systems of law have not been discussed in this article.
4. See Section 2 of the Act.
5. Ancestral property is the property that a person inherits from his father, father's father or father's father's father or any property that he gets from any of these three ascendants under a will or a gift where the testator or donor intended it to be treated as ancestral property in the hands of testate or donee (*Arunchala* v. *Murganatha*, 1954 S.C.R. 243). It includes any property that is acquired out of the income/or proceeds of sale, or with the assistance of ancestral property etc. and self-acquired property or separate property thrown in the joint family stock.

male the deceased's sons, grandsons and great grandsons (3 degrees in the line of male descent), natural or adopted, get an interest equal to that of their father. All those who get this right are called coparceners. So at any given time all the male members of the joint family who are within 4 degrees of male descent (head of the family, his sons, grandsons and great grandsons) form the body called coparcenary. One of the very important features of a coparcenary is that on the death of a coparcener, his interest in the coparcenary property devolves by survivorship on the other members of the coparcenary, and not by succession.

Section 6[6] of the Act, while keeping the general rule of survivorship, had added a very important proviso. It says that when any coparcener dies after the passing of this Act, leaving any of the female relatives mentioned in class I of the Schedule[7] or a son of a predeceased daughter, the deceased's share or interest in the coparcenary property would devolve by succession under this Act and not by survivorship. As a consequence of this proviso, the share of a coparcener, in a majority of cases, would devolve on his class I heirs by succession and not by survivcrship to the other coparceners, thereby improving the position of the female heirs of class I. For the purpose of determining the share of a deceased coparcener, Explanation I[8] to

6. "When a male Hindu dies after the commencement of this Act, having at the time of his death an interest in a Mitakshara coparcenary property, his interest in the property shall devolve by survivorship upon the surviving members of the coparcenary and not in accordance with this Act:

   Provided that, if the deceased had left him surviving a female relative specified in class I of the schedule or a male relative specified in that class who claims through such female relative, the interest of the deceased in the Mitakshara coparcenary property shall devolve by testamentary or intestate succession, as the case may be, under the Act and not by survivorship."

7. Son; daughter; widow; mother; son of a predeceased son; daughter of a predeceased son; son of a predeceased daughter; daughter of a predeceased daughter; widow of a predeceased son; son of a predeceased son of a predeceased son; daughter of a predeceased son of a predeceased son; widow of a predeceased son of a predeceased son.

8. Expl. I to Section 6: "For the purpose of this section, the interest of a Hindu Mitakshara coparcener shall be deemed to be the share in the property that would have been allotted to him if a partition of the property have taken place immediately before his death, irrespective of whether he was entitled to claim partition or not."

section 6 of the Act provides for national partition and allots the share to the coparcener which he would have got if the partition had taken place immediately before his death.

Under the Mitakshara law of partition, which does not seem to have been affected by the Hindu Succession Act, 1956, a mother or a grandmother, though not entitled to ask for partition of the coparcenary property, is yet allowed a share equal to that of the sons whenever there is a partition amongst the father and the sons or amongst the sons after the death of the father. Other females of the joint family are entitled to maintenance, and daughters to marriage expenses. In Madras the mother or grandmother is entitled to maintenance but to no share.[9]

Different views have been expressed on the question whether a share is to be provided for the mother while determining the share of the deceased coparcener in the coparcenary property at the notional partition envisaged in Explanation I. If the answer is in the affirmative, does the mother become entitled to get that share? The question has been viewed in the following different ways: (For clarity of elucidation the views have been illustrated with the help of a fact situation of a Mitakshara family consisting of father F, mother M, a son S and a son's wife SW in which S dies).

(a) Provision for a share is to be made for the mother but what she actually gets is her share as class I heir of S.[10] According to this view, deceased S's interest in the coparcenary property will be 1/3rd and M and SW, as his class I heirs, would get 1/6th each.

(b) In view of section 4 of the Act, the mother's right to claim a share at the notional partition is abrogated as it was merely in lieu of maintenance.[11] Applying this to the facts, the interest of S in the coparcenary property will be 1/2 and M and SW would get 1/4 each.

(c) The mother is entitled to a share at the notional partition and a further share as class I heir of the

9. *Sabramaniam* v. *Arunchalam*, *I.L.R.*, (1905) 28 Mad. 1.
10. Mulla's Hindu Law, pp. 781-82 (13th Ed.).
11. *Shiramabai* v. *Bhimgonda*, A.I.R. 1964 Bom. 263. See also Shivaramayya, B., Share to Female members at a Partition under Mitakshara law, 5 JILI 217.

deceased.[12] So M in our hypothetical example gets 1/3rd at the notional partition and another 1/6th being her share as class I heir of S.

(d) A mother is entitled to a share at the notional partition and therefore in view of explanation II of section 6,[13] she would not be entitled to a second share as class I heir.[14] Although M is entitled to a 1/3rd share at the notional partition, she does not get any share as class I heir, and so the whole of S's 1/3rd share would go to his widow SW.

And now for the second question whether, if provision for a share is made for the mother at the notional partition, she gets an indefeasible right to that share. Before the passing of this Act the Privy Council had held that till actual division of the share declared in her favour by a preliminary decree for partition of the joint family estate, a Hindu wife or mother was not recognized as owner.[15] But now the Supreme Court has held that the effect of sections 4 and 14 of the Act is that a preliminary decree having declared the right in favour of the mother (grandmother in the case), she becomes entitled to an absolute right in the property.[16] She gets this right even before actual (physical) division of the property. If the mother becomes entitled to an absolute right in the share provided for her, there is no reason why, by the same reasoning, why she should not be allowed to claim that share when provision is made for a share to the mother at a notional partition. The mother's right to get a share as class I heir is her statutory right and cannot be denied to her on the ground that thereby she would get a double share in the coparcenary property. Under section 6 as it

12. *Rangubai* v. *Laxman*, A.I.R. 1966, Bom. 169. The Court dissented from its earlier decisions and both are Division Benches decisions and Patel J. who was one of the judges in the two cases did not follow his earlier opinion.

13. Expl. II: "Nothing contained in the proviso to this section shall be construed as enabling a person who has separated himself from the coparcenary before the death of the deceased or any of his heirs to claim on intestacy a share in the interest referred to therein."

14. *Sidrappa* v. *Laxmi Bai*, (1965) Mys. LJ 625; for criticism of this view see author's exclusion of separated person under Section 6 of the Hindu Succession Act, 1956, 9 JILI, 93 at 98-100.

15. *Partapmull* v. *Dhanaboti*, A.I.R. 1936 P.C. 20.

16. *Munna Lal* v. *Raj Kumar*, A.I.R. 1962 S.C. 1493.

exists at present, the mother is bound to get a bigger slice of the coparcenary property. For example, in a joint family consisting of father, mother and several sons, and may be daughters also, in case of deaths of the sons the mother is the only class I heir. From the socio-economic point of view it is just as well, for the property would be going into the most deserving and safe hands. Being in possession of that property, the mother would not be a burden to the family or to the society and would be able to command better respect and treatment from her sons, daughters and daughters-in-law etc. After her death the property would ultimately go to the sons and daughters.

None of the views held in respect of section 6 of the Act can claim to be wholly acceptable. It should be so worded as to end the Matakshara joint family system. As it is worded, it has given rise to a spate of litigations, and the joint family system is being used as a device to reduce the incidence of income-tax, wealth tax, gift tax and estate duty. By giving shares under actual and fictitious partitions, joint families, actual and fictitious, have been able to circumvent the land ceiling laws of different states. The proposed legislation of ceiling on urban property would also meet the some fate. The joint family system comes handy in landlord-tenant disputes also. Legislation should end the principle of right by birth and devolution of property by survivorship.

SUCCESSION TO THE SEPARATE OF SELF-ACQUIRED PROPERTY OF MALES

Sections 8 to 13 of the Act provide for succession to the share of a deceased member of the Dayabhaga joint family and to the self-acquired or separate property, of a Hindu male dying intestate. The sections do not have any retrospective effect except in some cases where a male Hindu died before the passing of the Act and his property was inherited by a female having a limited estate in it. If the limited heir dies after the passing of the Act, the succession opens a second time. Though the male owner may have died before the passing of the Act, the succession to his property would be determined retrospectively by the provision of this Act.[17] In view of the Supreme Court ruling in this question, contrary views held by some of

17. *Daya Singh* v. *Dhan Kaur*, A.I.R. 1974 S.C. 665.

the High Courts previously has ceased to be good law.

Section 8 of this Act classifies the heirs in 4 categories—(i) relatives specified in class I of the schedule; (ii) relatives specified in class II of the schedule, (iii) agnates of the deceased, and (iv) cognates of the deceased.

Class I heirs succeed ro the property in preference to the heirs mentioned in class II, agnates and cognates. If there is only one heir belonging to class I, the whole of the property goes to him, and if there are more heirs than one in that category, it is divided according to the provisions of section 10. The mother, surviving sons, daughters and widows (if more than one, all the widows together) each take one share. Surviving sons, daughters and widow of a predeceased son by rule of representation take the share which predeceased son would have taken if he was alive. Similarly, the sons and daughters and widow of a predeceased son of a predeceased son takes the share which he would have taken if he was alive. The son and daughter of a pre-deceased daughter take the share which their mother (pre-deceased daughter), if alive, would have taken.

These provisions have improved the position of the female relations of the deceased; in a way, made it better than that of their male counterparts. The daughters in the family when married get some property in the form of dowry (in spite of Dowry Prohibition Act, 1961, the practice of giving and taking of dowry continues unabated) and at the time of the father's death they come in as equal sharers with their brothers and unmarried sisters in the property of the father. But the law does give to the father the testamentary capacity even in respect of his interest in the coparcenary property, whereby he can safeguard the rights of his children *vis-a-vis* married daughters.[19]

If the deceased does not leave behind any relative specified in class I, the property devolves on the relatives specified in class II of the schedule.[20] If there is only one relative belonging

18. Such a situation can arise only in respect of marriages performed before Hindu Marriage Act, 1955.
19. See Section 30 of the Hindu Succession Act, 1956.
20. I. Father.
    II. (1) Son's daughter's son, (2) Son's daughter's daughter, (3) brother, (4) sister.

to class II, the whole of the property goes to him and in case there are more than one relatives belonging to class II, the relation specified in the earlier entry succeeds in preference to the relation mentioned in any subsequent entry. Where there are more heirs than one belonging to the same entry, the property would be divided equally amongst them.

In the absence of class I and class II heirs, the property of the deceased would go to the agnates of the deceased, and failing them to the cognates. An agnate is a person related to the deceased by blood or adoption wholly through the male line. A cognate is a person related to the deceased by blood or adoption not wholly through male line but some female intervenees. Agnates and cognates mentioned in category III and category IV respectively are those agnates and cognates who are further removed from the agnates and cognates specified in class I and class II.

The rule of representation is followed in the case of class I heirs. The division of property is *per stirpes* (branches) and, amongst the members of the same branch, the distribution is made per capita.[21] Amongst Class II heirs the division of property is made per capita.[22] In all cases where two or more heirs succeed to the property together, they take the property as tenant-in-common and not as joint tenants.[23]

In case a male Hindu dies intestate without leaving any relation belonging to the aforesaid four categories, the property of the deceased would escheat to the State.[24]

Though equality of sexes has been recognized. In our law, the bias against the relations through females has been kept

---

III. (1) daughter's son's son's son (2) daughter's son's daughter (3) daughter's daughter's son, (4) daughter's daughter's daughter.
IV. (1) Brother's son (2) sister's son, (3) brother's daughter (4) sister's daughter.
V. Father's father; father's mother.
VI. Father's widow; brother's widow.
VII. Father's brother; father's sister.
VIII. Mother's father; mother's mother.
IX. Mother's brother, mother's sister.

21. See Section 10 of the Act.
22. See Section 11 of the Act.
23. See Section 19 of the Act.
24. See Section 29 of the Act.

alive. Third degree relations of the deceased through a male child are put in class I, whereas third degree relations through the female child are put in class II. Amongst the agnates and cognates, the cognates are not allowed to succeed till the whole lot of agnates, without any limit of degree of relationship, are exhausted. A cognatic relation, even one degree removed from the cognates mentioned in class II, cannot succeed to the property of his deceased relation as long as any agnate, no matter how many degrees removed from the deceased he may be, is in existence. In this respect the position of the cognates is worse than it was under the old law, which for purposes of inheritance, put a limit to agnatic relationship to 14 degrees and cognate relationship to 5 degrees. It would be well to enact legislation to restrict the list of heirs covering all the communities in India.

HINDU WOMEN'S PROPERTY AND ITS DEVOLUTION

Under the old Hindu law property held by a woman could be divided into (i) Stridhana and (ii) Non-Stridhana. In Stridhana, her right was absolute right except for some minor fetters. In non-Stridhana her rights were restricted in several ways: (i) she could not ordinarily alienate the corpus of the estate; (ii) on her death the property devolved, not on her heirs but on the heirs of last full owner, generally a male, and (iii) on her re-marriage she forfeited her rights in the husband's estate. The Hindu Women's Right to Property Act, 1937, gave some right to widow. In her husband's separate property she was given a share equal to that of the son; similar rights were given to the widow of the pre-deceased son and the widow of pre-deceased son of a pre-deceased son. In Mitakshara joint family property, the widow of a deceased coparcener took over the interest of her husband in the joint family property at the time of his death, her share or interest, however, being treated as non-Stridhana. The 1956 Act has repealed the 1937 Act. It has, in certain senses, reduced the quantity of the widow's share but has more than made up the loss by improving the quality of the estate taken by her. Section 14 of the Act,[25]

25. "Any property possessed by a female Hindu, whether acquired before or after the commencement of this Act, shall be held by her as full owner thereof and not a limited owner. Explanation (i) in this sub-

has revolutionized the position of a female by abolishing the limited estate, and converting it into an absolute estate in respect of all property, whether acquired by her before or after the commencement of the Act. In regard to the property acquired by her before the passing of this Act, the female must have been in possession of that property at the commencement of the Act. The expression 'property' connotes a bundle of rights exercisable by the owner in respect thereof and embracing within its purview both corporeal and incorporeal rights.[26] The word 'possessed' in the context means the state of owning or having in one's hand or power.[27] One of the characteristics of a limited estate is that the limited owner could alienate (mortgage, sell or gift) that property even without legal necessity but that alienation would be effective only during the lifetime of the limited owner and on the limited owner's death the property would revert to the heirs (called reversioners) of the last full owner. There is no doubt that a female owner can now dispose of (i) the property acquired by her after the passing of the Act, and (ii) the property acquired before the Act but in her possession at the time of the commencement of the Act. But in respect of the property which a female limited owner had acquired and disposed of before the passing of the Act, the old law applies, and reversioners can challenge such an alienation and get back the property after the death of the female limited owner, because it cannot be said that she was possessed of that property at the time of the commencement of the Act.[28]

Sub-section (2) of section 14 makes it clear that any limited

---

section, "property" includes both movable and immovable property acquired by a female Hindu by inheritance or devise, or at a partition or in lieu of maintenance or arrears of maintenance, or by gift from any person, whether a relative or not, before, at or after her marriage or by her own skill or exertion or by purchase or in any other manner whatsoever, and also any such property held by her as Stridhana immediately before the commencement of this Act. (2) Nothing contained in sub-section (1) shall apply to any property acquired by way of gift or under a will or any other instrument or under a decree or order of a civil court or under an award where the terms of the gift, will or other instrument or the decree, order or award strict estate in suh property."

26. *Dwarkadas* v. *Sholapur S.W. Co.*, A.I.R. 1954 S.C. 119.
27. *Gumalpura Tagina* v. *Sutra Veeravva*, A.I.R. 1959 S.C. 337.
28. *Radhe Rani* v. *Hanuman Prasad*, A.I.R. 1966 S.C. 216.

estate acquired by a female, either before or after the commencement of the Act, by the operation of transactions *inter-vivos*, by a testamentary disposition, by decree or order of a court or under an award shall not be enlarged into full ownership by operation of sub-section (1), if the gift, will or other instrument, decree, order or award had prescribed a restricted estate. The difference in the application of sub-sections (1) and (2) is explained by the Madras High Court[29] in the following words:

"The document, instrument, decree or award may, in certain cases, of its own force create a restricted estate in property and may in certain other cases only restate the restricted estate which the Hindu female possessed even prior to the date of the instrument, decree or award. Before applying sub-section (2), the proper question to ask is, does the instrument or decree 'prescribe' a restricted estate in the property, or does it merely acknowledge and recognise (and not prescribe) a pre-existing estate upon which the Hindu law had imposed restriction, because the holder of the estate was a woman? If, before the date of the deed or decree, she had no interest in the property and her only source of title is the deed or the decree, which confers upon her a restricted estate, section 14(2) will apply, and such restricted estate will not be enlarged into an absolute estate under section 14(1). If, on the other hand, the source of her title is independent of the instrument or decree and she held a restricted estate even prior to the date of the instrument or the decree, and all that the instrument or decree does is merely to recognise the pre-existing restricted estate to the female Hindu, then sub-section (1) of section 14 would certainly operate upon the restricted estate and expand it into an absolute one."

The heirs of a deceased female Hindu are set out in section 15, and the rules for distribution of her property amongst them are laid down in section 16. Most of the heirs are the same but are more numerous than those provided for a male Hindu. These heirs are the heirs to her own property, but property inherited by her from her father or mother reverts to the family of the father in the absence of son or daughter and, similarly, property inherited from her husband or father-in-law reverts

29. *Hussain Uduman* v. *Venkatachala*, A.I.R. 1975 Mad. 8.

to the heirs of the husband in the absence of her son or daughter or the children of any son or daughter.

The improvement in the female's rights of inheritance, and the conferring of absolute rights on them have not been received well in certain quarters. The chief arguments of the critics are: (i) that daughters, married and to be married, would take a part of the ancestral property out of the parental family and thereby reduce its quantum; (ii) that in case of re-marriage by the widow, property inherited from the former husband's family would go into the hands of the second husband; (iii) that the female generally illiterate is liable to be easily imposed upon and may not be able to safeguard her interest; (iv) that giving a share to daughter(s) would lead to friction between brothers and sisters; (v) that introducing so many females as heirs would lead to fragmentation of holdings. The answer to these is simply that the female is not only a daughter but also a daughter-in-law, who brings in as well as take away family property. As Prof. Derrett puts it, "Women are no longer fit objects for perpetual tutelage, and unless they are given responsibility they will never grow up emotionally and otherwise and will never achieve the equality which individuals have shown is potentially their due".[30] If distribution of property amongst brothers has not diminished their love and affection, why should the introduction of sisters be feared? Fragmentation of holdings is a natural consequence of all laws of succession, so the remedy has to be looked for somewhere else.

While commending the Act, it may be pointed that it is rather anomalous that when a female succeeds to a share in coparcener's interest in the coparcenary property, or to a self-acquired property of a male Hindu, she succeeds as an absolute owner with all rights of alienation, whereas a son or a grandson etc. succeeding to such a share takes it subject to (i) certain restrictions on his rights of alienation; and (ii) the right of his existing and after-born male descendants to take interest in such a share by birth.

DISQUALIFICATION TO INHERIT PROPERTY

Before the amendments were made in the Hindu law, several

30. Prof. JDM Derrett, "Section 14(2) of the Hindu Succession Act—A Disturbing Decision from Andhra Pradesh", 1969 Bom. L.R. 62.

disqualifications were recognized which disentitled an heir from inheriting the property of his deceased relation. Some of the disqualifications were removed by the Caste Disabilities (Removal) Act, 1850, Hindu Inheritance (Removal of Disabilities) Act, 1928, and by the present Act. The following disabilities, however, still exist:

(i) **Illegitimacy**: In the joint family property an illegitimate child, though entitled to maintenance, has no rights of inheritance amongst Brahmins, Kashatriyas, or Vaisyas.[31] The Shudra community takes a more humane view and places the illegitimate child on a better footing by recognising its rights of inheritance to the father's estate provided the mother was a Hindu and was in continuous and exclusive keeping of the father. The illegitimate son of a Shudra, however, is entitled to take one half of what he would have taken if he was legitimate.[32]

As far as the separate and self-acquired property of the deceased is concerned, Section 3(1)(J)[33] lays down the general rule that related would mean only related by legitimate kinship. The proviso to clause (J) however, provides that illegitimate children would be regarded as heirs of their mother and of each other. Therefore, an illegitimate child is entitled to inherit from his mother but not from his putative father (even where such relationship could be established) or father's family or even from any other relation of the mother. If there are more than one illegitimate children from the same mother, they would be heirs of each other. Some improvement has been made by Section 16 of the Hindu Marriage Act, 1955, in the status and rights of illegitimate children born of void or voidable marriages, subject to the condition that such a marriage has been annulled by a decree of nullity. Such children inherit from their father also. But this covers a very small category of illegitimate children. Illegitimate children falling under numerous other categories

31. Mitakshara, Ch. I, Section 12, V. 3.
32. Mitakshara Ch. I, Section 12 V. 2; *Gurnarian Das* v. *Gur Tehal Das*, A.I.R. 1952 S.C. 225.
33. "related" means related by legitimate kinship: provided that illegitimate children shall be deemed to be related to their mother and to one another, and their legitimate descendants shall be deemed to be related to them and to one another; and any word expressing relationship or denoting a relation shall be construed accordingly.

get protection only to the extent of a right to succeed to their mother's property.[34] The law as it stands now causes great hardship and does injustice to illegitimate children by imposing disabilities on them for no fault of theirs.

(ii) **Re-marriage by certain widows**: Widow of a pre-deceased son, widow of a pre-deceased son of a predeceased son and the widow of a brother, who are mentioned in section 24 of the Act, are disqualified to inherit if they are re-married at the time the succession opens. Father's widow (a step-mother) specified in entry VI of class II of the schedule is not mentioned in the category of disqualified widows even on her re-marriage. It seems to be an accidental omission. As a general rule, a female who joins her husband's family on marriage and becomes a widow, should be disqualified to inherit in her former husband's family on her re-marriage because she no more remains a widow and instead becomes the wife of another person. Other widows like daughter, mother, sister etc. who are blood relatives of a deceased person continue to be heirs even after their re-marriage, because their relationship with the deceased existed irrespective of their marital status.

(iii) **Conversion**: The rules relating to convert's succession have been further improved upon as now not only the convert and his children born before conversion but also the children and descendants born after conversion and reconverted to Hindu religion before the succession opens are entitled to succeed to their Hindu relations.[35] The only snag in the existing law is that the rule of reciprocity has not been followed. Though the convert is entitled to suceeed to his Hindu relations, his own property would devolve according to the personal law of his embraced religion and that law may not allow his Hindu relations to succeed to his property.[36]

(iv) **Murderer**: On grounds of public policy a murderer is disqualified to inherit the property of the person murdered. The disqualification is extended to the abetment of the offence. A

34. A study of the categories of illegitimate children left out of Section 16 of the Hindu Marriage Act, 1955, is made in author's article "Natural child of illegitimate parents." now ready for publication.
35. Section 26.
36. *K.P. Chandrasekharappa* v. *Govt.* of *Mysore*, A.I.R. 1955 Mys. 26.

person is also disqualified to inherit property in furtherance of the succession to which he or she committed the murder.[37]

(v) **Mental or physical defects**: Hindu Inheritance (Removal of Disabilities) Act, 1928, removed numerous physical and partly mental disqualifications but retained exclusion from inheritance on grounds of lunacy and idiocy if existing from birth. The present Act removes these grounds also. Now an heir cannot be excluded from inheritance on any ground whatsoever except those mentioned above.[38]

(vi) **Renunciation of worldly affairs**: This has not been indicated as a ground of exclusion but renunciation of the world and joining of a religious order has always been treated as tentamount to civil death because the very nature of the act itself implies absolute detachment from the temporal affairs of the world.

(vii) **Separated coparcener**: Any coparcener, who had separated from the coparcenary before the death of any other coparcener, is excluded from any share in the coparcenary interest of the deceased coparcener even though he may be class I heir of the deceased.[39]

(viii) **Testamentary succession**: This Act mainly deals with intestate succession and has only two sections—Section 6[40] and 30[41]—which have a bearing on testamentary succession.

Under the ancient Hindu Law, joint family property was the rule and separate property, if it did exist, was an exception. This probably explains why the idea of testamentary disposition was unknown to Hindu law. But as time passed separate

37. Section 25.
38. Section 28.
39. Section 6, explanation 2.
40. For text of Section 6, see foot note 6.
41. "Any Hindu may dispose of by will or other testamentary disposition any property, which is capable of being disposed of by him in accordance with the provisions of the Indian Succession Act, 1925, or any other law for the time being in force and applicable to Hindus."

Explanation : The interest of a male Hindu in a Mitakshara Coparcenary property or the interest of a member of a tarwad tavahi, illom, kutumba or kavaru shall, notwithstanding anything contained in this or any other law for the time being in force, be deemed to be property capable of being disposed of by him or by her within the meaning of this sub-section.

property gained prominence. In the nineteenth century definite recognition was given to the right of a Hindu to dispose of his property by will. The right of a Hindu to make a gift of his property was made the basis and was followed for fixing the restriction on the power to make a will.[42] Before the passing of this Act, a Hindu could dispose of by will his separate and self-acquired property. A Hindu governed by Dayabhaga law could dispose of by will his interest in the joint family property, but under Mitakshara law he could not do so in respect of his interest in the joint family property unless he was the sole surviving coparcener or he had got his interest separated by partition before the execution of the will. Even where he made a unilateral declaration of his intention to separate from the coparcenary and brought that fact to the knowledge of the other coparceners before his death, the will made by him of his interest in the coparcenary was held to be valid.[43] For execution and interpretation of wills the provisions of Indian Succession Act, 1925, are made applicable to Hindu wills also.

The proviso to section 6 and the Explanation to section 30 have given rise to some differences of opinion. Under the proviso the undivided interest of a Hindu would devolve by succession and not by survivorship only if he died leaving a female relative mentioned in class 1 or male relative claiming through such a female. A literal interpretation of the Explanation to section 30 seems to imply that it overrides section 6, giving unrestricted testamentary power to the Mitakshara coparcener irrespective of the heirs left by him.

Under Mitakshara law there are certain limitations on the right of a coparcener to deal with his undivided interest in the coparcenary property. He cannot make a gift or will of his undivided interest, and in Northern India he does not have the right to alienate his undivided interest even for valuable consideration. But a female owner has now absolute rights over the property acquired by her. As a consequence, a female mentioned in class I when she succeeds to an interest of a coparcener on his death, can deal with that interest without any constraints on her right of alienation. But the right of a male heir in class I is subject to certain restrictions on alienation *qua* his male

42. *Soorjeemoney* v. *Denobundee*, (1862) 8 MIA 123; *Tagore* v. *Tagore*, (1872) 9 Beng. L.R. 377.

43. *Raghavamma* v. *Chenchamma*, A.I.R. 1964 S.C. 136.

descendants. Moreover, a young widow without issue inherits the whole of the property of her husband including his interest in the joint family property. Having an absolute right in that property she may by her remarriage, take it to the second husband, which would, of course, not be to the liking of the husband's family. In Hindu families joint family funds have to be used disproportionately on marriages of daughters, sometimes voluntarily and many a time under compulsion, on dowries. On the death of the father, such a married daughter comes in as an equal sharer in the property of the father along with other sons and daughters. This leads to injustice to the sons and unmarried daughters of the deceased.

Maybe the legislature had these anomalous situations in mind when it gave to a coparcener the right to make a will of his coparcenary interest under section 30 of the Act. The need to make a will, it was thought, would arise only if a coparcener, visualizing the above-mentioned anomalous situations, tried to set things right during his life-time by exercising his power of testamentary disposition under section 30 of the Act. Considering that there are restrictions on the right of a coparcener to sell, mortgage or gift his undivided interest in the coparcenary property, it would again look anomalous that a coparcener is allowed an unrestricted right to dispose of by testamentary disposition what he could not do by any voluntary act during his life-time.[44]

The explanation to section 30 sets out the interest of a Mitakshara coparcener (and members of the other joint families mentioned in the section) but not of a member of a joint family governed by customary law (e.g. customary law of the Punjab), wherein the restrictions on disposition of the ancestral property are the same as that of a Hindu Mitakshara coparcener. It was held by the Punjab High Court that a person governed by the customary law of the Punjab has no right to bequeath his ancestral property and that section 30 had no application.[45]

44. See Chandrashekar Iyer, "Testamentary Succession under the Hindu Succession Act, 1956". A.I.R. 1957 J. 39; A.V. Subrahmanyerswara Sarma 'Testamentary capacity of a Mitakshara coparcener, Repugnancy between sections 6 and 30 of the Hindu Succession Act, 1956, A.I.R. 1957 J. 37.

45. *Kaur Singh* v. *Jaggar Singh*, A.I.R. 1961 Pb. 489; *Joginder Singh* v. *Kehar Singh*, A.I.R. 1965 Pb. 407 (F.B).

Explanation to section 30 needs amendment to avoid confusion and complications giving rise to a spate of litigations likely to result in course of time.

CONCLUSION

The Hindu Succession Act, 1950, has revolutionized the position of the Hindu female and it may be said that her position is better than that of a female governed by any other system of law. Traditions die hard, and it is alleged that in practice many women are either ignorant of their rights or are threatened and persuaded to forgo their rights under the Act. The Administration would do well to popularize and propagate the existence of these rights through the mass media and help females in effectively exercising rights given to them by law. Section 6 requires reconsideration by the legislature to do away statutorily with the right of survivorship and right by birth in Mitakshara joint family system. This will also go a long way towards removing the other anomalies in the Act. The list of heirs, too long at present, should be restricted to class I and class II heirs.

S. Venkataraman

CHAPTER IV

Intestate and Testamentary Succession among the Hindus

Succession signifies the devolution or rolling down of property from one person, on his demise, to another. It may be either testamentary or intestate. Testamentary succession gives effect to the intentions of the testator, as expressed in his will regarding the disposal of his property after his death. Intestate succession takes place in the absence of a will that is both valid and capable of taking effect. If a will fails even partially, the testator is deemed to have died intestate in respect of properties regarding which the will does not operate by reason of its partial invalidity.

"The law of succession is in truth an attempt to express the family in terms of property" remarks Richard O'Sullivan.[1] The family has other deeper and more enduring forms of expression than property, but there is an element of truth in the statement. Rules of succession are essentially conventional and therefore prone to change.

HISTORICAL BACKGROUND OF HINDU RULES OF SUCCESSION

Since ages Hindu life has centred round the joint family. Indeed, the joint family was the normal condition of Hindu society.[2] For centuries before the arrival of the British, succes-

1. O'Sullivan: The Inheritance of Common Law. Cf., Plucknett: A Concise History of the Common Law, 673 (Fourth edn.).
2. *Neelkisto* v. *Beer Chunder*, 12, MIA, 523, 540.

sion among Hindus throughout India, excepting Bengal, followed the lines laid down by Vijnaneswara in his work, the Mitakshara; in Bengal, it was regulated by the principles enunciated by Jimutavahana in his work, the Dayabhaga. Both systems had their moorings in religion, the Dayabhaga much more than the Mitakshara.

The Mitakshara defined heritage as wealth which devolved on another society by reason of his relationship to the owner. From this was deduced the principle of the right by birth of the son, son's son and son's son's son in the property of the holder; they were all regarded as extensions of himself, all being competent to render spiritual services to him. They, therefore, held the property in commensality. A right to claim partition, though originally non-existent, came to be recognized in course of time and eventually judicial decisions gave a member the right to separate himself from the family by merely making a unilateral declaration of his intention to separate.[3] According to the texts, so long as jointness held, property could not ordinarily be alienated even by the father. Other texts, which had recognized the father's power to alienate property acquired by him, were construed by the Privy Council as giving full power to the father to alienate his self-acquired property at his discretion.[4] A religio-juridical scaffolding was provided to the joint family. On the death of a member his interest devolved by survivorship. Women were, however, excluded. Property not held in common but in individual ownership devolved by succession. The Mitakshara was taken to recognize two distinct modes of devolution; survivorship and succession. The Dayabhaga, on the other hand, declared that the right of the heir to succeed arose not by birth but on the demise of the owner and property devolved by succession only.

A learned writer has observed that a proper understanding of the Mitakshara would show that it recognizes only one mode of devolution, a mode essentially akin to survivorship, and not two distinct modes.[5] Anyway, for all practical purposes, the position as stated above has become crystallized. Succession to property held in severalty was intimately linked with the

3. *Amritrao* v. *Mukundrao*, A.I.R. 1919 P.C. 91.
4. *Balwant* v. *Rani Kishore*, I.L.R. 20 All. 267 (P.C.).
5. I.S. Pawate: *Daya-Vibhaga*, 2nd edn., 1975, page 1.

principle: "He who inherits the property, also offers the pinda".[6] Manu declared: "To the nearest sapinda the inheritance next belongs".[7] The Mitakshara and the Dayabhaga interpreted the term 'pinda' differently, the former construing it as flesh and blood and the latter as balls of rice offered as oblations to the manes of the departed ancestors at the time of the sradha. The heirs under the Mitakshara were persons closely related by blood to the propositus; under the Dayabhaga, they were the persons most capable of exercising those religious rites which were considered to be beneficial to the deceased. Under both systems, physical and mental afflictions and diseases of a serious character, apostasy, etc., were held to disqualify a person from heirship.

A vedic enunciation that women were 'nirindriyas' and non-sharers made in the context of some sacrifice was held to postulate a general exclusion of women from succession except for special reasons, the widow, the daughter, the mother, the father's mother, and the father's father's mother. Though in the early vedic period there were indications of a theory of perfect equality between spouses,[8] the Smritis declared that a woman was never to seek independence and even her earnings would be at the disposal of her husband.[9] Manu allowed only 6 kinds of properties as a woman's stridhana.[10] Yajnavalkya in giving a list of stridhana property had added at the end of the word "adya" (and the rest). By a daring interpretation of that term, Vijnaneswara declared that stridhana should be understood in its etymological sense and it would include, in addition to the specifically enumerated items, property acquired by a woman by inheritance or at partition or by purchase, and that she would hold them in full ownership. The Dayabhaga, however, stuck to the orthodox position confining stridhana to the categories enumerated in the Smritis. According to the Dayabhaga, in the property coming by inheritance or partition, the woman would have only a limited estate. An inadequate appreciation of the place of the Mitakshara in matters of Hindu

6. Vishnu: XI–40.
7. Manu: IX, 187.
8. See *Vijayarangam* v. *Lakshman*, 8 Bom. H.C. 244.
9. Manu: VIII, 416; Dayabhaga, IX, 1, 19.
10. Manu: IX, 194, 195.

law practically throughout India led the Privy Council to reject the expanded definition of stridhana given in the Mitakshara and to affirm that women took only a limited estate in property obtained by inheritance or at partition.[11] The doctrine of woman's limited estate held sway in Hindu social life till its abolition by the Hindu Succession Act, 1956. Succession to stridhana was on totally different lines from succession to property of males. It depended on the status of the woman at her death—maiden, married or widow—the kind of property concerned, and the school of law to which she belonged. The rules were extremely confusing.

Generally, the systems of succession in vogue among Hindus were built with the male as the stock of descent, although in Kerala and some other places succession rested on the matriarchal principle with woman as stock of descent.

The Shastric Hindu law was never static. The Smritis were composed at different times, which enabled them to catch up with emerging facts, discard obsolete practices and incorporate new usages. The task of keeping law in harmony with contemporary life was continued by the great Commentators using such devices as the doctrine of *yuga dharma*, the principle of *loka vidvishtha* (jettisoning whatever was abhorrent to the public), the rule of *kali varjya* (practices prohibited in kali yuga), and principles of *yukti*, *nyaya* etc.

BRITISH ATTITUDE

Under the British rules, the role of Smritikars and Commentators passed on to the courts and the legislature. Judges tended to regard the Commentators as having said the last word on all the points dealt with by them. As observed by Mayne, "no voices were heard unless they came from the tombs". Legislative intervention was rare, hesitant and piecemeal because of fear of offending Hindu religious susceptibilities but also because of lack of legislator's credentials. Hindu law thus stopped growing and ceased to be responsive to new challenges. For nearly a century since 1850 there were few enactments bearing on Hindu intestate succession. The Freedom of Religion Act, 1850, which provided that so much of any law as impairs or affects any right of inheritance by reason of

11. *Bhugwandeen* v. *Myne Baee*, 11 MIA 487.

a person renouncing his religion or becoming a convert to another faith shall cease to be enforced as law. This negative legislation may have been designed to remove hurdles in the way of the prosetylzing activities of Christian missionaries. The Hindu Women's Rights to Property Act, 1937, though only a piecemeal legislation, had large repercussions on both Mitakshara and Dayabhaga laws of succession. The Act placed the widow, the widow of a predeceased son, and the widow of a predeceased son's predeceased son on par with the male issue of the last owner along with the male issue or in default of them. In regard to a person's separate property, the Act provided that (i) the widow along with the son would be entitled to the same share as a son; (ii) a predeceased son's widow would inherit in the same manner as the son; if there was no son surviving such a predeceased son, and, in like manner, as a son's son if there was surviving a son or son's son of such a predeceased son; (iii) the same provision *mutatis mutandis* applied to the widow of a predeceased son's predeceased son. A striking feature of the Act was that for the first time it directly arrested the operation of survivorship in Mitakshara coparcenary by substituting the widow in her husband's place with the right to claim partition. But in all cases, the widow would take only the limited interest known as a "Hindu woman's estate".

Though originally intended to cover all property, the legislation could apply by the time the Act came into force, only to non-agricultural property inasmuch as the Central legislature ceased to be, and the Provincial legislature became, vested with power to legislate on succession to agricultural property under the Government of India Act, 1935. The Act gave rise to a number of problems. For instance, the position of a widow taking the place of her husband in Mitakshara coparcenary *quoad* the family property was neither that of a coparcener nor that of a survivor. Nor could she be regarded as taking property by succession. In the circumstances, a majority of the High Courts regarded her interest as a special interest created by statute. Nevertheless, so long as she did not enforce partition she was held eligible for the benefit of survivorship on the death of a member along with the other coparceners, and if she herself died her interest would lapse to the other coparceners.

Whether unchastity, which disqualified a widow from taking as heir under Hindu law, would disqualify her from taking under the Act led to conflicting opinions.

IMPACT OF INDEPENDENCE

At the dawn of independence, rules of succession among Hindus were in a very unsatisfactory state. The difference between the Mitakshara and Dayabhaga systems, the existence of sub-schools serving to emphasise local differences, prevalence of the matriarchal system in some places, curbs on women's freedom to own property, perpetuation of the doctrine of women's limited estate, denial of equal rights with males in regard to heirship, the chaotic and complicated rules governing stridhana succession, the continued existence of Mitakshara coparcenary with its principles of right by birth of sons and devolution by survivorship which, however, well it might have served in other days when the country's economy was agricultural, had become unsuitable to a society switching over to industrial economy. The catalyst effect of the social goals envisaged in the Preamble to the Constitution, the guarantee of equality before law enshrined in Article 14, and abolition of discrimination on ground of birth or sex assured in Article 15 called for immediate overhaul of the rules of Hindu succession. The Hindu Succession Act, 1956, was Parliament's response to this.

SALIENT FEATURES OF THE HINDU SUCCESSION ACT, 1956

The Act seeks to provide a uniform law of succession to all Hindus. It has no links with religion. Blood relationship, tempered by natural love and affection, forms its base. All blood relations are heirs. None is disqualified from succeeding because of any disease, defect or deformity, or save as provided in the Act, on any other ground whatsoever. Women stand on a par with men in regard to heirship. Woman's limited estate is abolished. Rules of succession to woman's property are made simple, rational and uniform. Devolution by survivorship of the interest of a male Hindu in Mitakshara coparcenery is retained except where the intestate has died leaving a female heir of class I of the Schedule or a male representative of such heir in that class.[12] Unrestricted testamentary power is given to a Mitakshara coparcener in respect of his undivided interest.[13]

OUTLINES OF THE ACT

Classification of heirs as gotraja sapindas, somanodakas and bandhus under the Mitakshara and as sapindas, sakulyas and somanodakas under the Dayabhaga is scrapped, and the Act classifies the heirs into four groups: (i) heirs in class I of the Schedule; (ii) heirs in class II of the Schedule; (iii) agnates, and (iv) cognates. Property devolves in the first instance on the twelve heirs specified in class I, and failing them, upon the heirs in the second, third and fourth groups in that order as laid down in Sections 8 and 9. A striking feature is the provision for simultaneous succession by son, daughter, widow and mother among class I heirs. Eight others figure in this simultaneous succession by virtue of the doctrine of representation as applied to a predeceased son and a predeceased daughter. Class II heirs are listed under nine Entries and take in the order of the Entries. In Entry I, the father stands alone. In every other Entry certain persons are clubbed together for simultaneous succession. These are great-grandchildren, both male and female; brother and sister; sons and daughters of brother and sister; father's father and father's mother; stepmother and brother's widow; father's brother and sister; mother's father and mother's mother; and mother's brother and sister. Distribution among class I heirs is set out in Section 10, and among class II heirs in Section 11. Rules of preference relating to the order of succession among agnates and cognates, and those relating to the method of computing degrees of ascent and descent among them, are stated in Sections 12 and 13.

Section 14 provides that all property, in whatever manner acquired by a woman, will be held by her as full owner. Even property possessed by her at the commencement of the Act, whether acquired before or after the commencement, will be her absolute property. Succession to woman's property is regulated by Section 15, which groups the heirs under five Entries. Sons, daughters and children of predeceased son or

12. Section 6.
13. Section 30.

predeceased daughter, and husband are placed in Entry (a). They take first and simultaneously. In default of heirs in Entry (a) her property devolves on the heirs of her husband as stated in Entry (b), and failing them, the property goes to those in Entry (c), namely, her mother and father. In default of these, the property devolves on the heirs of the father (Entry d), and, finally, on the heirs of the mother (Entry e). Property inherited from her parents or from her husband or father-in-law shall, where the woman died without issue, revert to the heirs of the father in the former case and to her husband's heirs in the latter case. Computation of shares among the heirs shall be in accordance with the rules in Section 16.

The Act provides in Section 17 for modifications in the general scheme of succession in regard to Hindus governed formerly by systems founded on matriarchy.

Section 18 provides for preference of full blood to half blood, other things being equal. Section 19 states that normally coheirs shall take per capita and as tenants-in-common. Under Section 20, a child in the womb, if born alive, shall have the same right to inherit property as if it had been born before the death of the intestate. Section 21 states that the presumption in case of simultaneous deaths is, in the absence of evidence contra, that the younger survived the elder. Section 22 confers a preferential right analogous to a right of presumption in cases of devolution of property upon two or more heirs in class I of the Schedule. Section 23 makes special provision in respect of dwelling houses wholly occupied by members of the family of the intestate, restricting the right of a female heir in class I to claim partition so long as the male heirs in that class do not choose to effect a partition of the same. A right of residence is, however, given to a daughter other than one who is married and living with her husband.

WORKING OF THE ACT

The fundamental objective of uniform rules of succession for Hindus remains unrealised because of the Act itself. The Act does not apply to all Hindus nor to all property of a Hindu. Scheduled Castes and Scheduled Tribes stay outside the Act till the Central Government by notification in the Official Gazette otherwise provides (Section 2(2)). Again, the

Act does not govern succession to property of Hindu marrying under the Special Marriage Act or of the issue of such marriages (Section 5(1)). Devolution of tenancy rights in agricultural property is not affected by the Act (Section 4 (2)). Presumably, this is because tenancy rights are more closely allied to property rights than to personal rights, and because agricultural laws are a State subject. But a law providing for devolution of tenancy rights is essentially a law relating to succession which is within the competence of the Centre. To leave it to State legislation may result in perpetuating discrimination against females[14] or making it even more discriminatory.[15] Tenancy rights are not defined anywhere and it is possible for State legislation to so define the expression as to cover all interests in or relating to agricultural lands thereby keeping them out of the operation of the Hindu Succession Act.[16] Some States may not provide for devolution of tenancy rights in which case the personal law will step in; and where they have made such a provision each State may have chalked out a different line.

The retention of Mitakshara coparcenary (*vide* Section 6) not only perpetuates two different modes of devolution of property, but also effectively sustains discrimination and unequal rights between males and females. The son's right by birth operates to the prejudice of the daughter. For instance, if a deceased leaves behind family property worth a lakh of rupees and a son and a daughter, the son will take Rs. 75,000—Rs. 50,000 in his own right and Rs. 25,000 as heir to his father—whereas the daughter will get only Rs. 25,000. The plenary testamentary power given to a coparcener, instead of being used to set right or reduce the disparity between son and daughter, has been often used, to the writer's knowledge, to put the coparcenary interest of the testator beyond the reach of the daughter so as to deprive her of the share to which is

14. *Palak Dahri* v. *Dy. Director of Consolidation*, A.I.R. 1975 All. 410 (Section 30 of Hindu Succession Act cannot be invoked and bhumidhari cannot dispose of her interest by will).
15. *See* Section 171, U.P. Zamindari Abolition and Land Reform Act, 1951.
16. *Nahar* v, *Mst. Dukadhin*, A.I.R. 1974 (tenancy rights include bhumiswamin rights). *Uma Shankar* v. *Dy. Director of Consolidation*, A.I.R. 1973 All. 407 (tenancy rights include bhumidhari rights).

entitled under the proviso to Section 6. Again, nothing prevents a person from renouncing his interest in Mitakshara coparcenary in favour of the male coparceners, leaving the daughter high and dry. Another powerful weapon in his hands is his right to convert his self-acquisitions into corparcenary property. It is a matter of mere volition, and no formality or written instrument is needed. These devices could be used effectively by a father desiring to favour his son at the expense of his daughter.

The Mitakshara coparcenary is no longer what it was; its homogeneous character has been lost; Sapinda relationship through a Hindu marriage does not determine its composition. A son born to a Hindu by a Christian wife (married under the Special Marriage Act) but brought up as a Hindu can now be a member of Mitakshara coparcenary headed by his father.[17] Again every one of its special incidents—such as the right to partition, the right to restrain alienation, devolution by survivorship—has been eroded so much that a learned judge described it as a tottering structure liable to be sent toppling down at one blow and no one to shed a tear.[18] Nor can there be now any objection, based on the utility of the institution or sentiment, to its abolition. Individualistic trends within coparcenary have been steadily rising since the passing of the Hindu Gains of Learning Act, 1930. As to sentiment, even the most deep-rooted traditions have to yield to the relentless march of time.

Under the proviso to Section 6, any of the female heirs and a daughter's son specified in the proviso read with class I of the Schedule can succeed not merely to the separate property of the deceased but also to his interest in coparcenary property. Explanation I to the section provides that the interest of the deceased coparcener shall be deemed to be the share that would have been allotted to him if a partition had taken place immediately before his death irrespective of whether or not he was entitled to claim partition. The computation of such share depends on the number of persons entitled to shares if partition had in fact then taken place. The persons entitled to shares have

17. *Commissioner of Wealth Tax* v. *Sridharan*, (1976) 2 S.C.J. 482.
18. Per Viswanatha Sastri J., in *Paramanakam* v. *Sivaraman*, A.I.R. 1952 Mad. 419 (FB).

to be ascertained according to pure Hindu law inasmuch as the Act itself has not provided any guidelines. While incorporating the concept of notional partition in the definition of the interest of a Mitakshara coparcener in Explanation I, the Legislature has missed the fact that under the rules of partition in Bombay and North India, at a partition between father and son, the father's wife is entitled to an equal share with the son, whereas in South India she is not so entitled. A full bench of the Bombay High Court has affirmed that the right of the father's widow to a share is unaffected by anything in the Hindu Succession Act, as Section 6 provides for determining the interest of the deceased coparcener at partition.[19] In North India, the interest of the deceased coparcener that will pass under Section 6 proviso (as exemplified in the above illustration) is one-third, and in South India, one-half. The quantum taken by a daughter of the deceased by way of succession will thus vary according as the parties are governed by the rules of the North or the South. This detracts from the uniformity of law within the regions following the Mitakshara. It also discriminates between two equal heirs by giving an advantage to the mother of the deceased against his daughter in sharing his family property in North India.

Yet another approach to Section 6 proviso and the Explanations is seen in a case from Mysore.[20] In a joint family the father died in 1923 leaving his widow (W) and two sons. In 1961 one of the sons died leaving two widows (W1) and (W2), who sued for partition and possession of a moiety of the properties of the deceased. Under the Hindu law applicable to the parties, had the brothers separated immediately before the death of the deceased, W also would have got a share, with the result that the share of the deceased would have been one-third, liable, too, to be shared between W1, W2, and W. The Mysore High Court, invoking the principle behind Explanation II excluding a separated member from taking under the proviso, held that inasmuch as the mother was entitled to a share at the notional partition she could take only just that and was not

19. *Sushilabai* v *Narayan Rao*, A.I.R. 1975 Bom. 257 (FB); see also *Ananda Naik* v. *Haribandhu Naik*, A.I.R. 1967 Orissa 194; *Mallava* v. *Parvatevva* (1970) 2 Mys. L.J. 571.

20. *Sidrappa* v. *Laxmi Bai*, (1965) 1 Mys. L.J. 625.

competent to take again on the death of her son as she should be deemed to have separated under the statutory fiction. The reliance on Explanation II to reach the particular conclusion is unwarranted in view of the principle that an exception ought not to be stretched. Also, Explanation II contemplates a volitional and not notional separation. The words used are "has separated himself".

In implementing the proviso to Section 6, another anomaly may be noted. Suppose a coparcener makes a gift of his interest and dies. If he had left a son, son's son or son's son's son, the gift will not bind the latter as a coparcener cannot make a gift under the Mitakshara law. If, however, the coparcener had left along with his son a class I female heir, it is doubtful if the gift could at all be challenged in view of the principle that the heir cannot repudiate a transaction of the deceased unless the ground of attack was open to the deceased himself if alive. The object of the proviso to benefit female heirs will have been defeated by the operation of the general law principle.

Section 6 articulates the basic policy of intestate succession as formulated by the legislature. It classifies heirs into four groups and introduces simultaneous succession by class I heirs with equal rights to the sharers in quantum as well as quality. The exclusion of father and the inclusion of a person like the widow of a predeceased son's predeceased son may evoke criticism. Close blood relationship and natural affection would point to the inclusion and not to the exclusion of the father. The father is accorded a special status as reflected in his managership of joint family in the law of debts etc. There is no justification for excluding him. The widow of a predeceased son's predeceased son is found only in a few cases and her presence may not result in injustice. The mother's taking as full owner as a class I heir, according to some, may result in injustice to the children of the original holder, since on her death the share she had inherited from her son would pass not to those children only but also to her other heirs. A suggestion has been made that the mother should have only a limited estate in such property. This would flout the policy of giving absolute rights to females in all kinds of property and make the mother an inferior heir.

Strange results may ensure from the language used in

Section 15(1)(a) which states that sons and daughters and husband will be the first heirs to a woman's property. Husband, in the context, obviously refers to a living husband. Sons and daughters will include, where the woman had married more than once, her children by both marriages. If a person died leaving his wife and children, the widow would have a share equal to that of a child. If the widow remarries, has children by the second marriage and dies, her property, including what she got as her first husband's heir, will devolve not only on her children by both marriages *but also an her second husband*, a result inconsistent with the sentiment behind Section 15(2).

The provision in Section 23 regarding dwelling house is a statutory novelty that tends to discriminate against daughters by restricting their right to demand partition. Even where there is only a single male heir, he may successfully obstruct the right of the female heir to have a partition. The provision that a married daughter living with her husband has no right to reside in the family dwelling house even though she is co-owner along with the other heirs, is equally discriminatory. Again, the reference in the section to class I heirs of a female intestate is clumsy in that there is no such classification, as in the case of a male.

TESTAMENTARY SUCCESSION AND ITS BACKGROUND

A will is a solemn document by which a dead man entrusts to the living the carrying out of his wishes. Testamentary succession was not known to Hindus in early times. Under the influence of English concepts, courts recognized, first in Bengal where freedom of alienation of property was a normal feature in Hindu life, a person's power to dispose of property by will. Later, such power was recognized outside Bengal in respect of self-acquired or separate property of a Hindu.[21] Interest in coparcenary property could not, however, be conveyed by will since a coparcener had no disposing power over it. Under Section 38 of the Hindu Succession Act, 1956, a coparcener now possesses the power to dispose of such interest by will.

21. *M. Lachmia* v *Jagannadha Rao*, 2 MIA 54; *Nagalutchmee* v. *Nadaraja*, 6 MIA 309.

The Hindu Wills Act, 1870, insisted on written wills in respect to immovable property made after September 1, 1870 if the property was situated within Bengal or within the limits of the ordinary original civil jurisdiction of the High Courts in Madras and Bombay. An amendment to the Indian Succession Act, 1925, made in 1926, required every Hindu will made after January 1, 1927, to be in writing, signed by the testator, and attested by two witnesses.

REQUIREMENTS OF A VALID WILL

Every Hindu of sound mind and not a minor, whether male or female, can make a will. Writing is necessary though not registration. The legatee may be any person. A bequest may be made to an unborn person provided it does not offend the rule against perpetuities in Section 114 of the Indian Succession Act. Bequests for religious and charitable purposes stand outside the rule. Any condition restraining absolute alienation or partition of the property or interest absolutely conveyed is invalid. The bequest will take effect free from such restriction. A testator cannot create by his will a new line of inheritance inconsistent with the general law of inheritance.[22] A bequest may be made in favour of a class of persons answering to and included in a general description. The share of each member will depend upon the ultimate number of persons in the class at the relevant point of time. If, in regard to some members of the class, the bequest fails for offending the rule against perpetuities, the bequest will remain good as regards the rest.

REVOCATION AND ALTERATION OF WILLS

A will may be revoked or altered by the testator at any time and as often as he wants before his death, in accordance with Sections 70 and 71 of the Indian Succession Act. A will made by a Hindu is not revoked by his subsequent marriage, as in the case of Christians.

PROBATE AND LETTERS OF ADMINISTRATION

Ordinarily, the testator appoints by his will a person as executor to see the will carried into effect. No right can be established as executor or legatee in a court of law unless a

22. *Tagore* v. *Tagore*, 9 Beng. L.R. 377 (P.C.)

competent court shall have granted a probate of the will. Probate is granted on proof that the written instrument purporting to be the will of the deceased is indeed his lawful act. Probate is the official copy of the will with the certificate of its having been proved. If no executor has been appointed under the will, letters of administration are issued by the court. The executor or administrator of a deceased Hindu is his legal representative for all purposes and the entire estate of the deceased is vested in him.

CONSTRUCTION OF WILLS

The intention of the testator rules. Primarily the words used are considered, but their meaning may be affected by the surrounding circumstances. The court is "entitled to put itself in the testator's armchair" for this purpose. The old view was that "in construing a will . . . it may be assumed that a Hindu generally desires that an estate, especially an ancestral estate, shall be retained in his family, and it may be assumed that a Hindu knows that as a general rule women do not take absolute estates of inheritance which they are enabled to alienate".[23] The wheel has now turned full circle. The old assumptions have been jettisoned. After the enactment of the Hindu Succession Act, courts will be justified in assuming that a testator was fully aware of the radical changes effected in the Hindu law of succession and the spirit behind Section 14 of that Act—namely, that women take property in whatever manner acquired in full ownership.

CONCLUSIONS AND SUGGESTIONS

The Hindu Succession Act has been in force for just over two decades. Over the ground covered by it the Act is exclusive. But Mitakshara succession remains interlaced with Mitakshara Coparcenary and Partition laws. The broblems in implementing the provisions of the Hindu Succession Act have arisen mostly because of the difficulty in fitting the new Succession Act principles into the complicated and integrated structure of Hindu joint family law with its old principles. This is noticed particularly in operation of Section 6. The son's right by birth is a standing grievance of the daughter. Unless women's

23. *Mahomed Shamsul* v. *Shewakram*, 2 IA 7.

equal economic and property rights are fully recognized, they would continue to be treated as inferior to menfolk. Equality can be achieved by abolishing the ancient formula of right by birth and devolution by survivorship. The time is now ripe for it. Such a step will not only efface the discrimination between son and daughter, but will also ensure uniform laws of succession. A provision on the following lines is recommended:

(1) The Mitakshara Coparcenary with its incidents be abolished forthwith.

(2) In particular, and without prejudice to the generality of the foregoing provision, no Hindu may, except as otherwise provided in this Act, have any right to or interest in (a) the property held by any person during his lifetime solely by reason of birth in the family, or (b) the property belonging to a joint family based on survivorship.

(3) The provision in Section 4(2) relating to devolution of tenancy rights may lead to mischievous results and the exemption from the operation of the Hindu Succession Act may be scrapped.

(4) Father must be included in the list of simultaneous heirs in class I.

(5) Section 15(2) should incorporate a clause (c) providing that any property inherited by a female Hindu, married more than once, from any of her husbands shall devolve in the absence of any son or daughter of the deceased (including the children of any predeceased son or daughter) not upon the other heirs referred to in sub-section (1) in the order specified therein, but upon the heirs of that husband.

(6) Section 23 in respect of dwelling houses may be deleted.

It is desirable that a specified fraction of the property of a Hindu is kept beyond his testamentary power so as not to disappoint the expectations entertained by the heirs at law or defeat the reasonable claims for maintenance of any dependent of the testator who takes no benefit under the will, as when the testator leaves his property to outsiders and the benefit of Section 22 of the Hindu Adoptions and Maintenance Act, 1956, may not be available to him or her.

S.A. Ali

CHAPTER V

Inheritance Among Indian Muslims

None shall inherit but he who smites with spear.

—Ancient Arab saying

ORIGINS OF THE ISLAMIC LAW OF INHERITANCE

The pre-Islamic Arabs, locked in ceaseless inter-tribal wars, a vivid portrayal of which is to be found in the famous *Musaddas* of Khwajah Altaf Hussain Hali, regarded distribution of property as a compensation for active participation in wars. Women and children were thus excluded, and inheritance became a simple linear agnatic rule of thumb. This also provided the rationale for what we now technically call the 'case of the predeceased son', in other words, the denial to a male child a share in the property of his paternal grandfather simply because his father is dead—a practice which, in the twentieth-century notion of justice, looks both bizarre and repugnant. The practice of allowing only male members to inherit property possibly stemmed from a deep unconscious desire to prevent its fragmentation and erosion, which would be inevitable if women were permitted a share. It is a universal human desire, whether conscious or unconscious, to see that one's property remains as intact as possible and within the family, not only in one's own lifetime but even after death. The desire is rooted in the herd instinct, and manifests itself in all traditional societies. In India, it has taken the form of the joint family system; in Malaysia, the *adat* law of joint property. Interestingly, the same basic desire has sometimes led the people in opposite directions, as, for example, in adoption. The ancient practice of adopting a child appears to have arisen out of the need to replace a male missing link that would perpetuate the family and look after its property. But while other societies adopted children so that they could inherit the property and defend it better, the Arabs denied an adopted child the right to inheritance, as it involved the risk of the adopted child walking away with his share. Some writers, on the basis of the *Qur'anic* verse

> 33: *4* Nor has He made those whom you assert (to be) your sons,*

have concluded that pre-Islamic Arabs regarded the adopted son as a real son. I am inclined to think that such a view or practice was not common. There may have been stray cases of families following the Roman custom of adopting children for the purpose of inheritance. But, by and large, the concept of adoption is alien to the Judeo-Christian-Islamic tradition. The Hebrew Law Codes are silent on the practice of adoption, while in the Greek Testament it occurs only in the Pauline Epistles. In fact, the practice of adoption would have endangered the principle of maintaining property in the possession of the original tribe ...Among the Israëlites, the risk of childlessness was met in the earlier period by polygamy, and later by facility of divorce.[1]

The battle of Uhud in 3 A.H. occasioned the revelation of the rules of inheritance that we find in the fourth chapter of the *Qur'an*. The battle had left a large number of widows and orphans bereft of all means of sustenance. The inheritance law made women eligible for inheritance, and fixed specific shares for both male and female relatives. The chapter, appropriately called 'The Women', begins with the observation that men and women were created from a single being. This prepared the people psychologically to accept the right of women to inheritance. It then calls attention to orphans,[2] and reverts to the

* Maulana Muhammad Ali's translation has been used throughout.

1. See the article 'Adoption' in *Encyclopaedia of Religion and Ethics*, Vol. I, ed. by James Hastings. Edinburgh, 1908.
2. Polygamy was allowed to ensure care of a large number of orphans that a family might adopt, and not for its own sake. See *Qur'an* 4:3: "And if you fear that you cannot do justice to orphans, marry such women as seem good to you, two or three, or four; but if you fear that you will not do justice, then (marry) only one or that which your right hands possess. This is more proper that you may not do injustice."

rights of women, urging that they be given the bride-price as a free gift. It goes back to the subject of orphans, and, advancing the rights of women in stages, declares that

> For men is a share of what the parents and the near relatives leave, and for women a share of what the parents and the near relatives leave, whether it be little or much—an appointed share. (4:7)

The foundation for inheritance by women has been laid by this verse, though the quantum is left unspecified. The next three verses bring in the orphans again, and then come those two capital verses that are the pivot on which Islamic law of inheritance revolves:

> Allah enjoins you concerning your children: for the male is the equal of the portion of two females; but if there be more than two females, two-thirds of what the deceased leaves is theirs; and if there be one, for her is the half. And as for his parents, for each of them is the sixth of what he leaves, if he has a child; but if he has no child and (only) his two parents inherit him, for his mother is the sixth, after (payment of) a bequest he may have bequeathed or debt. Your parents and your children, you know not which of them is the nearer to you in benefit. This is an ordinance from Allah. Allah is surely ever Knowing, Wise.
>
> And yours is half of what your wives leave if they have no child; but if they have a child, your share is a fourth of what they leave after (payment of) any bequest they may have bequeathed or a debt; and theirs is the fourth of what you leave if you have no child, but if you have a child, their share is the eighth of what you leave after (payment of) a bequest you may have bequeathed or a debt. (4: *11-12*)

To distribute property strictly in accordance with the above revealed rules is the duty of every Muslim. Inheritance has thus been, along with *statut personnel* and *waqf*, as observed by Schacht, "in the conscience of Muslims, more closely connected with religion than other legal matters, and therefore generally ruled by Islamic law".[3]

Islamic law is, in principle, divine law. It is the manifestation of the Will of God. The *Qur'an* and the traditions of the Prophet offer a broad legal framework within which to work

3. Joseph Schacht, *An Introduction to Islamic Law*, London, 1964, p.76.

out details for specific problems, exercising reason in the absence of precedent. The Prophet himself, in a famous dialogue with a judge called Mu'adh bin Jabal approved of reason as a basis of sound judgement:

The Prophet : According to what shall you judge?
Mu'adh : According to the Book of God.
The Prophet : And if you find nothing there?
Mu'adh : According to the traditions of the Messenger of God.
The Prophet : And if you find nothing there?
Mu'adh : According to my reason.
The Prophet : Praise God who endows His Messenger's messenger with what His Messenger approves.

Iman Shafi'i (*d.* A.D. 820), the founder of the school of Islamic law that bears his name, said: "One who seeks knowledge without substantiation and argument is like the wood-gatherer at night who carries unknowingly a snake in the sheaf." Iman Ahmad bin Hanbal (*d.* A.D. 855), the founder of another school of Islamic law, warned: "Do not follow anyone unquestioningly in religious matters (excepting the Prophet and his companions)."

In fact, a great deal of reasoning and serious thinking have gone into the codification of Islamic law, finding solutions to all kinds of problems along the divinely ordained principles. "The grand superstructure of Islamic jurisprudence," says Syed Ameer Ali, "stands on the Koranic laws and the traditional sayings of the Prophet, but much of the coping stone was supplied at Bagdad, in Bokhara, in Syria, in Andalusia and Persia."[4]

The subject of inheritance received from the servants of Islamic jurisprudence far greater attention than did any other branch of Islamic law, as the great number of extant treatises on the subject testify. This was in keeping with a well-known saying of the Prophet that the laws of inheritance constitute half the knowledge, and in keeping also with the mundane demands—property often being a cause of friction.[5] In codifying

4. Syed Ameer Ali, Mahomedan Law (Tagore Law Lectures, 1884), Vol. I, Calcutta, 1912, p. 5.
5. The last Mughal king, Bahadur Shah Zafar, wrote: *Ba chashm-i ghaur jo dekha Zafar zamane men/to ya zamin ka ya zar ka ya hai zan ka*

the Islamic law of inheritance, they took great pains and went to great lengths, as, for example, in trying to determine whether a hermaphrodite was closer to male or a female.[6] Even a modern western scholar extols the care with which they have dealt with the subject:

> There is no aspect of the law in which the logical and technical excellences of the Islamic system are more advantageously displayed than in the law of inheritance.[7]

SCHOOLS OF ISLAMIC JURISPRUDENCE

We find today eight major schools of Islamic jurisprudence in the world. Four of them are Sunni, three—Ithna 'Asheri, Isma'ili and Zaidi—are Shi'a and the last one is Ibadi, which is followed by people in Oman and in certain parts of Algeria. The Sunni schools, Hanafi, Maliki, Shafi'i and Hanbali—all named after their founders—arose during the latter part of the eighth and the earlier part of the ninth century, and have continued to command till this day the allegiance of a vast majority of Muslims. The latitude that Islam offers for interpretation and extension of its laws according to the exigencies of time and circumstances have permitted these schools to take different stands, more noticeable in matters relating to inheritance. But even so, there is no divergence on fundamental principles as laid down in the *Qur'an*.

The school that predominates is the school founded by Imam Abu Hanifa (*d*. A.D. 767). It is this Hanafi school which a majority of Indian Muslims follows. A small minority of Sunni Muslims in South India, particularly in Kerala and Malabar, follows the Shafi'i school. Others follow the Shi'a law, established, long after the introduction of Hanafi law by Mahmud Ghaznawi, with the help of some South Indian and Moghul rulers and the Nawabs of Oudh. We shall first see the Hanafi formulation of the laws of inheritance, and then find out in what ways they differ from the Shi'a laws.

---

fasad (Look to the world, Zafar, carefully/And you will discover that all disturbances are rooted in land, wealth and women).

6. See *Hadaya*, translated by C. Hamilton, Lahore, 1957, for a fuller discussion.
7. J.N.D. Anderson, *Islamic Law in the Modern World*, London, 1959, p. 59.

As the *Qur'anic* verses cited above show, the property, by Arab customary law confined to direct male descendants was parcelled out among a large number of family members. This was justified on the ground that division of property, far from weakening the family's position, as was believed earlier led to greater family cohesion. "The property," remarks Muhammad Abu Zahra, "which a person owns in his life reverts to his family after his death. This is because the life of the family is considered to be an extension of his life, because the benefits in the family are mutual, and because cooperation between the members is an established thing which is made a duty by Islam."[8]

It was never the intention of Islam that the family property should remain within the family. We read in the *Qur'an*:

> It is prescribed for you, when death approaches one of you, if he leaves behind wealth for parents and near relatives, to make a bequest in a kindly manner; it is incumbent upon the dutiful. (2: *180*).

Bequest or *wasiyya*, according to Sunni law—but not according to Ithna 'Ashari law—can be only in favour of those who are not legal heirs, for the shares of the legal heirs are fixed. Traditions also support the view that bequests are for non-heirs. Abu Imama said: "I heard the Prophet say: 'Allah has already given to each entitled relative his proper entitlement. Therefore, no bequest in favour of a legal heir'. "[9] It is fortified by another tradition in the *Sahih* of Bukhari, reported by Sa'd Ibn Abi Waqqas, that bequests are not for relatives. One can make a bequest to any one not entitled to a share in one's inheritance, whether a Muslim or a non-Muslim, and such a bequest would be valid according to all schools of law. These schools, excepting the Shafi'i school, even recognize an apostate as a beneficiary of a bequest. The only condition is that *one cannot give in bequest more than one-third of the property*.

The *wasiyya*, an old Arab practice (see *Qur'an* 36:*50*), seems to have been on the wane in the Prophet's time. That is why the Arabs are exhorted in the *Qur'an* and in the traditions to

8. Muhammad Abu Zahra, 'Family Law' in *Law in the Middle East*, Ed. Majid Khadduri, Washington, 1955, p. 160.
9. Cited by N.J. Coulson, *Succession in the Muslim Family*, London, 1971, p. 214.

make bequests. A tradition in the *Sahih* of Bukhari asks people to write down their bequests and keep them under the pillow at the time of retiring. The *wasiyya* in pre-Islamic Arabia was not so much concerned with the distribution of property as with instructions to survivors,[10] but with the rise of Islam it assumed the form of instructions for the disposal of property within the prescribed limits.

It will be seen from the above discussion that one has the option to give away one-third of one's property to any person one likes, if that person is not otherwise entitled to a share in the inheritance; this is called *khilafa ikhtiariyya* or optional succession—option resting both with the giver and with the taker, the remaining two-thirds of the property must go to the heirs. This is *khilafa i jabariyya* or compulsory succession—the inheritors being duty bound to accept their shares that carry no liability.

We shall now proceed to examine how compulsory succession has been worked out in the Hanafi law and how it has been applied in India.

ISLAMIC LAW OF INHERITANCE IN INDIA

Islamic law, encompassing crimes, slavery, evidence, etc., which had been in vogue in India, though never in its totality, during Muslim rule was thrown into disarray during the British regime. Important matters were adjudicated upon by British magistrates and judges in accordance with the English law or local customary law, and religious matters and ceremonies were left to the *qadis*, *muftis*, *sadr-amin* and *sadr al-sudur*. Worse, there was no uniformity in the application of customary law and personal law. This anomaly was removed to some extent in 1937 when the Muslim Personal Law (Shari'at) Application Act No. 26 was passed. This law governs both Sunnis and Shi'as in specified matters, including inheritance, but excluding charities and charitable institutions, charitable and religious endowments, and all agricultural land which continues to be governed by custom, except in two States—Andhra Pradesh and Tamilnadu—where by later legislation

10. See article 'Wasiyya' in *Shorter Encyclopaedia of Islam*, ed. H.A.R. Gibb and J.H. Kramers, Leidan/London, 1953, p. 632.

agricultural land was brought under the purview of the Act.[11] A year later, in 1938, the Cutchi Memons, who are Hanafi and who were governed by the Hindu customary law in inheritance —like the Mapillas who followed the customary law of succession until the Muslim Personal law became applicable to them by the Mapilla Succession Act of 1918 and the Mapilla Wills Act of 1928—but who by an Act of 1920 had been given the option of filing a declaration that they wanted to be governed by Islamic law, were brought under the purview of the Muslim Personal Law by the Cutchi Memons Act X which laid down that "all Cutchi Memons shall in matter of succession and inheritance be governed by the Mohammedan law." Thus all Indian Muslims, in so far as succession and inheritance are concerned, are now governed by the Muslim Personal Law (Shari'at) Application Act, excepting those Muslims who marry under Special Marriage Act, 1954, and to whom Indian Succession Act, 1925 applies.

Determining inheritance shares according to Hanafi law is complicated, and in India it is subject to the provisions of other Acts. We cannot, therefore, go into all the details but have to be content with a broad outline of how shares are allotted.

Hanafi law divides those who can succeed to the estate of a deceased Muslim into four classes: (i) Sharers, (ii) Residuaries, (iii) Distant Kindred, (iv) Unrelated Successors.

Sharers: There are 12 sharers, or *Qur'anic* heirs. Nine of them are mentioned in the *Qur'an* (see 4: *11-12* quoted above) and three (grandfather, grandmother and grand-daughter) have been added by the traditions, *qiyas* or the principle of analogy, and *i jma'* or consensus. They are: (i) Descendants—daughter, son's daughter; (ii) Ascendants—father, grandfather, mother, grandmother; (iii) Collaterals—sister, consanguine sister, uterine brother, uterine sister; (iv) Heirs by affinity—husband, wife.

It will be noted that of these twelve sharers, eight are female who, along with the husband and uterine brother, were not entitled to any share under the pre-Islamic tribal law. The *Qur'an has fixed for them the following shares: 2/3, 1/2, 1/6, 1/3, 1/4, 1/8. The exact shares that would accrue to the sharers*

11. See Madras Act XVIII of 1949 and its amendment by Act XXVI of 1957; and Andhra Pradesh Act VIII of 1949.

would depend upon their number, and in working out the shares one has to keep in mind, apart from conditions that affect a person's succession, three broad rules:

(i) Descendants get preference over ascendants[12] (parents excluded and bracketed with descendants);

(ii) Higher ascendants go with the nearest collaterals;

(iii) Those nearer get preference over those remote.

It should also be noted that in certain circumstances six of the sharers become residuaries: father, nearest grandfather, daughter, son's daughter, sister and consanguine sister.

Residuaries: The residuaries are those entitled to a prescribed share in any residue left after the sharers have been allotted their shares, or in the whole estate if there is no sharer. The residuaries are: (i) male and female children of the deceased; (ii) male and female children of the son of the deceased; (iii) male and female children of the father of the deceased; (iv) male descendants of the grandfather in the agnatic line.

The son, although a residuary, is treated like a sharer—in fact sometimes more than a sharer—and is not excluded from inheritance. He is given a share either by excluding certain sharers (brothers, sisters, son's daughters), or by reducing the shares of certain sharers (husband, wife and mother) in such a way, that a residue is left over, or by reducing the daughter, a sharer, to the status of a residuary.

If there is a residue and no residuaries, it does not go to the distant kindred but is returned to the sharers in proportion to their shares, or given *in toto* to the lone sharer. This is called the 'Doctrine of Return' or *radd*, which is resorted to when the shares of the sharer do not add up to unity and a residue is left over. Husband and wife are an exception to this rule. As long as there is any other heir either among the sharers or among the distant kindred, the husband or the wife is not entitled to the residue, which otherwise goes to him or her.

If all the residuaries belong to one sex, the residue is distributed among them equally; if they are mixed, the *Qur'anic* rule

12. In an interesting study made by Rand Corporation in the United States in 1965, it was suggested that if the USA survived the third world war, it would "be better off without old and feeble" people, and that therefore it should make no provision for the care of the old.

of the male getting double the share of a female applies. In determining the order of priority, once more three rules have to be observed:

(i) descendants exclude all residuaries;
(ii) ascendants exclude all residuaries, excepting the descendants;
(iii) descendants of the nearer ascendants exclude those of the remote ascendants.

In allotting shares to the sharers and the residuaries it may sometimes be found that the shares add up to more than a unity. In such a case, one applies the 'Doctrine of Increase' or '*aul*—an ingenious device of reducing the shares—without their appearing to have been reduced as will be clear from a story later—to a common denominator which is increased to become the equivalent of the sum of the numerators, the numerators themselves remaining undisturbed. The fourth caliph 'Ali is credited with having originated this doctrine when once, while he was delivering a sermon from the *minbar* in a mosque, he was asked how much would a widow, whose husband had left behind his parents and two daughters, inherit. He promptly replied: "The wife's one-eighth becomes one-ninth." The event is famous as *al-Minbariyya*, and the formula, in accordance with the arithmetical rule described above, works out as follows:

Sharers	*Shares*		*Common denominator*		*By 'aul*
Father	1/6	=	4/24	=	4/27
Mother	1/6	=	4/24	=	4/27
Daughter	2/3	=	16/24	=	16/27
Wife	1/8	=	3/24	=	3/27

A more spectacular application of the doctrine of '*aul* by Caliph 'Ali is found in the story of a man leaving seventeen camels which were to be distributed among three persons in the proportion of 1/2, 1/3 and 1/9. He asked the first person, whose share amounted to 1/2 of 17 or less than 9, whether he would be happy if he got full nine camels. He said yes. Then the next man was asked whether he would be happy if he got six camels, which was more than his share of 1/3 of 17. He said yes. Then third man was asked the same question, and he also nodded yes. Caliph 'Ali then sent for a camel from the *bait al-mal*, added it to the string of the 17 camels, gave the first person 9 camels (1/2), the second 6 (1/3) and the third 2 (1/9) and sent the remaining camel back to the *bait al-mal*.

Distant Kindred: The distant kindred are persons related by blood, whether male or female, who do not figure as sharers or residuaries. They succeed when there are no sharers and residuaries, and get the residue when the husband or the wife is the only heir out of the sharers or residuaries as explained above.

In determining the order of priority, the same three rules as given for the residuaries apply. Thus all distant kindred are divided into four classes which, in order of priority, are: (i) descendants, (ii) ascendants, (iii) descendants of the parents, (iv) descendants of the grandparents.

In allotting shares to the distant kindred, there is a conflict of opinion between the Hanafi jurists, Imam Abu 'Abdullah Muhammad al-Shaibani (*d.* A.D. 805) and Abu Yusuf (*d.* A.D. 798)—both disciples of Imam Abu Hanifa—the former taking into consideration the blood and sex of the ancestral links, and the latter going by the blood and sex of the entitled heirs alone. This results in a considerable difference in shares. Indian courts have accepted the view of Imam Muhammad al-Shaibani in allotting shares to the distant kindred, holding it to be nearer to the principle of justice, equity and good conscience.

Unrelated Successors: In the absence of sharers, residuaries and distant kindred, the estate goes, by virtue of *wala'*[13] or friendship to—in that order—

(a) a person who may have entered into a contract with the deceased to assist him by paying any amount on his behalf, like fine or ransom; or, in the absence of such a person, to,

(b) a kinsman, acknowledged as such by the deceased, not through the person of the deceased but through another person; or in the absence of such a kinsman, to,

(c) the person to whom the deceased has bequeathed his entire estate, technically called the 'universal legatee' (as noted above, the *shari'at* does not allow anyone to

13. A master, by *wala'*, was entitled to inherit the estate of his freed slave if no blood relation of the slave survived. Slavery having been abolished by law everywhere—in India by Act V of 1843, though it continued clandestinely at least until early 1920s—there is no question now of a master succeeding to the estate of his slave.

bequeath more than one-third of one's estate so that the direct relatives can benefit, but when there are no direct relatives a bequest for the entire estate is valid); or, in default of the above successors, to,

(d) the Public Treasury (the substitute, in India as elsewhere, of the traditional *bait al-mal*) by escheat.

The broad rules of inheritance given above belong to the Hanafi school of law. The Shi'a rules differ on several points. We shall now delineate the principal areas of differences.

HOW SHI'A RULES DIFFER

The Sunni schools do not differentiate between various types of properties: to them 'property' is a term that covers both movable and immovable property, whether inherited or acquired by the deceased, to which every heir is entitled according to the quantum of the share. In Shi'a law, however, a childless widow has no share in the land, whether it is agricultural or non-agricultural, belonging to her husband. But she is entitled to a share in anything that the land might contain, like a structure or tree. In India, a childless widow has been held as one who does not have a child at the time of her husband's death, though Bailey holds that "when the wife has had a child by the deceased she inherits out of all that he has left; and if there was no child she takes nothing out of the deceased land, but her share of the value of the household effects and buildings is to be given to her."[14]

Islamic law makes provision for the child in the womb. According to Abu Hanifa, the shares of four sons should be reserved in such a case, as the possibility of quadruplets cannot be ruled out. Al-Shaibani puts the number at three, and wants the shares of three sons or daughters, whichever is greater, to be reserved. It is the view of Abu Yusuf, which has prevailed, that the share of one son or one daughter, whichever is greater, should be held in reserve, and security taken from those who would have to surrender their shares if more than one child is born that they would look after the extra child or children and give the share due on the child's attaining maturity. Shi'a law stipulates reservation of the shares of two sons, and in this

14. Neil B E. Bailey, A Digest of Moohumudan Law, Part Second, Lahore, 1958, p. 295.

respect it is supported by the Hanbali and Shafi'i schools. Thus, if a son is the only heir, he would get 1/3, and 2/3 will be reserved.

Hanafi law has three classes of heirs—sharers, residuaries and the distant kindred. Shi'a law dispenses with the third one. In Hanafi law, the sharers exclude the residuaries and the latter exclude the distant kindred, but Shi'a law lumps the sharers and residuaries by blood—the heir by marriage (*mutia* or temporary marriage does not confer the rights of inheritance) being considered as heir by blood—together and then divides them into three classes in order of preference:

(i) parents, children and their descendants (howsoever lower down on the scale);
(ii) Grandparents (howsoever higher up on the scale); brothers and sisters and their descendants (howsoever lower down on the scale);
(iii) Paternal and maternal grand uncles and aunts of the deceased and of his parents and grandparents (howsoever higher up on the scale) and their descendants (howsoever lower down on the scale).

Hanafi law recognizes twelve sharers, but Shi'a law treats three of them—true grandfather, true grandmother and son's daughter—as residuaries.

Hanafi law applies the 'Doctrine of Increase' to all the heirs, and in applying the 'Doctrine of Return' excludes the husband and wife only. Shi'a law, on the other hand, limits the 'Doctrine of Increase' to daughters, sisters and consanguine sisters and reduces their shares by the amount in excess.[15] Thus, if a wife dies leaving behind her husband, mother and two daughters, the shares are:

for husband	1/4 =	3/12
for mother	1/6 =	2/12
for daughters	2/3 =	8/12 reduced to unity = 7/12

As for the 'Doctrine of Return', while the Hanafi practice is to exclude the husband and wife only while any other heir is present, the Shi'a practice excludes also the following conditionally:

15. Bailey, *op. cit.*, Part Second, p. 395.

Mother	*Excluded when there is*	father and one daughter and (a) at least two brothers including consanguine brothers; or (b) one brother and two sisters, (c) four sisters including full or consanguine sisters.
Uterine brothers and sisters	,,	a sister or sisters.
All other heirs	,,	any heir entitled to a share by dual relationship.

According to Shi'a legal theory, the estate should not go to the *bait al-mal* or public treasury if there is no heir, but by *wala'* to the Imam and through him to the poor. In India, however, the estate escheats to the government.

BARS TO INHERITANCE

Succession takes place only after the death of a person whose estate is to be divided among his successors, or when that person is *mafqud* or missing for a sufficient length of time to warrant the presumption of death. Abu Hanifa wanted the maximum life-span of 120 years to elapse before a missing person could be declared dead. His disciples, al-Shaibani and Abu Yusuf, reduced the life-span to 110 and 105 years respectively. The Shi'a law, like the Shafi'i and Hanbali law, lays down a period of 4 to 10 years of waiting before declaring a person dead—a practice now found in Egypt, enforced by Egyptian Law No. 25 of 1920 (Articles 21 and 22), and in the Sudan. In India, according to the provisions of Sections 107 and 108 of the Indian Evidence Act of 1872, a missing person is taken as dead when seven years have elapsed since the date of disappearance, whether it is a person whose estate is to be inherited or one who inherits it.

Determining the exact time of a person's death is most important, for failure to do so might result in the disinheritance of some. If, for instance, a person dies a few minutes before his son, the son's son is entitled to inherit his grandfather's estate. But if it is wrongly shown that a person died after his son's death it would result in the 'case of the predeceased son' referred to at the very beginning of this chapter. Muslim jurists have therefore taken pains to frame rules to ensure that the exact time of a person's death is determined. They have laid down, for example, that where two persons die simultaneously, the older one should be considered to have died first.

Of the bars to inheritance recognized by all schools of Islamic law, only homicide is now legally tenable in India, the bar of slavery having been removed by Abolition of Slavery Act V, 1843, and the bar of the difference in religion and apostasy by Caste Disabilities Removal Act XXI, 1850, which states:

> So much of any law or usage now in force . . . as inflicts on any person forfeiture of rights or property, or may be held in any way to impair or affect any right of inheritance by reason of his or her renouncing or having been excluded from the communion of any religion or being deprived of caste shall cease to be enforced as law . . .

The apostasy of husband or wife, which had not been covered adequately by the latter Act, was dealt with clearly by the Dissolution of Muslim Marriages Act, VIII passed on 17th March, 1939, Section 4 of which states:

> The renunciation of Islam by a married Muslim woman or her conversion to a faith other than Islam shall not by itself operate to dissolve her marriage.

It should be noted that this Section mentions the wife but not the husband whose apostasy continues, as before, to dissolve the marriage. But what exactly is apostasy is difficult to define.[16] In a famous case over half a century ago, in which a wife took a second husband arguing that her first husband, a Hanafi, had turned apostate by joining the Ahmadiyya sect, the Madras High Court ruled that she was guilty of bigamy as the Ahmadiyya was a Muslim religious movement.[17] Since then in several Arab countries the members of the Ahmadiyya movement have been declared non-Muslims on a liberal interpretation of apostasy—or shall one say a narrow interpretation of Islam? The latest country to join the Arabs—not very readily but choosing between Scylla and Charybdis—is Pakistan where the National Assembly passed in 1974 a Bill known as Constitution Amendment Bill.

16. *Narantakath* v. *Parakkal*, (1922) 45 Mad. 986.
17. It appears it is one of the difficulties that have so long delayed the framing of comprehensive laws relating to apostasy in Egypt.

Clause 3 of this Bill reads as follows:

(a) A person who does not believe in the absolute and unqualified finality of the Prophethood of Hazrat Muhammad (peace be on him) or claims to be a Prophet after Hazrat Muhammad (peace be on him) or recognises such a claimant as a prophet or religious reformer or *Muslih* is not a Muslim.

(b) The following has been added to clause 106 of the Pakistan Constitution where mention has been made of the following non-Muslim sects, namely, Christian, Hindu, Sikh, Buddhist and Parsi communities or Scheduled Castes:

and persons of the Qadiani group or the Lahori group who call themselves Ahmadis.

(c) The following explanation to be added to Section 295-A of Pakistan Penal Code:

Prescribes punishment for a Muslim who professes, practises or propagates against the concept of finality of the Prophethood of Hazrat Muhammad as set out in clause 3 of Article 260 of the Constitution.[18]

India, in spite of appeals from Dar al-'Ulum, Deoband, has not declared the Ahmadis as non-Muslims. It would be interesting to see what verdict an Indian High Court would hand down if the question came before it. If an Ahmadi were to argue that both by inner conviction and outward appearance, and by adhering to religious duties enjoined by Islam, he was a Muslim, and wished to be governed by the Muslim Personal Law, would the court treat him as a non-Muslim? If he was held a non-Muslim, what other personal law would he be governed by? Would the court still require one to be an orthodox Muslim for being governed by Muslim Personal Law?[19] Or will it refuse to scrutinize the sincerity of a

18. This sub-clause is anomalous, for in sub-clause A it has been made clear that anyone not believing "in the absolute and unqualified finality of the Prophethood of Hazrat Muhammad (peace be on him) . . . is not a Muslim." The question of "punishment for a Muslim" in sub-clause C therefore does not arise. Rather than attributing it to bad drafting, one could take it as a subtle attempt to pacify the orthodox as well as save the Ahmadis.

19. In *Raj Bahadur* v. *Bishan Dayal*, 4 Alld. 343, orthodoxy was held a prerequisite for the application of personal law.

Muslim believer or look into his observance of religious rites and ceremonies, and consider, instead the mere profession of religion a sufficient proof?[20]

The Caste Disabilities Removal Act was meant to protect an apostate who, according to the principle of the traditional Islamic law (that a Muslim does not inherit from a non-Muslim and a non-Muslim does not inherit from a Muslim) had forfeited his right of inheritance by changing his religion. The Act, does not however, protect any other relative of an apostate who may be affected by his apostasy. An apostate is entitled to inherit according to the inheritance law of his original religion even after abandoning that religion, but his own estate will be inherited by his successors according to the inheritance laws of his new religion, and his relatives belonging to his original religion will have no claim over his property. Thus the Hindu brother of a Muslim widow who had converted to Islam failed in his claim to be her legal heir when she died intestate.[21]

Regarding homicide, there are traditions saying "The killer inherits nothing".[22] But there was a difference of opinion among Islamic schools of law whether the traditions referred to both intentional and accidental killing, and whether a father or a teacher, who beat a child as admonition could be treated as a killer. Abu Hanifa, unlike his two disciples, held that such a father or teacher was a killer. He also refused to differentiate, contrary to Shi'a law, between intentional and accidental killing. Criminal law in India, cases of homicide are decided in accordance with the Indian Penal Code, and if the court holds a person guilty of homicide he does not inherit. According to an important judgement given a decade ago by the Pakistan High Court,[23] the effect of homicide on inheritance does not remain confined to the killer but extends to others:

> Under the principles of justice, equity and good conscience, a murderer or his progeny cannot be allowed to benefit by his crime of murder. The murderer may be the father alone but if the descendants claim through him even though not

20. In *Abdul Razack* v. *Aga Mohammad Jaffar*, 21 Cal. 666, the simple profession of religion was considered sufficient.
21. *Chandrasekhar* v. *Government of Mysore*, A.I.R., 1955, Mys. 26.
22. Quoted in Joseph Schacht, The Origins of Muhammad Jurisprudence, London 1953, p. 159.
23. *Beguman* v. *Saroo*, P.L.D. (1964) Lah. 451.

> merely from him their title becomes tainted, as the source or the channel through which the inheritance has to flow becomes blocked and extirpated by reason of the crime committed by that source.

A final bar to inheritance, according to Shi'a law, arises out of illegitimacy. An illegitimate child does not inherit from any side, unless the father acknowledges the paternity of the child, which would entitle the child to inherit from the father alone without the father being entitled to any share in the child's inheritance. Hanafi law, on the other hand, recognizes mutual inheritance between an illegitimate child and the mother and maternal relations. Section 125 of the new Code of Criminal Procedure confers, however, the statutory right upon an illegitimate child to demand maintenance allowance from the father as long as the child is unable to maintain himself.[24]

REFORMS IN MUSLIM PERSONAL LAW

In the Symposium on Muslim Personal Law held at New Delhi on 9 January, 1964 on the occasion of the XXVI International Congress of Orientalists, some of the speakers advocated changes in Muslim Personal Law relating to polygamy, unilateral divorce and disinheritance of orphaned grandchildren. While the reluctance of the orthodox to change established practices and entrenched beliefs is understandable, those participating in the seminar were surprised that a modern thinker coming from one of the advanced countries of Asia, asked the famous question: "If the law, the Divine Law, has to march with the times, what do the times have to change with"? Prof. Seyyed Hossein Nasr's argument was that for a Muslim it is not the material and dialectal processes but the human will that governs the world. He added: "If you change the law in 1964, in 1974 you will have exactly the same problem".

When the Adoption of Children Bill was introduced in

24. Interestingly, the Madras High Court in a recent judgement (*K.M. Adam* v. *Gopala Krishnan*, A.I.R. 1974 Mad. 232 granted Rs. 100.00 per month to Gopala Krishnan—an illegitimate child by a Hindu mother—against his Muslim father by applying Section 20(2) of the Hindu Adoption and Maintenance Act of 1956 which confers, contrary to Islamic law, upon an illegitimate child the right to claim maintenance from the father.

Parliament in 1972 the Muslim community in India feared that it was but another step in the direction of piecemeal replacement of existing personal law by secular law envisaged in our Constitution in Article 25(2)(a):

> Nothing in this Article shall affect the operation of any existing law or prevent the State from making any law—regulating or restricting any economic, financial or other secular activity which may be associated with religious practice;[25] and, more importantly, in Article 44: "The State shall endeavour to secure for the citizens a uniform civil code throughout the territory of India".

Several meetings and conventions since have demanded the withdrawal of the Bill and also an assurance from the government that the personal law of the Muslims will not be changed. No government can effectively enforce a law by overriding public opinion. Dicey put it aptly: "Public opinion is always in advance of the law". Unfortunately, Muslim religious leaders and intellectuals have never been widely consulted, with one exception,[26] in regard to changes in the Muslim Personal Law. The Muslim leaders have, on the other hand, refused to listen even to those proposals for reform which demand of them no more than tempering law with mercy, for that is just what trying to secure property for an orphaned grandchild or an adopted child, amounts to. In fact, mercy has so often been stressed in the *Qur'an* that one can only expect that the Muslim religious leaders would heartily welcome, indeed themselves advance, proposals for healthy reforms based on humanitarian grounds, within, of course, the divinely ordained framework.

Of the four issues on which reform is being sought, I shall deal with only two-orphaned grandchild and adopted child—the other two—unilateral divorce and polygamy[27]—being out-

25. However, by Clause 1 of Article 25, "all persons are entitled to the freedom of conscience and the right freely to profess, practise and propagate religion.
26. Dr. Zakir Hussain, then Vice-President of India, called a meeting—probably at the instance of Pandit Jawaharlal Nehru—of Muslim religious leaders and intellectuals to find out their reactions to changes in Muslim Personal Law. Their almost unanimous resentment at the very idea was conveyed to Pandit Nehru who shelved the proposed changes.
27. Polygamy is little talked of now, since the statics have shown that it is prevalent more among non-Muslims than among Muslims.

side the scope of this paper.

ORPHANED GRANDCHILD

Although an orphaned grandchild is not recognized as a *Qur'anic* heir, there is nothing in the *Qur'an* to suggest that such a child cannot benefit by bequest. In fact, the *Qur'an* supports the cause of the orphans so forcefully in 4:*10*—"Those who swallow the property of the orphans unjustly, they swallow only fire into their bellies. And they will burn in blazing fire", that it is quite in keeping with its spirit to ensure that an orphaned grandchild is not left out in the cold when succession opens. If we look to the *Bukhari*—which is next to the *Qur'an* in importance—for guidance, we find the following in the chapter on inheritance called *Kitab al-fara'id:*

> Zaid (bin Thabit Ansari) says that grandsons are like sons, and when there is no son the grandsons equal sons, (that is) grandsons inherit like the sons and like them exclude (certain heirs).

The problem of saving an orphaned grandchild from disinheritance has been solved in Egypt, Morocco, Pakistan,[28] Syria and Tunisia by what Sir J.N.D. Anderson has described as an ingenious device "not affecting the structure of the Islamic law of intestate succession which it leaves completely untouched, while it yet makes provision for orphaned grandchildren".[29] This simple device is to allow an orphaned grand-

---

Anyway, polygamy has been partially curbed with the restriction placed on all Indian government servants not to have more than one wife.

28. In Pakistan, an orphaned grandchild's share is not restricted to one-third of the estate. Section 4 of the Muslim Family Laws Ordinance, 1961, states: "In the event of the death of any son or daughter of the *propositus* before the opening of succession, the children of such son or daughter, if any living at the time the succession opens, shall *per stirpes* receive a share equivalent to the share which such son or daughter, as the case may be, would have received, if alive". Pakistan thus clearly honours Islamic law, which supposedly governs all legislation, more in the breach than in observance.
29. J.N.D. Anderson, 'Recent Reforms in the Islamic Law of Inheritance' in *International and Comparative Law Quarterly*, 4th Series 14 (1965), p. 358.

child to inherit a maximum of one-third of the estate, treating it as a bequest, since Islamic law allows a person to make a bequest of a maximum of one-third of the estate to a non-heir. While Egypt and Pakistan allow children of both the son and daughter of the deceased to inherit, the other three countries do not make any provision for the children of the daughter of the deceased.

ADOPTED CHILD

The ancient Arab tribal structure *'asabiyya*—allegiance to the group of agnates—ensured continuity of family strength. Adopting children and giving them the rights of inheritance would have thrown the *'asabiyya* system overboard. They were not allowed, therefore, to have a share in the estate. Now when the *'asabiyya* system is hardly operative anywhere, adopted children are being given the rights of inheritance, as in Nagri Sembilan in Malaysia where Section 24(d) of the Small Estates (Distribution) Ordinance (No. 34 of 1955) empowers the Collector to "give effect to 'customary adoption where they are satisfactorily proved'. This is a redical departure from Islamic law which gives no right of succession to adopted children.".[30] In India, law requires a Muslim who adopts a child and yet wishes to be governed by Muslim Personal Law to file an application to this effect, failing which the customary law of adoption applies. This law should be revised, and every Muslim who adopts a child should be made to file a declaration that one-third of his estate would go as bequest to the adopted child or children on his death. There should be no opposition to this proposal, since a Muslim who does not wish to give any part of his property to an adopted child may well abstain from adopting. However, the provision in the adoption of Children Bill, 1972,[31] that an adopted child will be treated in every way as a natural-born child, and that an adopted child will be considered as belonging to the religion to which the child was born[32] is quite another proposition, which Muslims do not find acceptable. Treating

30. M.B. Hooker, *Adat Laws in Modern Malaya*, London, 1972, p. 211.
31. This Bill is obvicusly meant for Muslims and other minorities, since the Hindus are governed by Adoption and Maintenance Act, 1956.
32. As reported by I. Divakaran in the *Hindustan Times*, dated 26 February, 1975.

an adopted child as a natural-born child not only goes against the clear *Qur'anic* statement,[33] but affects the Islamic law of marriage, and might in certain cases harm a child needing a home. For instance, a Muslim might be willing to adopt a boy in the hope of getting him married to his natural daughter, but if the law prevents him from doing so, he would eschew adoption, defeating the very purpose of the Bill is "to provide proper homes and families for abandoned, destitute and neglected children".[34]

The other provision regarding the religion of the child militates against reason. If the religion of an adopting family is different from that of an adopted child, how can he fully share the religious celebrations with the other members of the family, or how, by himself, can he carry out and enjoy his own religious ceremonies? The child will simply be doomed to alienation, and adoption is likely to end up in frustration and fiasco, if the aim of the draftsman was to prevent conversion, this could be done by disallowing a family to adopt a child from a different religious community. In India, there is quite a large number of destitute children and orphans in every community to choose from.

One last point. The law relating to apostasy, as it exists in India, is anomalous. According to Section 4 of the Dissolution of Muslim Marriages Act already quoted, apostasy on the part of the wife does not dissolve the marriage, but the conversion of the husband does. The result is that whereas an apostate Muslim wife remains entitled to inherit from her husband, the husband loses the right to inherit from his wife. The law needs to be amended to bring both husband and wife on par and confer the same rights of inheritance on both.

33. 33: *4* quoted at [the beginning of this chapter which seeks to show that the natural and artificial cannot be equated.

34. The quotation is not directly from the Bill, but has been supplied by a very dependable Indian Jack Anderson.

B. Shivaramayya

CHAPTER VI

The Indian Succession Act, 1925

It may be pointed out at the very outset that legislation dealing with succession may appropriately be considered 'social legislation'. By social legislation is meant, legislation intended to curb social evils, such as, to take only two examples—untouchability and dowry—or legislation intended to remove social and legal disabilities arising out of irrational prejudices or legislation to protect the weaker sections of the population, two outstanding examples of which in India are untouchables and women,[1] oppressed over centuries. The traditional Hindu and Muslim laws were based on non-equalitarian values.[2] For example, the traditional Hindu law denies to woman the right of inheriting property, and Muslim law, although not going to that extreme, restricts her share to half of a male heir. In the Indian context a statute which confers equal rights of inheritance may, therefore, be justly regarded as social legislation.

The precursor of the succession law now in force was the Indian Succession Act, 1865. The main class of persons to whom it was intended to apply was the Europeans—who were either domiciled in India or had immovable properties in India. As Ilbert forcefully pointed out, "the exceptions (to the applicability of the Act) are so wide as to exclude all natives of India".[3]

Also in 1865, the Parsee Intestate Succession Act was

1. In matriarchal societies, as in Kerala, women enjoyed equal or even superior rights. But such cases are exceptions rather than the rule.
2. See Yogendra Singh, Modernization of Indian Tradition, (1973), 96.
3. Ilbert, Government of India, 362 (3rd ed.).

passed.[4] Other laws were enacted from time to time for other communities—such as the Hindu Wills Act, 1870, the Probate and Administration Act, 1881, the Succession Certificates Act, 1889, and the Native Christian Administration of Estates Act, 1901.

The Indian Succession Act, 1925, consolidating all these Acts, applies, broadly speaking, to Europeans, Ango-Indians, Jews, Armenians, and Parsis generally, to Hindus partially and to Muslims to a negligible extent.

The Act of 1925 also draws a distinction between the Presidency towns of Madras, Bombay and the territory governed by the Lieutenant Governor of Bengal and the rest of India[5]—a distinction which has its roots in history rather than in logic.

BACKGROUND OF THE INDIAN SUCCESSION ACT

Of the Indian Succession Act, 1925, Professor Fitzgerald has this to say: "The Indian Succession Act is not a code but merely a consolidation—a shapeless mass, that is to say, of legal matter, much of it obscure or obsolete or badly drafted and all of it calling aloud for revision. It would be an easier and more *grateful* topic to criticise the Act . . ."[6]

All in all, the Indian Succession Act, 1925, is a sad remainder of the neglect of the Directive Principle of State Policy outlined in Article 44 of the Constitution.[7]

INTESTACY

The consolidation of the various Acts in the Indian Succession Act, of 1925, resulted in two sets of provisions relating to the intestate succession: one applicable to Europeans, Ango-Indians, Jews, Armenians, Indian Christians, and to persons marrying under the Special Marriage Act, 1872 or the Special Marriage Act, 1954, and the other applicable to Parsee intestates.

The general provisions relating to succession are based on the Statute of Distribution which governed the succession to

4. Act XXI of 1865. For details, see Paruck, The Indian Succession Act 54-57 (5th ed. Joshi, 1966).
5. See Sections 57, 212 and 213.
6. *Review* 44 Law Quarterly Rev. 247 (1928).
7. "The State shall endeavour to secure for the citizens a uniform civil code throughout the territory of India."

personal property in England, the notable features of which are: (1) that there is no discrimination based on sex among the heirs—between, for example, the sons and daughters of an intestate; (2) that there is no distinction between persons related by full blood and persons related by half blood; and (3) that relations by adoption are not recognised.

The absence of discrimination based on sex is, no doubt, a great advance when viewed in the overall context of laws applicable to other communities in India. But the benefits of the Indian Succession Act, 1925, have not reached many even among the limited number of Christians in India, because of the narrow interpretation put on Section 29 in *Kurian Augusty* v. *Devassy Alley*.[8]

APPLICABILITY OF THE GENERAL PROVISIONS OF THE INDIAN SUCCESSION ACT

Prior to Independence, the princely States and foreign possessions, such as Pondicherry and Goa, had their own laws for Christians. In the former Native States of Travancore and Cochin, there were diverse laws of succession applicable to Christians based on customs and statutes like The Travancore Christians Succession Act[9] and the Cochin Christian Succession Act,[10] though differing in some particulars, are both based on customs and Hindu law and both discriminate against women.[11]

The question is: Should not, in Independent India, the Indian Succession Act, 1925 be deemed to have repealed the laws in the former princely States? The question came up for consideration before the Travancore-Cochin High Court in *Kurian Augusty* v. *Devassy Alley*[12] in which the plaintiffs (sister's sons of the deceased) would have been entitled to a share under the Indian Succession Act, 1925. The plaintiffs relied on Section 6 of the Part B States (Laws) Act, 1951[13] which reads:

> If immediately before the appointed day there is in force in any part B State any law corresponding to any of the Acts

8. A.I.R. 1957 Tr-Co.1.
9. A.I.R. 1957 the Travancore Christian Succession Act, 1092 (M.E) (1916 A.D).
10. The Cochin Christian Succession Act, 1097 (M.E.) (1921 A.D.).
11. For details see, Sivaramayya, Women's Rights of Inheritance in India, 190-93 (1973).
12. A.I.R. 1957 Tr-Co. 1.
13. Act 3 of 1951.

or Ordinances now extended to that State that law shall, save as otherwise expressly provided in this Act, stand repealed. . .

The court recognised that if the Travancore Christian Succession Act was a law corresponding to the Indian Succession Act, then it stood repealed by the Indian Succession Act. But, relying on Section 29 of the Indian Succession Act,[14] it held that "the Indian Succession Act is not intended to interfere with the personal law of the communities which have settled laws of their own". In the result Christians in Travancore were held to be exempt from the Indian Succession Act, 1925 and were to be governed by their personal laws.

The phrase "any other law for the time being in force", read in the context of sub-section (2) suggests, first, that any other law *must specifically*, and not merely by implication, provide for the exclusion of the Indian Succession Act,[15] and, secondly, it must be "any other law for the time being in force," not in princely states, but in what was known as *British India*, as in *Prem Chand* v. *Leelawati*.[16] The interpretation put by the Travancore-Cochin High Court substantially nullifies Section 6 of the Part B States (Laws) Act, 1951. The result is the great diversity in the laws applicable to Christians in Kerala, many of which discriminate against women in matters of succession.

The Indian Succession Act, 1925 has not been extended to the former French territory—Pondicherry. Therefore, the native Christians of Pondicherry, who have not renounced their personal law in favour of the French Civil Code (renoncants) and to whom the Indian Succession Act does not apply, are governed by the Hindu Customary law—based on the laws of Manu.[17]

14. Section 29 of the Indian Succession Act lays down: 29(1) This part shall not apply to any intestacy occurring before the first day of Jan. 1866 or to the property of any Hindu, Buddhist, Sikh or Jaina. (2) Save as provided in sub-section (1) or by another law for the time being in force, the provisions of this part shall constitute the law of British India in all cases of intestacy.
15. For example, Section 5 of the Punjab Laws Act, 1872, which unambiguously states that custom shall be the rule of decision, save where it is contrary to justice, equity and good conscience, has not been declared void.
16. A.I.R. 1956 H.P. 17.
17. Subash C. Jain, *The French Legal System in Pondicherry: An Introduction*, 12. J.I.L.I. 507, 601, 1970; *David Annoussamy*, *Pondicherry: Babel of Personal Laws*: 14. J.I.L.I. 420, 423 (1972).

Christian women of Pondicherry, thus, suffer the disabilities of the customary Hindu law in regard to succession.

ADOPTION AND THE INDIAN SUCCESSION ACT

It was pointed out earlier that the provisions relating to intestacy in the Indian Succession Act were based on the Statute of Distribution which governed the succession to personal property (as distinguished from real property). Since the institution of adoption did not exist in England before the Twentieth century and was not prevalent among the Christians in India, the Act did not provide for adoptive relationships.

Occasionally, the rights of adopted children were canvassed before courts as being within the purview of the Act, as in the Rangoon case *Makhin* v. *Ma Ahma.*[18] The court, however, held that since the Act did not recognise an adopted child as an heir, the plaintiff was not entitled to any share in the property in her capacity as an adopted daughter but that as the niece of the deceased she was entitled to half the property of the deceased. Later, the Allahabad High Court in *Ranbir Karan Singh* v. *J.C. Bhattacharji,*[19] ruled to the same effect relying on Section 24 of the Act, which lays down that "kindred or consanguinity is the connection or relation of persons descended from the same stock or common ancestor", and on Section 25 (1), which lays down that "lineal consanguinity is that which subsists between two persons, one of whom is descended in a direct line from the other, as between a man and his father, grandfather and great-grandfather, and so upwards in the direct ascending line, or between a man and his son, grandson, great-grandson and so downwards in the direct descending line".

From these decisions it is clear that the Indian Succession Act does not contemplate an adopted child's share on intestacy. As for non-Hindus, there is no enactment which enables them to adopt a child. The Adoption of Children Bill, 1972[20] intends to rectify this serious lacuna in the law, but at the time of writing it appears to be extremely doubtful that the Bill would be enacted into law.

A more anomalous feature is that when two Hindus marry

18. A.I.R. 1934 Rangoon 72.
19. I.L.R. 1940 All. 100; A.I.R. 1940 All. 134.
20. Bill No. XVIII of 1972, as introduced in the Rajya Sabha.

under the Special Marriage Act, 1954, they are entitled to adopt under the Hindu Adoptions and Maintenance Act, 1956, but the adopted child is not entitled to succeed to their property on intestacy under the Indian Succession Act, 1925.[21]

OTHER LACUNAE

According to Section 33 of the Indian Succession Act, 1925, if the intestate has left a widow and any lineal descendants, the share of the widow is one-third, the remaining two-thirds being distributed among the lineal descendants. If, on the other hand, the intestate dies without any lineal descendants, the share of the widow is half. Even if the intestate has left behind a wife and only one child, her share is reduced to one-third. In some common law jurisdiction, the anomaly is rectified and the property is distributed equally.[22] The Act should be amended to remove this unsatisfactory aspect of the law.

Section 33-A of the Act lays down that where the intestate dies leaving a widow but no lineal descendant, and the net value of the estate does not exceed Rs. 5,000, the whole property is to belong to the widow. If the net value of the estate exceeds Rs. 5,000, she is entitled to a sum of Rs. 5,000, in addition to her share in the residue. However, the operation of the Section is not applicable to the property of: (i) an Indian Christian, (ii) any child or grandchild of male who is or was at the time of his death an Indian Christian, and (iii) any person professing Hindu, Buddhist, Sikh or Jaina religion the succession to whose property is, under Section 24 of the Special Marriage Act, 1872, regulated by the provisions of the Act. The object of Section 33-A is to confer better rights of succession on the widow. The exceptions, therefore, are illogical and should be deleted.

Moreover, under the existing Act, if a pre-deceased son

21. For details, see Sivaramayya, Adoption: An anomaly under the Indian Succession Act, 1960 S.C.J. 201(J); Derrett, Introduction to Modern Hindu Law, 176 (1963).
22. For example, in New York State article 4-1.1(1)(2) of the Estates, Powers and Trusts Law provides: "A spouse and only one child or a spouse and only the issue of deceased child, money or personal property not exceeding in value two thousand dollars and one half of the residue to the spouse and the balance thereof to the child or to his issue *per stirpes*."

leaves a widow (who has not remarried), she is not entitled to represent her husband. In other words, a widowed daughter-in-law is not entitled to succeed. It may have been logical for the Indian Succession Act, 1865, originally intended for Europeans, to exclude relations by marriage. Such exclusion does not result in much hardship in England because of the prevalence of marriage settlements, the higher social status of women, the larger opportunities available for women to engage in professions, and the greater frequency of widow-remarriages. But in Indian conditions a different approach is necessary. As the Act is applicable to the succession of properties of persons who solemnize their marriage under the Special Marriage Act, 1954, the need for change in the law is greater.

PARSI INTESTATE SUCCESSION

The Parsi Law of succession contains the rule that in the case of a male intestate the share of female heir is half that of a male heir of the same degree. Section 51(1) of the Indian Succession Act, 1925 states:

Subject to the provisions of sub-section (2), the property of which a male Parsi dies intestate shall be divided—

(a) Where he dies leaving a widow and children, among the widow and children, so that the share of each son and of the widow shall be double the share of each daughter, or

(b) Where he dies leaving children but no widow, among the children, so that the share of each son shall be double the share of each daughter.

Sub-section(2) of Section 51 reads:

> Where a male Parsi dies leaving one or both parents in addition to children or a widow and children, the property of which he dies intestate shall be divided so that the father shall receive a share equal to half the share of a son and the mother shall receive a share equal to half the share of a daughter.

But, curiously, the property of a female Parsi intestate will be divided equally among the widower and children.[23] The discrimination against female heirs is indefensible, and the sections should be amended on the basis of equality of sexes.

23. The Indian Succession Act, 1925, Section 52.

Jyotsna Shah

CHAPTER VII

Welfare of Children under Indian Laws

Children in India have not received the attention they deserve, largely because of lack of resources for investment in special services for children, but even more than that because of lack of unawareness on the part of the community in general of the needs of children at various stages. This is evident from the fact that among the institutional services for children of all categories there is a preponderance of those which are residential and consequently separate children from their families (at greater cost to the public exchequer) than those that are non-residential and at the same time less costly.

There is no integrated approach to the welfare needs of children, they are touched upon incidentally in both civil and criminal legislation, there being no statutory measures for the care, protection and treatment of the physically, emotionally or mentally handicapped children, let alone comprehensive social security or social defence programmes. The child is left to the charitable and philanthropic instincts of the people. Even the Omnibus Children Acts of the Union and State Governments are more punitive than protective, with the paraphernalia of the liveried police, the awe-inspiring court, the remand and detention homes. Only a few States can boast of remand and detention homes that are not crude and primitive; others leave neglected and destitute children to fend for themselves, and send delinquent children to prisons without any qualms. The Union

Government has still to discover the need for a Model Children Act.

It is against this background that this paper surveys the legislation affecting children—the civil code, the criminal procedure code, labour laws, and special laws for the education, health and welfare of children. A review of the manner of application of these laws in various States is outside the scope of this paper. It may be hoped that even the bringing together of the various laws affecting children will be of some assistance to those engaged in the field of child welfare.

THE CONSTITUTION AND CHILD WELFARE

A. **Directive Principles:** The legislation pertaining to children at any given time reflects the consciousness and concern of the community for its children. It will be worthwhile to review such legislation in independent India in the context of the Directive Principles of State Policy relating to the welfare of children in Part IV of the Constitution of India:

(i) The State shall endeavour to see that the tender age of children is not abused and that children are not forced by economic necessity to enter into vocations unsuited to their age and strength, and that childhood and youth are protected against exploitation and moral and material abandonment (Article 39).

(ii) The State shall make provisions for maternity relief (Article 42).

(iii) The State shall endeavour to provide for free and compulsory education for all children until they complete the age of 14 years (Article 45).

(iv) The State shall promote with special care the educational and economic interests of the weaker sections of the people, and in particular, of the Scheduled Castes and Scheduled Tribes and shall protect them from social injustice and all forms of exploitation (Article 46).

(v) The State shall regard the raising of level of nutrition and the standard of living of its people and the improvement of public health as among its primary duties (Article 47).

B. Fundamental Rights: In Part III, dealing with Fundamental Rights, the Constitution of India provides as follows:

(i) Untouchability is abolished and its practice in any form is forbidden (Article 17).

(ii) Traffic in human beings and *begar* etc. is prohibited (Article 23).

(iii) No child below the age of 14 years shall be employed to work in any factory or mine or engaged in any hazardous employment (Article 24).

(iv) Nothing in this Article (15 on Right to Equality) shall prevent the State from making any special provision for women and children [Article 15(3)].

NATIONAL POLICY FOR CHILDREN

A. Parliament's resolution: The duty of the State towards children having been laid down in the Constitution, Parliament adopted a resolution on a National Policy for Children in 1974 giving further substance to the needs of children (India is also a party to the United Nations Declaration of the Rights of the Child). The Resolution, in part, reads:

"It shall be the policy of the State to provide adequate services to children, both before and after birth and through the period of growth, to ensure their full physical, mental and social development. The State shall progressively increase the scope of such services so that, within a reasonable time, all children in the country enjoy optimum conditions for their balanced growth."

B. Concrete measures: To attain these objectives the following measures were indicated:

(i) All children shall be covered by a comprehensive health programme.

(ii) Programmes shall be implemented to provide nutrition services with the object of removing deficiencies in the diet of children.

(iii) Programmes will be undertaken for the general improvement of the health and for the care, nutrition and education of expectant and nursing mothers.

(iv) The State shall take steps to provide free and compulsory education for all children upto the age of 14 for which a time-bound programme will be drawn up consistent with the availability of resources. Special efforts will be made to reduce the prevailing wastage and stagnation in schools, particularly in the case of girls and children of the weaker sections of society. The programme of informal education for pre-school children from such sections will also be taken up.

(v) Children who are not able to take full advantage of formal school education shall be provided other forms of education suited to their requirements.

(vi) Physical education, games, sports and other types of recreational as well as cultural and scientific activities shall be promoted in schools, community centres and such other institutions.

(vii) To ensure equality of opportunity, special assistance shall be provided to all children belonging to the weaker sections of the society, such as children belonging to the Scheduled Tribes and those belonging to the economically weaker sections, both in urban and rural areas.

(viii) Children who are socially handicapped, who have become delinquent or have been forced to take to begging or are otherwise in distress, shall be provided facilities for education, training and rehabilitation and will be helped to become useful citizens.

(ix) Children shall be protected against neglect, cruelty and exploitation.

(x) Facilities shall be provided for special treatment, education, rehabilitation and care of children who are physically handicapped, emotionally disturbed or mentally retarded.

(xi) Children shall be given priority for protection and relief in times of distress or natural calamity.

(xii) Special programmes shall be formulated to support, encourage and assist gifted children, particularly those belonging to the weaker sections of society.

(xiii) Existing laws should be amended so that in all legal disputes, whether between parents or institutions, the interests of children are given paramount consideration.

(xiv) In organizing services for children, efforts would be directed to strengthen family ties so that full potentialities of growth of children are realized within the normal family, neighbourhood and community environment.

C. **Priorities**: In formulating programmes in different sectors, priority shall be given to those relating to:

(i) preventive and promotive aspects of child health;

(ii) nutrition for infants and children in the pre-school age along with nutrition for nursing and expectant mothers;

(iii) maintenance, education and training of orphaned and destitute children;

(iv) creches and other facilities for the care of children of working or ailing mothers; and

(v) care, education, training and rehabilitation of handicapped children.

The National Policy Statement gives expression to our aspirations for children's welfare. Such resolutions serve to remind ourselves of the tasks still to be accomplished. However, unless aspirations get translated into achievements, it would be wrong to be complacent.

THE CIVIL CODE AND THE CHILD

There is no single piece of legislation defining or safeguarding the position of children in the civil laws of the country. This often places the child in a helpless condition. Clauses relating to the duty of maintaining minor children are incorporated in the Criminal Procedure Code. But there is no provision under which an orphan or destitute child can be given in adoption; the draft bill on the subject has been pending for almost a decade. The authority to deal with children is divided among different courts, and there is no proper coordination of data being presented to them. The legislative enactments on various subjects do not carry cross-references. We do not yet have family courts, which should include children's courts, for all civil or criminal matters relating to families and children. The guardianship issue is dealt with vaguely. Even for children in institutions, we do not have facilities of "social welfare information exchange" to collect the relevant data about families or children dealt with by public agencies.

We discuss below some of the laws that have a bearing in

the position of a child, specially those pertaining to marriage, divorce, adoption, maintenance, minority and guardianship.

THE HINDU MARRIAGE ACT, 1955 (NO. XXV OF 1955)

(a) **Age at Marriage**: This act regulates marriages among Hindus. One of the conditions required is that at the time of marriage the bridegroom should be above 18 years and the bride above 15 years. Violation of this condition can lead to imprisonment for 15 days or fine up to Rs. 1000 or both. If the bride has not completed 18 years, the consent of parents or guardian is required for the marriage. Violation of this condition is liable to a fine of Rs. 1000. No person who has not completed 21 years of age can function as a guardian for purposes of marriage. Notwithstanding anything stated in this law, if it considers a marriage arranged by a guardian not to be in the interest of the bride is competent to issue stay orders (Section 5).

(b) **Condition of marriage**: A marriage is declared void under Section 12(6), if any of the conditions stipulated in Section 5 are violated and if permission is obtained by force or fraud. The application for declaring the marriage void has to be made within one year of the use of force or the knowledge of fraud [Section 12 (2)].

(c) **Legitimacy of offsprings**: On a marriage being declared void or resulting in divorce, the offsprings of the marriage will be treated as a legitimate (Section 14).

(d) **Custody of children**: In any proceedings under this Act, the court may make a decision about the custody, maintenance and education of minor children after consulting the wishes of the child. The orders can be modified periodically and even withdrawn. Interim orders can also be given (Section 26).

THE CHILD MARRIAGE RESTRAINT ACT, 1929 (ACT XIX OF 1929)

This Act was passed in response to a demand by a section of the population for legislation to check the evil of child marriage prevailing at the time. Popularly known as the 'Sarda Act', it provides penalties for child marriage. A man over 18 years of age but less than 21 years marrying a girl of less than

15 years can be punished with imprisonment for 15 days or with a fine of Rs. 10C0 or with both (Section 3). If a man over 28 years of age marries a girl under 15 years of age, he is liable to 3 months' imprisonment and fine. The priest who performs the marriage, as also those who organise the marriage, are also punishable with imprisonment for 3 months if they cannot prove that they had had no hand in such a marriage (Section 5).

When a minor gets married, parents or guardians giving permission for the marriage or neglecting to prevent the marriage, are liable to imprisonment upto 3 months and fine. However, Section 6(1) forbids a woman to be sentenced to imprisonment. Under Section 6(2), unless proved otherwise, it is presumed that the persons having the custody of the minor have negligently not prevented marriage.

The court does not take cognizance of the offence of child marriage one year after such marriage.

The Central Act of 1929 was non-cognizable, but the State of Gujarat amended it in 1964 and made it cognizable.

The Child Marriage Restraint Act, 1929 is a classic example of legislation outstripping public opinion and public education. In spite of the Act, marriages of minor continued to take place on a large scale, rendering the statute a dead letter. Only social education and creation of strong public opinion can eradicate child marriage. Gujarat has made earnest efforts in this direction by appointing six Child Marriage Prevention Officers with powers to prosecute offenders.

THE HINDU ADOPTION AND MAINTENANCE ACT, 1956

This Act applies to Hindus, Baudhs, Jains and Sikhs but not to Scheduled Tribes.

(a) **Adoption**: The Act makes a Hindu male, if he is not a minor or a lunatic competent to take a child in adoption subject to the condition that if he has wife living, he must consult her before adopting a child, except in the event of the wife having renounced the world, or having been declared a lunatic by the court, or having ceased to be a Hindu (Section 7).

A Hindu woman, who is not a minor or a lunatic, can ta ke a child in adoption if she is unmarried or divorced or if a co urt has pronounced her husband a lunatic.

Under Section 9, only the parents or the guardian can give a child in adoption. If the father is dead or has renounced the world or changed his religion or has been declared a lunatic, the mother is competent to give the child in adoption. If both the parents are dead or have abandoned the child or are lunatic, or if the parents have not been heard of or their whereabouts are not known, the guardian of the child can, with the prior permission of the court, give the child in adoption. Before giving permission, the court has to verify the wishes of the child as far as possible and take a decision solely in the interest of the child after making sure that the adoption has not been arranged for pecuniary considerations.

Under Section 10, a person already adopted, a married person, or a person who has not completed 15 years of age cannot be taken in adoption. A husband and wife, or a husband, or a wife are barred from adopting a child if they, or he, or she have/has a living son or daughter. A male adopting a female child should be older than the girl at least by 21 years. Similarly, a woman taking a male child in adoption should be at least 21 years older than the boy.

No child can be adopted by two or more persons who are not husband and wife. The adopted child enjoys all the privileges of offspring as if he/she was born in the adopted family. All his/her rights in the family of birth are extinguished.

An adoption, once effected, cannot be undone. Taking or giving money by either side concerned in adoption is illegal and offenders are liable to six months' imprisonment and fine.

(b) **Maintenance**: Under Section 20 of the Act, a legitimate as well as an illegitimate child is entitled to maintenance by the father or mother so long as the child is a minor. The heirs of a deceased Hindu are obliged to maintain the dependents of the deceased. The court has been given the discretion under Section 23 to determine the amount of maintenance allowance with due regard to the value of property, position and status of both the parties, reasonable needs of the claimants, and the number of persons entitled to maintenance. The amount of allowance may be altered on account of change in circumstances.

THE GUARDIAN AND WARDS ACT, 1890

In the interest of or for the welfare of a minor, the court can appoint a guardian of the minor's person or property, or remove a guardian who has not been appointed by will of the deceased parent or guardian or by the court itself. An application for guardianship of the person or property of a minor is to be made to the district court in the place where the minor lives, whereupon the court may direct that the person who has custody of the minor shall produce him at the place and time required, and the court issues orders for the temporary custody or shelter of the person and property of the minor (Section 12). If the minor is a female, she is not to be compelled to appear in public except in accordance with the prevailing customs. While making orders, the court takes into consideration the age, sex and religion of the minor and the character and capacity of the proposed guardian, and the wishes of the deceased parents, if any, and the preference of the minor if the minor is old enough to make an intelligent preference. No person can be appointed a guardian against his will.

The court does not appoint a guardian, if

(i) a minor is a married female and her husband is fit to be the guardian;

(ii) the minor's father is alive and is not unfit to be the guardian;

(iii) the minor's property is under the superintendence of the Court of Wards, which is competent to appoint a guardian of the person of the minor.

The Act also prescribes the duties, rights and liabilities of a guardian in respect of the person and the property of a minor. Guardianship can be terminated, if in the opinion of the court the guardian has failed in his duty or has neglected to take proper care or has given ill-treatment to the minor or is otherwise incapable of discharging the duties of guardian.

THE CRIMINAL PROCEDURE CODE AND THE CHILD

The Code of Criminal Procedure enacted in 1884, and later modified in 1889, contained special sections dealing with children up to the age of 21 years. Section 29(B) provided for the trial of any person under 15 years of age, by any competent authority under the Reformatory Schools Act, 1897. Section 309 provided that when sentencing a person under 15 years to imprisonment, the court might direct that such a person be confined in State reformatory to acquire suitable discipline and training. Section 562(1) made specific provision for the release of persons under 21 years of age on probation on certain conditions instead of being sentenced to imprisonment, taking into consideration the physical and mental condition of the child and the circumstances in which the offence was committed.

The Criminal Procedure Code, 1973, as amended has been in force since April, 1974. It contains several provisions applicable to children. The main sections of the revised Code are summarized below:

(1) **Competent Courts:** Any offence, not punishable with death or imprisonment for life, committed by any person, who, on the date when he appears or is brought before the court, is under the age of 16 years, may be tried by the court specially empowered under the Children Act, 1960, or any other law for the time being in force providing for the treatment, training and rehabilitation of youthful offenders (Section 27).

The section is substantially the same as Section 29B of the old Code. Only, the reference to the Reformatory Schools Act has been substituted by reference to the Children Act, 1960 or State Children Acts.

(2) **Age:** The age limit of a juvenile has also been raised from 15 years to 16 years with a view to fitting it into the Children Act, 1960. The expression "custody, trial and punishment" has been substituted by the expression "treatment, training and rehabilitation", since it is inappropriate to use the term "punishment" in relation to children.

(3) **Restoration of a female child:** Upon a complaint, made on oath, of the abduction or unlawful detention of a woman or a female child under the age of 18 years, for any unlawful purpose, a district magistrate, a sub-divisional magistrate or a magistrate of the first class may make an order for the immediate restoration of such a woman to her liberty or of such a female child to her husband, parent, guardian or other person having lawful charge of the child and may compel compliance with such order, using such force as may be necessary (Section 98).

(4) **Maintenance of wife, children and parents**: If any person, having sufficient means, neglects or refuses to maintain (a) his wife, unable to maintain herself, or (b) his legitimate or ielegetimate minor child, whether massied or not, unable to maintain itself or (c) his legitimate or illegitimate child (not being a married daughter) who has attained majority, where such child is by reason of any physical or mental abnormality or injury unable to maintain itself, or (d) his father or mother, unable to maintain himself or herself, then a magistrate of the first class may, upon proof of such neglect or refusal, order such a person to pay a monthly allowance for the maintenance of his wife or such child, father or mother, at a rate not exceeding a total of Rs. 500. The magistrate may, however, order the father of a minor female child, if married, to continue to pay such allowance until she attains majority, if he is satisfied on evidence that the husband of the minor female child is not possessed of sufficient means (Chapter IX, Section 125).

(5) **Police officer's power to demand attendance of witnesses:** A police officer making an investigation-may order in writing the attendance before himself of any person within the territory of his jurisdiction who on the basis of information received, appears to be acquainted with the facts and circumstances of the case. He cannot, however, order a person under the age of 15 years or a woman to attend at any place other than the one in which such a person or women resides (Section 160).

(6) **Prosecution for offences against marriage**: No court shall take cognizance of an offence punishable under Chapter XX of the Indian Penal Code except upon a complaint made by some person aggrieved by the offence or with the court's leave, by some one close in behalf of the aggrieved person if this person is an idiot or a lunatic or is a woman who, according to the local customs and manners, ought not to be compelled to appear in public (Section 198).

(7) **Compounding offences**: The offences specified as punishable under the Indian Penal Code compounded by persons so entitled. However, the person, otherwise competent to compound an offence, is under the age of 18 years or is an idiot or a lunatic, any person competent to contract on his behalf may, with the permission of the court, compound such offence under Section 320(1), 4(a).

(8) **Release on Probation of good conduct**: Two categories of convicts can be let out on probation of good conduct if it appears to the court before which the person is convicted, regard being had to the age, character or antecedents of the offender and to the circumstances in which the offence was committed, that it is expedient that the offender should be released on his entering into a bond with or without sureties, to appear and receive sentence when called upon to do so during such period (not exceeding 3 years) as the court may direct and in the meantime to keep the peace and be of good behaviour (Section 360). The two categories are: (i) persons under 21 years of age who are convicted of offences punishable with imprisonment for a term of upto seven years or with fine; and (ii) men under 21 years and women of any age who are convicted of offences punishable with death or life sentence but have no record of provious conviction.

The provisions of the Probation of Offenders Act, 1958, have been incorporated in the Criminal Procedure Code to facilitate their wider application by criminal courts.

The reference to the Reformatory Schools Act, 1897 in Section 546(2) of the old Code (to which the present sub-section corresponds) has been substituted with the reference to the Probation of Offenders Act, 1958, and Children Act, 1960, or "any other law for the treatment, training and rehabilitation of youthful offenders" (Section 360(x)).

(9) **Restrictions on imprisonment of youthful offenders**: If in a case the court could have dealt with (a) an accused under Section 360 or under the provisions of the Probation of Offenders Act, 1958, or (b) a youthful offender under the Children Act, 1960, or any other law for the time being in force for the treatment, training or rehabilitation of youthful offenders, but does not do so, it has to record in its judgement the special reasons for not having done so (Section 361).

Children may be allowed bail for non-bailable offences. When person accused or suspected of a non-bailable offence is arrested or detained without warrant by an officer in charge of a police station or appears or is brought before a court other than the High Court or Court of Sessions, he may be released on bail, but not if there appear reasonable grounds for believing that the person has been guilty of an offence punishable with death or imprisonment for life; but even in such a case the court may, if person is under the age of 16 years, or is a woman, or is sick or infirm release the person on bail (Section 437).

(10) **No bond required from a minor**: When a person required by any court or officer to execute a bond is a minor, the court or officer may accept, in lieu thereof, a bond executed by a surety or sureties (Section 448).

THE INDIAN PENAL CODE AND THE CHILD

A child below 7 years is exempted from criminal liability. In the case of a child between 7 years and 12 years, the court has the discretion to decide whether he is sufficiently mature.

Nothing done by a child under seven years of age is an offence (Section 82). The exemption does not, however, extend to offences under special or local laws.

Nothing done by a child above seven but under twelve years is an offence if he has not got sufficient maturity of understanding to judge the nature and consequences of his conduct on that occasion (Section 83).

However, wherever the Children Act is enforced, the child, as defined under the Act, is not treated as an offender and cannot be sentenced to imprisonment.

CHILDREN ACTS

(1) **History**: The first law relevant to the welfare of children and young people was the Apprentice Act passed in 1850. Although it was punitive in nature, it sought to provide better treatment for children between 10 and 18 years of age. The Reformatory Schools Act, 1876, modified in 1897, provided for special courts which could order three to seven years' detention and training instead of imprisonment.

It was not until 1919-1920 that a move to formulate a Children's Act was made on the Indian Jails Committee (1919-20) recommending that child offenders (or non-offenders) should not be kept in prisons. The Committee emphasized the need for special treatment for minor and youthful offenders to reform and rehabilitate them. It recommended, *inter alia*, the creation of children's courts for hearing all cases against children and young offenders, the return of a child offender to his parents if the home was a decent one, and the making of commitments of children and young persons to prisons illegal.

Madras, Bengal and Bombay Presidencies enacted their Children Acts in 1920, 1922 and 1924, respectively. These Acts were passed to provide for (a) the custody, trial, maintenance, welfare, education and punishment of young offenders, and (b) for the protection of children and young persons who are destitute, or in moral danger, or in need of care and protection.

Subsequently, the Central Provinces and Berar, and Travancore (a princely state) enacted Children Acts. After independence, some more States followed. Bombay enacted a new Children Act in December, 1948; West Bengal followed suit by enacting new Children Act in 1959. In 1960, the Government of India passed a Children Act for the Union Territories. Many other States, empowered by the Constitution to pass and enforce their own Children's Acts framed new acts on the lines of the Central Children Act of 1960.

(2) **Definition of child**: Section 2(c) of the (Central) Children Act, 1960 defines child as a boy who has not completed the age of 16 years and a girl who has not attained the age of 18 years. A majority of States have now adopted this definition with some variations. For example

(i) In the Madras Children Act, 1920, "child" means a person under the age of 14 years, while those above 14 years but under 18 years are classed as "young persons".

(ii) The Bombay Children Act, 1948, defines "child" as a boy or a girl who has not attained the age of 16 years. The Madhya Pradesh Children Act, 1969, the East Punjab Children Act, 1949, and the Uttar Pradesh Act, 1951 all follow the same definition.

(iii) The West Bengal Children Act, 1959, and the Saurashtra Children Act, 1955, define "child" as a person who has not attained the age of 18 years.

The various labour laws and the Suppression of Immoral Traffic in Women and Girls Act, 1956, provide further variations on the definition of "child".

(3) **Definition of neglected child**: Section 2(b) and (1) of the (Central) Children Act, 1960, and Section 40 of the Bombay

Children Act, 1948, and other State Acts define the following types of children as "neglected":

(a) a child with no parent or guardian or shelter;

(b) a child with no legal means of livelihood;

(c) a child found begging or doing a job which goes against his welfare;

(d) a child in the care of parent or guardian who, due to criminal practice or drinking habit or madness or disease or cruelty or wickedness or for any other reason is either unfit to take care or incapable of taking care of the child;

(e) a child who is known to live with a prostitute or with a brothel-keeper or with a drunkard or has connections with a confirmed criminal;

(f) a child who takes shelter or lives in a house used for prostitution or who often visits such places;

(g) a child who has the possibility of having connections with bad people or has the possibility of losing his character, or has the possibility of earning a living through criminal acts;

(h) a child who is used to intoxicants;

(i) a child who does not listen to the proper advice of parents or guardians or is uncontrollable by any one.

(4) **Definition of delinquent child**: A delinquent child is one found guilty by the competent court. Some State legislatures define a "Youthful Offender" as any person under the age of 18, who has been convicted of an offence punishable with imprisonment.

(5) **Competent authority**: According to (Central) Children Act, 1960, the following are the competent authorities:

(i) Child Welfare Boards: The Government may constitute for any area one or more child welfare boards, each consisting of a chairman and such other members (one of whom must be a woman) as Government thinks fit to appoint to exercise powers and discharge the assigned duties in regard to neglected children (Section 4).

(ii) Children's Courts: The Government may constitute for any area one or more children's courts each consisting of a magistrate designated as senior and as many other magistrates (atleast one of whom must be a woman) as the Government may think to appoint to constitute a bench, to exercise the powers and discharge the duties assigned to such courts in relation to delinquent children.

In the absence of board or a children's court in any area, the powers conferred on the competent authority are exercised by—

(i) the district magistrate,

(ii) a sub-divisional magistrate, or

(iii) a first class magistrate (Section 7).

Section 6(3) of the Children Act prescribes special knowledge of child psychology and child welfare on the part of members of child welfare boards and magistrates of children's courts.

The Hyderabad Children Act, the Madhya Pradesh Children Act, The Madras Children Act, the Mysore Children Act, the Uttar Pradesh Children Act, the Bombay Children Act, and the West Bengal Children Act provide for only juvenile courts to deal with both neglected and delinquent children.

Opinion is divided on whether it is in the interest of children themselves to label them as "destitute" or "delinquent" at the stage of initial processing. Nor is there unanimity on which system is better for dealing with children—the dual set-up, as in India, or the single set up, as in the Scandinavian countries, where juvenile courts have been dispensed with and child welfare boards deal with all children below a certain age. The recent policy in Britain also (since the passing of the Children and Young Persons Act, 1969, of England and Wales) favours a "non-statutory" processing of all children below a certain age. However logical the separation of various categories of children for treatment in institutions or outside may be but experience shows that a dual system of "competent authority", as under the (Central) Children Act, 1960, does not work out very well. It is worthwhile considering why children below a certain age should not be spared handling by the police, juvenile courts or other statutory agencies, nor is there any reason why cases of simple poverty and destitution, or even orphanhood, should not be left to local governments to deal with them appropriately in the light of special circumstances of each child. A society in which the system of extended family prevails and where community concern for the welfare of its members is not totally lacking, many favour such a measure.

(6) **Institutions under the children acts**: The (Central) Children Act, 1960 provides for the following institutions:

(i) observation home for temporary accommodation, maintenance and medical examination and treatment, with facilities for useful occupation of inmates. (This corresponds to the Remand Home provided in the State Acts.)

(ii) children's home providing neglected children with accommodation, maintenance and educational facilities for the development of their character.

(iii) special school to receive delinquent children and provide them with accommodation, maintenance and educational facilities for character development. (Some States have approved or certified schools for neglected and delinquent children).

(iv) after-care organization for children released from children's homes or special schools so as to help them live an honest, industrious and useful life.

The State Government may establish similar homes or may recognize such homes run by volunteer organisations as meet government standards. Additionally, the various Children Acts recognise the following institutions:

(i) Fit persons, institutions, and approved places, the government prescribing the conditions for the recognition of institutions or associations as fit persons' institutions and approved places for taking care of children, or preventing cruelty to children, or bringing up children in conformity with the religion of each child.

(ii) voluntary homes maintained wholly or partly by voluntary efforts receiving children.

(iii) places of safety, which include remand homes or other suitable places or institutions the occupiers or managers of which are willing to receive children temporarily.

(7) **Special offences in relation to children**: Children Acts specify punishable offences by adults in relation to children such as:

(i) cruelty to a child;

(ii) permitting a child to live at a house of prostitution;
(iii) employing a child for begging;
(iv) being drunk while in charge of a child;
(v) giving liquor or dangerous drugs to a child;
(vi) allowing a child to stay in a place where liquor, opium or ganja is sold or employing a child for sale of these articles;
(vii) inciting or encouraging a child to gamble or take part or share in gambling on public road;
(viii) receiving in mortgage articles from a child;
(ix) encouraging a child to run away;
(x) publishing news about a child involved in proceedings of a juvenile court.

When an adult and a child are brought together before a court on the charge of begging, the cases are separated, the child's case being transferred to the juvenile court of the area. A child found begging under the Beggary Control Act is also be referred to the juvenile court of the area.

Normally, juvenile courts or children's courts function very informally and do not permit a lawyer to appear on behalf of the child. Since this practice has been challenged as violating the fundamental right of defence through a counsel, it is suggested that the Government should make available the services of a defence counsel at government cost.

A very desirable feature of the children Acts ever since they were involved viz. the honorary magistrate of the juvenile courts has been taken away by the revised Criminal Procedure Code 1973. This feature needs to be reintroduced.

The guardianship issue is left vague in children Acts or rules both of the Centre and of the States. Neither is it clear who should be regarded as a guardian of a destitute child placed in an institution by a court's order.

After-care organizations though made mandatory under the (Central) Children Act, have not been functioning, with the result that discharged children are left very much to the voluntary sector, without much follow-up action.

(8) **Probation of young offenders**: Probation means conditional suspension of punishment. Thus, probation itself does not constitute punishment; the original offence remains punishable throughout the period of probation, and the offender is actually

to be punished if he violates the conditions of probation.

Probation is a method to be applied on a selective and individual basis. To determine conditions of probation, it is necessary for the court to investigate the case, the offenders' personal traits, familial and social circumstances and other factors, including the potential of the offender's social rehabilitation. The method of treatment of offenders by probation officers can be individualized and made flexible to suit changing circumstances in the course of probation.

Probation is a form of treatment within the community. It does not disrupt the offender's relationships with his family, friends or occupation. Moreover, there is no stigma attached to probation treatment.

The (Central) Children Act, 1960, applicable to the Union Territories, contains the following provisions concerning probation:

(i) When a child is arrested, the police has to inform the parents as well as the probation officer in order to enable the latter to gather information regarding the antecedents and family history of the child and other material circumstances likely to be of assistance to the children's court for making an inquiry (Section 19).

(ii) When a children's court is satisfied on inquiry that a child has committed an offence, it may direct under Section 21(1), the child to be released on probation of good conduct and placed under the care of his parent, guardian or ony other fit person on executing a bond, with or without surety as that court may require, for a period not exceeding three years. Under sub-section (2) of the same section the court may further stipulate that during probation the child shall remain under the supervision of the probation officer named in the order. The duties of probation officers as described in Section 53(2) are:

  (i) To inquire, in accordance with the direction of the competent authority, into the antecedents and family history of any child accused of an offence with a view to assist the authority in making a decision;

  (ii) to visit neglected and delinquent children at such

intervals as necessary or desirable;

(iii) to report to the competent authority on the behaviour of neglected or delinquent child;

(iv) to advise and assist neglected or delinquent children and, in suitable cases, endeavour to find them suitable employment;

(v) to see in the event of a neglected or delinquent child being placed under the care of any person on certain conditions, that such conditions are being complied with; and

(vi) to perform such other duties as may be prescribed.

Similar provisions have been made in the State Children Acts of Tamil Nadu, Maharasthra, Uttar Pradesh, Karnataka and West Bengal.

It is interesting to note that the probation officer is required to work for both neglected and delinquent children. In the Children Act, there is no mention of probation officers as such, but it can be inferred that 'authorized person' means 'probation officer'.

(9) Supervision and control of voluntary agencies dealing with children: For the control of voluntary social welfare agencies, the Union Government has enacted two laws: the Licencing (Women's and Children's Institutions) Act, 1956, which authorizes State Governments to make rules to implement this Act; and the Orphanages and other Charitable Homes (Supervision and Control) Act, 1960, Act which repeals the earlier law. This is a Central legislation which may be made operative in a State by a resolution of the state legislature concerned. The Act specifically provides that:

(i) the minimum standards regarding boarding lodging, clothing, sanitation, health and hygiene which, having regard to the institution's resources and to the conditions of the locality in which the recognized home is situated, are observed.

(ii) the education and/or training provided for the inmates of the home is of the required quality.

The Act leaves it to State governments to constitute boards of control which must consist of three members of the State legislature, five members of the managing committees in the State, the officer in charge of social welfare work in the State, and six members to be nominated by the State Government. The duty of the Board is to supervise and control generally all matters relating to management of homes in accordance with the provisions of the Act, and exercise such other powers and perform such other functions as may be prescribed by or under this Act (Section 7).

Children Acts also have provisions for controlling institutions established under the Acts. States which have adopted Orphanage Supervision and Control Act may face problem of co-ordinating two sets of controlling laws. To obviate the difficulty, the (Central) Children Act, 1960 provides that the Orphanages and other Charitable Homes (Supervision and Control) Act, 1960, will not apply to children's homes, special schools, or observation homes established and maintained under the Children Act.

LABOUR LAWS AND CHILDREN

Historically, child labour is a concomitant of industrial civilization. The term 'child labour' refers both to an economic practice and to its attendant social evil. As an economic practice, child labour means gainful occupation and material contribution to the income of the family. As a social evil, the term denotes the exploitation of children.

In the early stages of industrialization, women and children always provided a large supply of cheap labour. Machines did not require much physical strength or mental maturity. An indifferent public opinion paid little heed to the plight of children. Absence of adequate educational facilities contributed to the evil. Children worked long hours under insanitary working conditions, causing damage to the health and physical growth of children. Later social awareness of the evil led to the protection of children from exploitation through legislation.

The Directive Principles of State Policy in the Constitution of India forbid the employment of children below 14 years in a factory or mine or in hazardous work.

The following labour laws regulate the employment of children:

(1) The Plantation Labour Act, 1951, which is a Central Act. Under Section 24 of the Act, "no child who has

not completed his twelveth year shall be required or allowed to work in any plantation".

(2) The regulation of shops and establishment is a States' subject. The minimum age prescribed by the various States is not the same. In Andhra Pradesh, Kerala, Punjab, Tamil Nadu and Uttar Pradesh, it is 14 years; in other States it is 12 years.

(3) The Factories Act, 1948, prohibits the employment of children below 14 years.

Similar restrictions on the employment are to be found in Indian Merchant Shipping Act, 1923, Mines Act, 1951, and other laws. As we envisage compulsory education for children upto the age of 14 years, it will be necessary to lay down a uniform minimum age for employment at 14 years in all labour laws. Where, under special circumstances, employment below that age is not prohibited, there should be restrictions on the number of hours, time, place and nature of work.

In agriculture and in cottage industries, as well as in the handicrafts, boys generally join their fathers as apprentices to learn the family trade. However, there are several other fields wherein the tender age of children is exploited and they are made to work under deleterious conditions.

PROTECTION OF WOMEN AND GIRLS

The Indian Penal Code, passed in the latter part of the nineteenth century, contained some penal provisions for the safety and protection of women, and children against kidnapping and abduction. With minor variation, these provisions have remained. Similar provisions find a place also in the various States' Children Acts.

The Government of India being a signatory to the International Convention of 1921 on human traffic, the major Presidencies of Bengal, Bombay and Madras, in 1923, 1923 and 1930 respectively passed Acts for suppression of immoral traffic.

THE SUPPRESSION OF IMMORAL TRAFFIC IN WOMEN AND GIRLS ACT, 1956

India again signed rhe International Convention of 1949, and in 1956 put on the statute-book the Suppression of Immoral Traffic in Women and Girls Act. Although it is a Central Act which repeals the States acts and is applicable to the whole country, the implementation of the Act is the responsibility of State Governments. The Act envisages a comprehensive scheme of suppressing immoral traffic in women and girls by penalizing traffickers and controlling the activities of prostitutes near public places. It also provides for the setting up of 'Protective Homes' and shelters at the State and district levels. Voluntary organisations may establish such homes, subject to a licence issued by a State Government on being satisfied that the home would meet the prescribed standards.

PENAL OFFENCES UNDER THE ACT

The Act provides for the following offences:

(i) keeping a brothel or allowing a premises to be used as brothel (Section 3);

(ii) procuring, inducing or taking women or girls for prostitution (Section 5);

(iii) detaining a woman or a girl in a premises where prostitution is carried on (Section 6);

(iv) carrying on prostitution in, or in the vicinity of, public places (Section 7);

(v) seducing or soliciting for the purpose of prostitution (Section 8); and

(vi) seducing a woman or a girl in custody (Section 9).

The legislation seeks to curb commercialized vice. Women and girls rescued from brothels are to be sent to protective or corrective homes. The Act also provides for the setting up of non-official advisory bodies to assist special police officers, who, while making search of any premises, are required to be accompanied by two responsible persons of the locality, one of whom has to be a woman (Sections 13-15).

The Suppression of Immoral Traffic Act, 1956, suffers from several loopholes, with the result that hardly any convictions take place except under Section 8. The Act calls for a thorough revision.

MATERNITY BENEFIT ACT

The Maternity Benefit Act, 1961, regulates the employment in certain establishments for certain periods before and after child birth; and provides for maternity and certain other benefits.

Every pregnant woman is entitled to maternity benefits, at prescribed rates, for the period of actual absence preceding and for six weeks following the day of delivery. She is also entitled to medical bonus, leave for certain illnesses, nursing breaks, etc. During her absence or pregnancy, she cannot be dismissed or discharged by the employer.

Factories employing women in good numbers are required to set up creches for infants and young children.

CONCLUSION

The foregoing necessarily brief review of both civil and criminal legislation affecting children leads to the conclusion that there is no consistent or integrated approach behind it, children being treated incidentally in the course of handling other matters. There are no cross-references in the legislation to various other relevant provisions of special laws. Based on unco ordinated data produced before them, the courts cannot but be casual while dealing with children's cases. The laws do mention that in family disputes the courts will safeguard the 'welfare' of the child, but they do not lay down any uniform procedure. The child is faced with the formality-ridden awe-inspiring court where even adults feel nervous. We have so far no 'family affairs court' with its friendly cordiality and well-meaning 'conciliators'. No specialization or special training is required of magistrates or judges dealing with family problems or children. There is hardly anything like 'free legal aid' to children or families who cannot afford the services of lawyers. Moreover, proceedings in both criminal and civil suits are intolerably long.

There is no uniform civil code for all citizens. The issue of guardianship of destitute and homeless children is not faced squarely either in the civil code or in children Acts. There is no legal authority for giving a destitute child in adoption or foster-care. The draft legislation on the subject is yet to materialize.

In the (Central) Children Act, 1960, the competent authority dealing with children is split, on to deal with delinquent and another to deal with destitute children. This defeats the very purpose of the Children Acts not to stigmatize the child. It is desirable that all children below a certain age should be processed through a non-statutory, non-penal medium.

The revised Criminal Procedure Code of 1973 abolished the institution of 'honorary magistrates' of juvenile courts, evolved over the past five decades. Thus the atmosphere of informality that prevailed in the juvenile court with the presence of two non-official members on the Bench (one of whom had to be a woman) has disappeared.

It is strongly recommended that a high-level committee be set up by the Union Law Commission to examine the various civil and criminal laws and procedures affecting children to see how far they are in conformity with the Directive Principles of State Policy and with the resolution on the national policy for child welfare.

M.P. Singh

CHAPTER VIII

Legal Framework of Adoptions Amongst Hindus

Adoption of children as a socio-legal institution has existed since the beginning of their legal system. Giving and taking of a child is a futile exercise if law does not recognize it and invests it with some consequences. It is through a legal fiction that the child of one becomes the child of another as if he was his natural-born child. In what manner and the extent to which the fiction applies differ from system to system.

Why Hindu law introduced this fiction and how the institution of adoption became part of the Hindu society is a matter of controversy. Traditionally, adoption has a religious significance: a Hindu must have a son to perform religious ceremonies after his death for the place of his soul. But there is also a secular aspect of adoption: one's desire for the continuation of his name and lineage and the desire, too, of having some one to inherit his property. The present law, however, does not distinguish between sacramental and secular adoptions; both are governed by the same law.

THE CURRENT LAW OF ADOPTION

Till December 21, 1956, adoptions among Hindus were regulated by uncodified law based on Smritis, Commentaries, judicial decisions, and local customs when the Hindu Adoptions and Maintenance Act, 1956 (hereinafter referred to as the Act), came into force. The Act consolidates and codifies the earlier customs and case laws with some significant changes, and now governs all adoptions except those made before the commencement of the Act.[1] The Act extends to the whole of India except the State of Jammu and Kashmir.[2] The word "Hindu" has been broadly defined as one who is (i) Hindu by religion in any of its forms or developments including a Virashaiva, a Lingayat or a follower of the Brahma, Prarthana or Arya Samaj, or (ii) Buddhist, Jain or Sikh by religion, or (iii) not a Muslim, Christian, Parsi or Jew by religion. However, a person is not covered in (iii) if it is proved that "such person would not have been governed by the Hindu law or by any custom or usage as part of that law in respect of any of the matters dealt with" in the Act,[3] had the Act not been passed. Unless the Central Government, by notification in the official gazette, otherwise directs, the Scheduled Tribes are not covered by the word "Hindu", and are therefore outside the provision of the Act.[4]

ADOPTIONS

An adoption can be made "by or to a Hindu" only in accordance with the provisions of the Act, and any adoption made in contravention thereof shall be void. A void adoption cannot create in the adoptive family any rights which the adopted person could not have acquired except by reason of the adoption, nor can it destroy the rights of any person in the family of his birth.[5]

The prerequisites of a valid adoption are discussed below:

(i) **Who may adopt**: Both male as well as female Hindus are competent to adopt a child, subject to certain conditions which differ between males and females. Even among males a distinction has been drawn between one who has a wife living and one who has not. The latter can adopt a son or a daughter if he (i) is of sound mind[6] and (ii) is not a minor.[7] But an

1. The Hindu Adoptions and Maintenance Act, 1956 (hereinafter cited as HAMA) Section 30. See also *Dhaniraiji* v. *Chandraprabha* (1975) 1 SCC 612.
2. HAMA. Section 1.
3. Section (2)
4. Clause(2)
5. Section 5.
6. For soundness of mind no test has been laid down. The onus of proving unsoundness lies on the person who alleges unsoundness. The

additional condition has been imposed on the male who has a wife living. He must have the consent of his wife unless she (i) has completely and finally renounced the world, or (ii) has ceased to be a Hindu, or (iii) has been declared by a court of competent jurisdiction to be of unsound mind. If a person has more than one wife living at the time of adoption, the consent of all the wives is necessary unless the consent of any one or more is rendered unnecessary for any of the three above-mentioned reasons.[8]

Like the male, a female can adopt a son or a daughter. If the female is unmarried, she can adopt subject to the same conditions as a male having no wife, viz., (i) she must be of sound mind and (ii) must not be a minor. But if she is married, she cannot adopt unless (i) her marriage has been dissolved, or (ii) her husband (a) is dead, or (b) has completely and finally renounced the world, or (c) has ceased to be a Hindu, or (d) has been declared by court of competent jurisdiction to be of unsound mind.[9] Thus it is clear that so long as marriage subsists a female cannot adopt even with the consent of her husband unless the husband suffers from any of the above-mentioned disabilities.

This distinction between the position of a married male and that of a married female may not have any practical consequence because in any case an agreement between the two is absolutely essential for a valid adoption.[10] Nevertheless, the law is apparently discriminatory in that while the husband has only to persuade the wife to give her consent, the wife has to persuade the husband to adopt. And since the Act does not insist on any particular form of consent, the husband may say that the presence of the wife at the time of adoption implied or

onus may, however, shift where, for example, it is shown that the adoptive father was found to have been a lunatic—*Gopi* v. *Madan Lal*, A.I.R. 1970 Raj. 190.

7. According to Section 3(c) of the HAMA "minor" is a person who has not completed the age of 18 years.
8. HAMA, Section 7.
9. Section 8.
10. A wife who refuses to give her consent may prevent her husband from adopting a child. See J.D.M. Derret, A Critique of Modern Hindu Law, N.M. Tripathi Pvt. Ltd., Bombay. 130-31 and footnote on 131, 1970.

proved her consent. It must be admitted, though, that the Act is an improvement on the earlier position when the husband could adopt even against the express dissent of the wife, but a woman could not adopt at all, except in some parts of the country and on the express authority of her deceased husband, and then, too not to herself but to her husband.

There are few more conditions, laid down in Section 11, to be satisfied by the person taking in adoption. They are:

(i) if the adoption is of a son, the adoptive father or mother by whom the adoption is made must not have a Hindu son, son's son or son's son's son (whether by legitimate blood relationship or by adoption) living at the time of adoption;

(ii) if the adoption is of a daughter, the adoptive father or mother by whom the adoption is made must not have a Hindu daughter or son's daughter (whether by legitimate blood relationship or by adoption) living at the time of adoption;

(iii) if the adoption is by a male and the person to be adopted is a female, the adoptive father must be at least twentyone years older than the person to be adopted.

(iv) if the adoption is by a female and the person to be adopted is a male, the adoptive mother must be at least twenty-one years older than the person to be adopted.

In (i) and (ii) the word "Hindu" is very material. If a son or a daughter has renounced Hinduism and has converted to any other religion and there is no son or grandson or great grandson, the father or the mother as the case may be has the right to take a son in adoption. The same considerations would apply in case an adopted son becomes a convert to any other religion.

Although the law relating to the competence to adopt appears quite clear and free from ambiguity, it is not actually so. Some genuine difficulties have been found and pointed out. One of them is with respect to those Hindus who marry under the Special Marriage Act, 1954. Such Hindus can adopt a child in accordance with the provisions of the Act, but, if they die intestate their property does not go to the adopted child because the Indian Succession Act, 1925, which governs the succession of property of such Hindus, does not recognize an adopted child as heir; nor can such a child become a member of the Hindu joint family because the adoptive father ceases to be a member of the family on marrying under the Special Marriage Act.[11]

Doubt has also been raised with respect to the capacity of a widowed mother-in-law to adopt a child when a child of the same sex has already been adopted by her widowed daughter-in-law. On a plain reading of the Act there should be no bar on her because in the background of the confused position under the old law, the legislature should be presumed to have authorized every widow to adopt to herself. But in view of *Sawan Ram's Case*,[12] it appears that the mother-in-law is competant to adopt because the daughter-in-law does not adopt to herself but also to her deceased husband, and that being so, the child adopted by the daughter-in-law becomes the grandchild of the mother-in-law and therefore she is barred by section 11(i) and (ii). However, adoption by mother-in-law does not debar the daughter-in-law to adopt.

The Act is silent on the capacity of a *Sanyasi* to adopt. However, there being no disability in him, he can adopt in the same manner as any other male Hindu.[13]

(ii) **Who may give in adoption**: A child may be given in adoption only by his or her father or mother or guardian. If the father is alive, then only he can give the child in adoption subject to the consent of the child's mother. Mother's consent, however, is not necessary if she (i) has completely and finally renounced the world, or (ii) has ceased to be a Hindu, or (iii) has been declared by a court of competent jurisdiction to be of unsound mind.[14] The Act clearly excludes the adoptive father from the definition of "father"[15] and it is submitted

11. This anomaly was first pointed out by Dr. B. Sivaramayya in "Adoption: An Anomaly under the Indian Succession Act", SCJ 20 (1960). See also Derret, *Ibid.* at 128 and Paras Diwan, Modern Hindu Law, 194-95 (Allahabad: ALA 1972).
12. *Sawan Ram* v. *Kalawati*, A.I.R. 1967 SC 1761.
13. See Derret, supra f.n. 11 at 131 and Diwan, supra f.n. 12 at 195. For some other anomalies, see Derret, at 132-35.
14. HAMA, Section 9(2).
15. *Ibid.*, Explanation (i).

that a putative or stepfather is also excluded.[16] Therefore only a person who begets a child in a valid wedlock[17] can give the child in adoption.

A question might arise, as it did under the old law, whether a father, who himself was adopted after his marriage,[18] can give in adoption his children born prior to his adoption? The old law supplied an affirmative as well as a negative answer to this question.[19] The Act being silent, it can be argued that since on adoption all the ties of a person in the family of his birth are severed, the negative answer is more sound.[20] However, denial of authority to such a person would not be very reasonable if his wife and children followed him on his adoption and continued to live with him in the family of his adoption.

A mother can give a child in adoption only if the father (i) is dead, or (ii) has completely and finally renounced the world, or (iii) has ceased to be a Hindu, or (iv) has been declared by a court of competent jurisdiction to be of unsound mind.[21] Just as a woman whose husband is not dead and does not suffer from any disability is incompetent to take in adoption, so she is also incompetent to give in adoption if her husband is alive and does not suffer from any of the above mentioned disabilities. As in the case of father, so also in case of mother, only a natural mother (neither a stepmother[22] nor an adoptive mother[23]). However the mother, can give in adoption even her illegitimate child.

16. Diwan, supra at 198. On the anology of Dhanraj's case, infra f.n. 24, where the Supreme Court has held that a step mother is excluded from giving a child in adoption, it may be said that the same will be the position of the father.
17. Valid marriage would include a voidable marriage and also a void marriage declared null and void by a court. See Section 16 of the Hindu Marriage Act, 1956.
18. A married person can be adopted if the custom or usage applicable to the parties permits such adoption: HAMA, Section 10(iii).
19. See *Martand* v. *Narayan,* 1939 Bom. 305 and *Sharad Chand* v. *Shanta Bai*, 1944 Nag. 266.
20. See Diwan, supra f.n. 12 at 198.
21. HAMA, Section 9(3).
22. *Dhanraj* v. *Suraj Bai*, (1975) 2 SCC 251.
23. HAMA, Section 9, Explanation (i).

A guardian[24] can give a child in adoption only if the parents[25] of the child (i) are dead, or (ii) have completely and finally renounced the world, or (iii) have abandoned the child, or (iv) have been declared by a court of competent jurisdiction to be of unsound mind, or (v) are not known.[26] Although the guardian's authority to give a child in adoption is as wide as that of the parents, he can exercise it only with the prior permission of the court.[27] Before granting permission the court should be satisfied that the adoption is for the welfare of the child. After giving due consideration to the wishes of the child, in the light of the age and understanding of the child, and after making sure that the applicant has not received or agreed to receive any payment or reward in consideration of the adoption except such as the court may sanction.[28] Since the acceptance of any payment or reward in consideration of any adoption is punishable,[29] it may be presumed that the court will sanction only such payments as are necessary for the welfare of the child. The punishment provision also suggests that the validity of an adoption will not be affected by the acceptance of money or reward as consideration for the adoption. The provision for punishment constitutes a check on undesirable practices which could develop into trafficking in human beings under cover of adoption.

A guardian can give the child in adoption even to himself.[30]

(iii) **Who may be adopted**: The Act permits the adoption of males as well as of females. But no person is capable of being

24. Guardian, according to Explanation of Section 9 (ia) is "a person having the care of the person of a child or both of his person and property and includes—
    (a) a guardian appointed by the will of the child's father or mother, and
    (b) a guardian appointed or declared by a court."
25. Parents means father and mother who are competent to give a child in adoption.
26. HAMA, Section 9(4).
27. "Court means the city civil court or a district court within local limits of whose jurisdiction the child to be adopted ordinarily resides." HAMA, Section 9, Explanation (ii).
28. HAMA, Section 9(5).
29. *Ibid.*, Section 17.
30. *Ibid.*, Section 9(4).

taken in adoption unless the following conditions are fulfilled:

(i) he or she is a Hindu;
(ii) he or she has not already been adopted;
(iii) he or she has not been married; and
(iv) he or she has not completed the age of fifteen years.

Conditions (iii) and (iv) may be waived if the custom or usage applicable to the parties permits the adoption of married persons or of those who have completed the age of fifteen years.[31] A person cannot be adopted simultaneously by two or more persons.[32]

The old law was very complicated about the competence of persons to be adopted. Females could not be adopted except in certain areas in the south where adoption of females was permitted by custom.[33] The law also insisted that the person to be adopted must be of the same caste as that of the adoptive family and that he must be a nearest sapinda and must not be one whose mother the adoptive father could not have legally married. Similarly, disabled, deformed, orphan, abandoned, fondlings and illegitimate children could not be adopted under the old law. The present law has done away with all these disabilities. It has not only been simplified but also liberalized and modernized to help solve certain social problems, such as casteism and illegitimate children.

(iv) **Ceremony of Adoption**: The law does not prescribe the performance of *datta homam* or any other religious ceremony for adoption. But it clearly says that "the child to be adopted must be actually given and taken in adoption by the parents or guardian concerned or under their authority with intent to transfer the child from the family of its birth or in case of an abandoned child or a child whose parentage is not known, from the place or family where it has been brought up to the family of its adoption."[34] The ceremony of giving and taking is absolutely necessary whether the adoption is of a minor or of an adult.[35] The performance of this ceremony cannot even be

31. *Ibid.*, Section 10. See also *Housbai* v. *Jijabai,* A.I.R. 1972 Bom. 98 and *Dhanraj* v. *Surajbai*, (1975) 2 SCC 251.
32. HAMA, Section 11(v).
33. See *Brijendra* v. *Chitra*, A.I.R. 1961 M.P. 173.
34. HAMA, Section 11 (vi).
35. *Dhanraj* v. *Surajbai*, A.I.R. 1973 Raj. 7.

delegated to some other person though, of course, some one may be expressly authorized to give and take if the persons giving and taking the child are incapable of doing so because of some physical disability or infirmity.

The fact of adoption need not be recorded in writing and if so recorded, need not be registered. However, if the person giving and the person taking in adoption have recorded the fact of adoption and have got it registered, then, unless otherwise provided, the presumption is that the adoption has been made in compliance with the provisions of the Act.[36] Thus, though the registration cannot be a substitute for the ceremony of giving and taking, it is helpful in proving the ceremony.

EFFECTS OF ADOPTION

The effects of an adoption are mentioned in Section 12 of the Act. Because the interpretation of this section has caused serious controversy, it is proper to reproduce the section.

It reads:

> An adopted child shall be deemed to be the child of his or her adoptive father or mother for all purposes with effect from the date of adoption and from such date all the ties of the child in the family of his or her birth shall be deemed to be severed and replaced by those created by the adoption in the adoptive family:
>
> Provided that—
>
> (a) the child cannot marry any person whom he or she could not have married if he or she had continued in the family of his or her birth;
>
> (b) any property which vested in the adopted child before the adoption shall continue to vest in such person subject to the obligations, if any, attaching to the ownership of such property, including the obligation to maintain relatives in the family of his or her birth;
>
> (c) the adoptive child shall not divest any person of any estate which vested in him or her before the adoption.

On a plain reading of the section it seems clear that the adopted person is treated as if he was born in the adoptive family and not in the family which gave him in adoption. All his relationships in and through the family of his birth are

36. HAMA, Section 16.

snapped and new relationships in and through the adoptive family are established. For purposes of succession on paternal as well as maternal side as well as for purposes of Hindu joint family and coparcenary he is treated to be the natural child of his adoptive parent or parents as if he was not born in the family of his birth.

This interpretation has become controversial with respect to the effects of adoption made by a widow. Under the old law a widow could adopt only on behalf of and to her husband and therefore the adoption was deemed to have been made by the deceased husband himself. Strictly speaking, in such cases the adopted child was deemed to have been in the womb of the adoptive mother at the time of the death of her husband. Thus the adoption was antedated from the time of the death of the widow husband. This was called the doctrine of "relation back". This had certain consequences. For example, those who got the estate of the deceased either by inheritance or by survivorship or through transfers not for legal necessity or benefit of the estate could be divested of that estate on a valid adoption by his widow. For sometime it appeared that the words "with effect from the date of adoption" in Section 12 had abrogated the doctrine of relation back and that proviso (c) had done away with its effects. But in *Sawan Ram* v. *Kalawati*[37] the Supreme Court refused to accept such an unqualified approach to Section 12. The main question in the case was whether a person adopted by a widow should be treated as the adopted son of the widow alone or of the both widow and deceased husband. The court held that the person was the adopted son of both on two grounds. First relying on the words "by or to a Hindu" in Section 5(1) it said:

> On the face of it, adoption to a Hindu was intended to cover cases where an adoption is by one person, while the child adopted becomes the adopted son of another person also.[38]

Secondly, emphasizing the words preceding the provisions of Section 12, it observed:

37. A.I.R. 1967 SC 1761. Prior to this decision some High Courts had also taken a similar view. See, *Ankush Narain* v. *Janabai*, A.I.R. 1966 Bom. 174; *Subhash* v. *Thagi*, A.I.R. 1967 All. 148 and *Hanumantha* v. *Hanumayya* (1964) 1 An.W.R. 156.
38. *Sawan Ram* v. *Kalawati*, *ibid.*, at 1764-65.

> It is well recognised that, after the female is married, she belongs to the family of her husband. The child adopted by her must also, therefore, belong to the same family. On adoption by a widow, therefore, the adopted son is to be deemed to be a member of the family of the deceased husband of the widow.[39]

Clarifying the position of proviso (c) of the section the court observed:

> It appears that by making such a provision, the Act has narrowed down the rights of an adopted child as compared with the rights of a child born posthumously. Under the Shastric law, if a child was adopted by a widow, he was treated as a natural born child and, consequently, he could divest other members of the family of rights vested in them prior to his adoption. It was only with the limited object of avoiding any such consequence on the adoption of a child by a Hindu widow that the provisions in clause (c) of the proviso to Section 12 and Section 13 of the Act were incorporated. In that respect the rights of the adopted child were restricted. It is to be noted that this restriction was placed on the rights of a child adopted by either a male or a female Hindu and not merely in case of adoption by a female Hindu. This restriction on the rights of the adopted child cannot, therefore, in our opinion, lead to any inference that a child adopted by a widow will not be deemed to be the adopted son of her deceased husband.[40]

The Supreme Court reiterated this stand in *Sitabai* v. *Ramchandra*,[41] without, however, referring to *Sawan Ram*. In this case a widow had an illegitimate son (born during her widowhood) as well as an adopted son, both of whom laid claim to joint family property. The Supreme Court reversed the judgment of the High Court and upheld the adopted son's claim. In doing so Ramaswami J., *inter alia*, said:

> The scheme of Sections 11 and 12, therefore, is that in the case of adoption by a widow the adopted child becomes absorbed in the adoptive family to which the widow belonged. In other words the child adopted is tied with the

39. *Ibid.*, 1765.
40. *Ibid.*
41. A.I.R. 1970 SC 343.

relationship of sonship with the deceased husband of the widow. The other collateral relations of the husband would be connected with the child through that deceased husband of the widow .... It is true that Section 14 of the Act does not expressly state that the child adopted by the widow becomes the adopted son of the husband of the widow. But it is a necessary implication of Sections 12 and 14 of the Act that a son adopted by the widow becomes a son not only of the widow but also of the deceased husband ... In other words the result of adoption by either spouse is that that the adopted child becomes the child of the spouses.[42]

The two judgements highlight the fact that a Hindu widow, particularly a widow in a joint family, cannot be equated with a widow in any other system or with a spinster or a divorcee.[43] A widow has certain rights in the family which a divorcee or a spinster does not have. The type of relationship which the widow creates for the adopted child cannot be created by a spinster or a divorcee. Her adopted child has relatives both on the maternal and the paternal sides, while the adopted child of a spinster or a divorcee may not have any relative except his adoptive mother or, at the most, relatives on the maternal side. A son adopted by a widow in a joint family becomes coparcener with other members of the coparcenary. Refusal to admit him as coparcener may apart from shackling the widow's right to adopt, disrupt the family structure.

Section 13 says that adoption does not deprive the adoptive father or the adoptive mother of the right to dispose of his or her property by transfer *inter vivos* or by will.[44] But by an agreement between the adoptive father or mother and the person giving the child in adoption, the right of disposal of property may be restricted.[45]

CANCELLATION OF AN ADOPTION

A valid adoption once made can't be cancelled by the adop-

42. *Ibid.*, at 347-48 Emphasis supplied.
43. See Diwan, *ibid.* at 213. He advocates that a widow should not be treated differently from a spinster or a divorcee.
44. HAMA, Section 13.
45. *Ibid.*

tive father or mother or any other person. Nor can the adopted boy or girl renounce his or her status as such and return to the family of his or her birth.[46] However, the Supreme Court has held that if a customary adoption made prior to the commencement of the Act was revocable under that custom, then revocation is valid even after the commencement of the Act.[47]

CONCLUSION

In addition to simplifying and modifying the law, the Act has heralded an era of social change. It is based on egalitarian principles and excepting one or two minor instances of discrimination based on sex, it washes the ugliness of the earlier law. We have no detailed sociological data concerning the impact of the Act on actual social behaviour, but its application has posed no serious problems or difficulties. That it has not spunned litigation is an indicator of its smooth working.

The Act has been criticised for not providing for state supervision of adoptions. State intervention may be helpful in checking misuse of the law. A bill titled The Adoption of Children Bill, 1972, pending in Parliament, takes care of this matter.[48] The passage of the bill will be a long step in the direction of a uniform civil code envisaged by Article 44 of the Constitution, because it will apply to all persons. Muslims opinion is opposed to it because adoption is inconsistent with Koranic law. However, since the Bill does not make adoption mandatory but only seeks to regulate those that do take place, such Muslims as refrain from adopting will not be affected.[49]

46. *Ibid.*, Section 15.
47. *Dhaniraiji* v. *Chandraprabha*, (1975) 1 SCC 612.
48. See Sections 4, 8, 9, 10, 11, 12, 13, 14, etc. of the Adoption of Children Bill, 1972.
49. Tahir Mahmood, in "Muslim Law", *Annual Survey of Indian Law*, 227-28; The Indian Law Institute, New Delhi, 1973, 227-28, suggests that the proposed law is neither inconsistent with Muslim Law nor imposes any compulsion on Muslims.

S.D. Gokhale

CHAPTER IX

Guardianship of Minors under the Hindu Law

Since 1956, the guardianship of minors among Hindus is governed by the Hindu Minority and Guardianship Act, 1956, read with the Guardians and Wards Act, 1890. Prior to the Act of 1956, the matter came within the purview of the Hindu Law, since very early times minors have been a subject of concern among Hindus. A minor was called a Poganda by Narada.

(1) Manu declares that "the King shall protect the inherited (and other) property of a minor, until he has returned (from his teacher's house)/or until he has passed his minority."

(2) Minority under the Hindu Law terminates at the age of sixteen, whether at the beginning or at the end is not clear. The rule is based on the text of Narada: "A child is comparable to an embryo upto the eighth year. A youth who has not yet reached the age of sixteen is called Poganda. Afterwards he is no longer a minor and independent in case his parents are dead."

(3) According to the Dayabhaga School, the age of majority is attained at the beginning of the sixteenth year, while according to the views of all others, it is on the completion of the sixteenth year. This controversy was set at rest by the passing of the Indian Majority Act, 1875, which applies to all persons domiciled in India and to all matters except marriage, dower, divorce and adoption. According to this Act, every minor of whose person or property a guardian has been appointed by any court and every minor of whose property the superinten-

dence has been assumed by a Court of Wards is deemed to have attained his majority at the completion of the twenty-first year; and in all other cases, at the completion of the eighteenth year.

Under the Hindu Law, there are three types of guardians: (i) natural guardians, (ii) guardians appointed by a father's will (testamentary guardians), and (iii) guardians appointed under the Guardians and Wards Act, 1890. The father is the natural guardian of a minor, and after him the mother. The husband is the guardian of a minor wife. The power of a natural guardian, if he is a father and a Karta or a manager of a joint Hindu family, are wide.

Under Hindu Law, there are mainly two types of property: separate property, and joint family property. The male members of a joint family constitute a coparcenary. Members of a coparcenary have no fixed shares in the joint family property, shares increasing in case of death in joint family and decreasing in case of birth in the joint family. The eldest male member is the Karta of the joint family. His powers to alienate the joint family property were defined by the Privy Council as follows in *Hanooman Parsaud* v. *Musamat Babooee*. The power of the manager for an infant heir to charge an estate not his own, is under the Hindu Law, a limited and qualified power. It can only be exercised rightly in a case of need or for the benefit of the estate. The actual pressure on the estate, the danger to be averted, or the benefit to be conferred upon it, in the particular instance, is the thing to be regarded. Their lordships think that the lender is bound to enquire into the necessities for the loan, and to satisfy himself as well as he can with reference to the parties with whom he is dealing, that the manager is acting in the particular instance for the benefit of the estate. But they think that if he does so inquire, and acts honestly, the real existence of all alleged, sufficient and reasonably credited necessity is not a condition precedent to the validity of his charge and they do not think that under the circumstances, he is bound to see to the application of the money. Thus the manager could alienate joint family property for legal necessity or benefit of the estate.

(4) Thus, under Hindu Law, as in force before 1956, a *de facto* guardian of a minor could dispose of, or deal with, the

property of a Hindu minor.

Under the old Hindu Law, the mother had no right to make a will and appoint a testamentary guardian for the person and property of a minor.

Under the personal law of the Hindus, when the father is alive, he, and not the mother, is entitled to the custody of a minor child of whatever age. But in *re Muruga*, it was held that where the father had taken a second wife, the custody of a minor girl of very tender years was to be given to her mother.

(5) Under the old Hindu Law, the Father as the Karta of the joint family is entitled to manage the whole coparcenary property including the minor's interest. The mother is not entitled to the custody of the undivided interest of her minor son in the joint property (because such property is not separate property), though she is entitled to the custody of his person and of his separate property, if any. In *Bindaji* v. *Mathurabai*, it was held that if all the sons were minors, the court might appoint a guardian of the whole of the joint property until one of them attained majority.

The Shastraic Hindu Law was not uniform. There were differences between different schools of Hindu law, all rooted in ancient divergent customs and traditions. The Government of India therefore decided to codify the Hindu Law. However, only four measures towards codification were enacted: (i) The Hindu Marriage Act, 1955; (ii) The Hindu Succession Act, 1956; (iii) The Hindu Minority Guardianship Act, 1956; and (iv) The Hindu Adoptions & Maintenance Act, 1956.

THE HINDU MINORITY AND GUARDIANSHIP ACT, 1956

The purpose of the Act was to amend and codify certain parts of the law relating to minority and guardianship among Hindus. It came into force on 25 August 1956. It extends to the whole of India except the State of Jammu and Kashmir. It applies to every person domiciled in India and wherever residing who is not a Muslim, Christian, Parsi or Jew by religion (Section 3). In effect this section covers even those non-Hindus who do not profess any of the four above-mentioned faiths. The law thus does not leave any one in a state of religionlessness.

This enactment replaces the traditional Hindu Law of guardianship hitherto applicable to Hindus by virtue of any text, rule or interpretation, or any custom or usages having the force of law. Thus, both the provisions of the Dharmashastras and the judicial precedents are nullified for the sake of uniformity and progressive outlook (Section 5 (a)).

It may be noted that the Act does not supplant but supplements the Guardians and Wards Act, 1890. Section 8(5) of the Act provides that the Guardians and Wards Act, 1890 shall apply to and in respect of applications under section 8(2) preferred by the natural guardian for previous permission of the court to mortgage or charge, or transfer by sale, gift, exchange or otherwise, any part of the immovable property of the minor or for leasing minor's property for more than 5 years or for more than 1 year beyond the date on which the minor will attain majority. Again Section 8(6) of the Act provides that Court means the City Civil Court or a District Court or a Court empowered under section 4A of the Guardians and Wards Act, 1890. This law did not interfere with the rights of the natural guardian of a minor Hindu except in so far as it empowered the court to appoint a guardian in certain situations.

Section 4(a) of the Hindu Minority and Guardianship Act, 1956 defines 'minor' as a person who has not completed the age of eighteen years. It defines guardian (Section 4(b)) as a person having the care of the person of a minor or of his property or of both. It divides guardian into four classes: (i) natural guardian, (ii) testamentary guardian, (iii) court guardian and (iv) a person empowered to act as such by or under any enactment relating to any court of wards. The last type of guardian did not form part of the traditional Hindu Law.

The provisions relating to the natural guardian in this Act are generally on the same lines as the traditional Hindu Law. However, a significant and welcome change is introduced by section 6(a) of the Act. Whereas, under the old Hindu law, a father was the natural guardian of a minor Hindu of whatever age and the mother had no right to be recognized as a natural guardian, section 6(a) of the Act provides that the custody of a minor who has not completed the age of five years shall ordinarily be with the mother. This is in keeping with the modern spirit which recognizes that the mother is better suited by nature to be the natural guardian of a child of tender age. Another departure from the traditional Hindu Law has been made in respect of the powers of the natural guardian. Whereas the traditional Hindu Law gave the natural guardian full power to alienate the minor's property for legal necessity or benefit of estate, this Act makes the exercise of that power subject to the permission of the court which is enjoined not to grant such permission except in case of necessity or for an evident advantage to the minor. Thus, the power of the natural guardian to dispose of or to deal with the minor's property for the benefit of the estate (for example, to protect the estate from some threatened danger or destruction) has been taken away. Section 8 makes alienation without court's permission voidable at the instance of the minor or any person acting for him. The same section also provides that application for permission to part with minor's property will be governed by the procedure laid down in Section 29 of the Guardians & Wards Act, 1890. Thus the effect of Section 8 of the 1956 Act is to bring on par the natural guardian and the court-appointed or court-declared guardian in the matter of alienation of the minor's property.

Section 9(4) of the Act vests the Hindu mother entitled to act as a natural guardian of her legitimate or illegitimate minor child with power to appoint a testamentary guardian in respect of the minor's person or property or both. Section 7 of the Act declares that the natural guardianship of an adopted minor son passes on adoption to the adoptive father, and after him to the adoptive mother.

Section 10 makes a minor incompetent to act as the guardian of the property of any minor. This means that a minor can be the guardian of the person of any minor; for example, a minor husband of his minor wife.

Another timely change brought about by Section 11 of the Act in the traditional Hindu Law is the deprivation of the powers of *a de facto* guardian to deal with the minor's property. It lays down in express terms that after the coming into operation of the Act no person shall be entitled to dispose of or deal with the property of a Hindu minor on the ground of his or her being the *de facto* guardian of the minor.

The Hindu Minority and Guardianship Act, 1956 and the

Guardians and Wards Act, 1890 together make the minor's welfare the primary and paramount consideration of the court in deciding matters of minors and their guardianship. The state is *pater patriae* and as such has jurisdiction to do all acts and things necessary for the protection of minors who, by reason of their natural immaturity are incapable of forming a rational judgement on proposals made to them, and are therefore incapable of entering into valid contacts. A minor thus needs a guardian to protect his interests. That is why law casts a duty on the court to appoint a guardian when it is satisfied that it would be minor's welfare to appoint or declare a person as a guardian of the minor's person or property or both Sections 7 and 17 of the Guardians and Wards Act, 1890 provide the criteria for the appointment of a guardian. Section 17 directs the court, in a matter of appointing a guardian to the age, sex and religion of the minor; the character and capacity of the proposed guardian and his nearness of kin to the minor; the wishes, if any, of a deceased parent and any existing or previous relations of the proposed guardian with the minor; and, if the minor is old enough to form an intelligent preference, the minor's preference. In a case, it was held that where the father is of unsound mind, the mother can be appointed guardian of the minor in preference to the brother (Section 7). Under the Hindu Minority and Guardianship Act, 1956, also the welfare of the minor Hindu is made the statutory paramount consideration in appointing a guardian (Section 13).

It is necessary to note that under Section 12 no guardian can be appointed for the minor's undivided interests in joint family property, because the peculiar nature of the Hindu joint family property itself provides for the management of the minor's interest by the Karta of the joint family. Every coparcener in a Mitakshara joint family (this name is derived from the celebrated commentary of Vijnyashwar on Yagnyavalkya Smriti) acquires a right by birth in the joint family property, which is managed by the eldest male member of the family known as the Karta.

It will be seen that the Hindu Minority and Guardianship Act has brought about a number of salient changes in the traditional Hindu Law:

(1) It has abrogated the traditional Hindu Law including

the Smriti Law and relevant judicial precedents.

(2) To alineate the minor's property by making it subject to court's permission.

(3) It brings on a par the powers of natural guardian, the testamentary guardian and the guardian appointed or declared by court.

(4) It vests the Hindu mother with power to appoint a testamentary guardian for her legitimate or illegitimate children.

(5) It makes voidable, at the instance of the minor, any disposal or immovable property, by natural guardian in contravention of the set limits.

(6) It vests in the court the power to sanction disposal of the minor's immovable property, and only if there is a necessity or if the court is satisfied that the disposal of the property is to the evident advantage of the minor.

(7) It abrogates the power of a *de facto* guardian to deal with minor's property.

(8) It makes the welfare of the minor the paramount consideration of the court.

It would be relevant to consider the question of guardianship in marriage and adoption. Section 6 of the Hindu Marriage Act, 1955, gives a preferential list of persons who can give consent to marriage where consent is necessary. The section also lays down that such a guardian must himself have completed 21 years of age. The consent of a guardian is necessary where the bride is below 18 years.

In the matter of adoption, Section 9 of the Hindu Adoptions & Maintenance Act, 1956, provides that where the parentage of the child is unknown, the guardian of the child may give the child in adoption, with the previous permission of the court, to any person including the guardian himself.

It will be seen that the Hindu Minority & Guardianship Act marks a forward step in the modernization of Hindū Law by enlarging the rights of the mother, by curbing the powers of a natural guardian in order to protect the interest of the minor, and by making welfare of the minor a paramount consideration. Thus, this enactment can rightly be considered a welfare measure for the minor.

ADOPTION OF MINORS

Although adoption does not replace the biological relationship between the child and its natural parents, it does reconstitute a stable family through the enduring ties which it creates. Adoption is to be regarded as the most complete means whereby family life can be restored to a child deprived of its natural family. It was inevitable, therefore, that adoption should become one of the effective instruments of social action.

(1) **The Hindu Adoption and Maintenance Act, 1956**. The ancient law of adoption for Hindus was awfully dissimilar and uncertain; different schools of Hindu Law followed different authorities, which were in their turn interpreted differently by Hindu law commentators and courts. In order to bring about uniformity in different schools of Hindu Law the Government of India decided to codify Hindu adoption laws in the Hindu Adoptions and Maintenance Act, 1956. For the first time, uniformity has been ensured in the adoption law throughout India, irrespective of the school of Hindu law operating in that locality.

(2) **The Guardianship and Wards Act, 1890**. In India, in the absence of a secular adoption law it is not possible for a non-Hindu to adopt a child. Muslim, Parsees, Jews, and Christians interested in adopting a child have to take recourse to the Guardianship and Wards Act, 1890, by virtue of which they are appointed legal guardians of a minor till the latter attains the age of eighteen. The ward has no right to the family name or to the coparcenary property. The guardians are usually advised to make a will in the name of the child during their lifetime to provide the child the necessary financial security.

A new development is the adoption of Indian children by foreigners. Foreigners, like Indian non-Hindus, have to take recourse to the Guardianship and Wards Act. The prospective adopting parents have to petition the High Court to grant them guardianship of a child. On the petition having granted, the child is removed out of India, and possibly adoption takes place in that country under the law of that land. In absence of a valid adoption agreement between the two countries, the procedure is rather risky, for adoption laws differ from country to country. Before placing a child under the guardianship of a foreigner it is imperative to ensure that adoptive parents fulfil the necessary legal requirements of their country, and also to ensure that the child's adoption is completed in its adoptive country. Or else, the child may find itself without legal status and without security.

The above procedure did not provide for evaluation and matching of the needs of the child with those of the parents. The High Court had to decide without professional intervention or social welfare assistance. In the absence of a proper enquiry by a competent welfare agency in the parent's country to assess the suitability of the adoptive parents, it was not possible to ensure the assimilation of the child in the new community so that as an adult he/she could confidently face serious questions such as marriage and employment. It was also observed that even legal procedures were not always followed strictly; in some cases children on remand and commitment under the Bombay Children Act were given in adoption under the Guardians and Wards Act by some of the well-known child welfare agencies in Bombay.

With a view to streamlining the procedure, the Indian Council of Social Welfare moved the High Court of Bombay to issue a notification appointing the Indian Council to assist the High Court in this matter. The High Court was pleased to amend the Rules, adding a new Rule 361-B and issued the following notifications on 10 May 1972.

"Application by foreigner for appointment as guardian of person or property of minor—Rull 361-B. When a foreigner makes an application for being appointed as the guardian of the person or property of a minor, the Prothonotary and Senior Master shall address a letter to the Secretary of the Indian Council of Social Welfare, informing him of the presentation of the application and the date fixed for the hearing thereof. He shall also inform him that any representation which the Indian Council of Social Welfare may make in the matter would be considered by the court before passing the order on application. A copy of the application shall be forwarded to the Secretary of the Indian Council of Social Welfare along with the letter of the Prothonotary and Senior Master."

A Case Reviewing Committee, consisting of experts in the

legal and social welfare field, scrutinizes each position and gives its observations, which the court duly considers before passing an order. After the child leaves the country the parents and the supervising agency in that country have to send periodic follow-up reports of the child's adjustment in its new country till its regular adoption in accordance with the law of that land.

It is absolutely necessary to make sure that the socio-legal processes involved in inter-country adoptions provide adequate safeguards. The European Convention on this subject laid down the main guidelines in this behalf, some of which are reproduced below:

(1) That adoptions are the best substitute for care by the child's own parents or close relatives, provided that adoption is based fundamentally on the welfare of the child.

(2) That sufficient consideration should be given to possible alternative plans for the child within his own country before inter-country adoption is decided upon, since there are various hazards inherent in transplanting a child from one culture to another.

(3) That increased efforts should be made in each country to examine at as early a stage as possible whether certain children should be adopted within the country, rather than remaining indefinitely in institutions.

(4) That efforts should be made in each country to find adoptive homes within the country for children with certain mental or physical defects and for children whose family background presents an obstacle to adoption.

(5) That extremely careful consideration should be given to all possible alternatives before a child is removed from his own relatives for adoption, that a parent, regardless of social and legal status, should have the opportunity for full consideration of what is involved, including legal and psychological consequences before a decision is made that adoption is the best plan for the child; that concepts of modern child and family welfare should prevail over economic and social factors.

(6) That those who have ties, legal or emotional, to the

child should be helped to understand thoroughly the meaning of adoption in the culture of the new country; that the child, if old enough, should also be prepared for the implications of adoption and life in the new country; that unless this can be done and the consequences accepted by all the concerned, the child should not be considered suitable for inter-country adoption.

(7) That an adequate home study of the perspective adopters should be completed before a child is suggested to, or placed with, a couple with a view to inter-country adoption, as well as an adequate study of the child's background, physical condition and personality development; that it is recognised that a home study of the adoptive parents may have a limited value when the parents are living in temporary setting so that there are often valid reasons for not considering such couples as prospective adoptive parents unless they live in one setting for a sufficient length of time where they can be studied by a social worker who is sufficiently familiar with their culture, and an appraisal, of them in their own home community can be obtained, before a child is suggested to or placed with them.

(8) That the process of matching together child and adoptive parents in inter-country adoption should be a shared responsibility between the child welfare agency which makes the home study of the prospective adopters and the child welfare agency responsible for the child, with the participation of the specialised international social welfare agency acting as intermediary between the two. All relevant factors which are accepted as valid in matching child and adoptive parents in local adoptions shall be taken into consideration with special attention to the factor of religion.

(9) That before legal adoption is completed, there must be a trial period of not less than 6 months under the supervision of a social worker attached to a qualified agency, able to understand the cultural patterns of the prospective adopters and the child; in the case of older children this period should be longer.

That there is opposition to proxy adoptions except

under certain exceptional circumstances where prospective adoptors and child have lived together for a reasonable time and established a satisfactory parent-child relationship.

(10) That care must be given, before the adoption plan is finalised, that pertinent documents necessary to complete the adoption are available particularly that all necessary consents are in a form which is legally valid in both countries; that it must definitely be established that the child will be able to immigrate in the country of the prospective adopters and can subsequently obtain their nationality.

That care must be given to assuring adequate protection of the child in his new country, and that in view of the difficulty or exercising guardianship functions across national boundaries, the value of the former legal guardianship needs to be examined; that legal responsibility for the child in the new country should be established promptly.

That steps should be taken to assure that the adoption is legally valid in both countries.

The change in emphasis from viewing adoption primarily as a means of providing childless couples with heirs to the current practice to see it as a possible solution for children deprived of normal home life makes it necessary to draw adoption work into the framework of social services administered and staffed by qualified professionals. It is not generally recognized that the task of assessing the need of a child for adoption, of assessing the suitability of couples as adoptive parents, of matching child and parents, and of helping them through a trial period of living together until adoption is completed can be handled only by qualified persons. Experience shows that when unqualified persons, howsoever well-meaning, become involved, there is a risk, because of their ignorance of the social, psychological and legal factors in inter-country adoptions, that adoptions may not callest to tragedy turn out to be in the best interests of children, natural parents and adoptive parents. The best solution would seem to be to have a national law on adoption of children irrespective of religion or nationality.

The Adoption of Children Bill, 1972, pending before the

Parliament, is an important welfare oriented measure, which ensures maximum security to the child whether adopted by Indians or foreigners. The Indian Council of Social Welfare, along with Indian Council for Child Welfare, All India Women's Council and Guild Service voiced strong support to this Bill. All efforts should be made to have it placed on the statute book as early as possible.

A.S. Bedi

CHAPTER X

Juristic Framework for Protection of Morals in India

This paper seeks to review the juristic framework for protection of morals in India, especially the constitutional norms, the offences affecting public morals under the Penal Code, The Young Persons (Harmful Publications) Act, 1956, The Cinematograph Act, 1952, and to highlight the problems connected with its implementation.

CONSTITUTIONAL NORMS

Our founding fathers had emphasized the importance of moral values even in the struggle for independence. With the advent of freedom major concern was focussed on economic growth with social justice and on reconstruction of the society so that India took its proper place in the comity of nations. It was realized that the underpinning of moral values is the removal of inequalities and the ushering in of a new social order. The new goals were set down thus in the Constitution of India. "The State shall strive to promote the welfare of the people by securing and protecting as effectively as it may a social order in which justice, social, economic and political, shall inform all the institutions of the national life"[1] and further, the "State shall in particular, direct its policy towards securing . . . that childhood and youth are protected against exploitation and against moral . . . abandonment".[2]

1. Directive Principles of State Policy, Part IV, Article 38.
2. *Ibid.*, Article 39(f).

So concerned were the Constitution-makers about the interests of the general public that they sought to strike a balance between the conflicting ideals of individual freedom and social good and even qualified the freedom of speech and expression, the matrix of all freedoms.[3] The Directive Principles of State Policy also emphasize the welfare of the people and enjoin the State to protect childhood and youth against moral abandonment. In fine, the Constitution makes it the duty of the State to safeguard public morality.

INDIAN PENAL CODE AND MORALS

It is essential for the maintenance of public morality that the moral fabric of the individual and of family be strengthened. This cannot be done by law alone, for law has its limitations. Hence the Indian Penal Code only provides certain checks against moral exploitation and deviation from well-accepted decencies. In this way, it indirectly upholds the community mores—including the sex mores.

It thus makes assault or use of physical force on a woman with intent to outrage, or knowing that it is likely that he will thereby outrage, her modesty a criminal offence. But a woman's modesty is not merely her sex; it is the sense of shame stemming from aversion to certain things and acts forcibly taking off a girl's clothes, or seizing her by the arm or making amorous overtures against her wishes, for example, would fall within the prohibition. The law thus seeks to protect women against indecent behaviour cf others which is offensive to public morality.

Under Section 509 of the Indian Penal Code assault or criminal force is not essential; it would suffice to make any word, sound, gesture or exhibition of any object an offence if the intention is to insult the modesty of a woman. Any intrusion upon her privacy to insult her modesty would thus be a crime. A person who sent by post a letter containing indecent overtures to a woman was held guilty.

3. Constitution of India, Art. 19(1): "All citizens shall have the right—(a) to freedom of speech and expression . . . (2) Nothing in sub-clause (a) of clause(1) shall affect the operation of any existing law, or prevent the State from making any law, in so far as such law imposes reasonable restrictions on the exercise of the right conferred by the said sub-clause in the interests of decency of morality . . ."

The underlying policy of many provisions of the Penal Code is to provide protection to girls and women by preventing sexual commerce on the part of persons who corrupt morals by taking advantage of others' youth or inexperience. Kidnapping of a girl under eighteen,[4] kidnapping or abducting any woman with the intent or knowledge that she is likely to be compelled to marry against her will or forced or seduced to illicit intercourse[5] procuration of minor girl;[6] or importing[7] into India a girl under twentyone years with intent that such girl may be, or knowing that it is likely that she will be forced or seduced to illicit intercourse; fraudulent ceremony of marriage;[8] and taking or enticing away any woman who is and whom the accused knows or has reason to believe to be the wife of any other man, from that man with intent that she may have illicit intercourse,[9] are all offences.

Every community has its sex mores and any departure therefrom necessarily is punishable. So sexual immoralities and perversions in the form of adultery,[10] rape,[11] cohabitation by deception,[12] and unnatural offences[13] of homosexuality and bestiality entail heavy penalties.

OBSCENITY AND LAW

Law's attempt to check obscenity is based on the belief that anything which has the tendency to inflame passion or lust or incite sensuality is likely to have a pernicious effect upon public morality.

With a view to preventing and suppressing the circulation of obscene publications, many nations met in a conference in Geneva on August 31, 1923, under the auspices of the League of Nations. The conference, attended also by India, drafted a convention on the suppression of circulation of and traffic in

4. Section 363.
5. Section 366
6. Section 366-A
7. Section 366-B
8. Section 496
9. Section 498
10. Section 497
11. Section 375
12. Section 493
13. Section 377

obscene publications. The Indian Penal Code already contained provisions against purveyors of obscenity; but in order to effectively implement the convention, The Obscene Publications Act, 1925 was passed.

Obscenity is not defined in the Code; but the courts have uniformly applied the *Hicklin's* test: "The test of obscenity is this, whether the tendency of the matter charged as obscenity is to deprave and corrupt those whose minds are open to such immoral influences and into whose hands a publication of this kind may fall.[14] In a case relating to D.H. Lawrence: *Lady Chatterley's Lover*, the Hicklin's test and Section 292 I.P.C. were questioned as violative of the free-speech guarantee. The Supreme Court held that the law against obscenity, being in the interests of decency and morality, is protected by Art. 19(2) of the Constitution.

The following propositions may be culled from the judgment:

(1) The Hicklin's test has been uniformly applied in India and need not be discarded.

(2) The court has to weigh the claims of freedom against those of the interest of decency and morality in each case.

(3) It is not necessary to compare one book with another to find the extent of permissible limits.

(4) (a) Although the work must be taken as a whole, any obscene matter must be considered by itself to judge whether it is gross and whether it is likely to deprave and corrupt those into whose hands the work is likely to fall.

(b) The interests of our contemporary society and particularly the influence of the book on it must not be overlooked.

(c) Where obscenity and art are mixed, art must so preponderate as to throw the obscenity into shade, or the obscenity so trivial and insignificant that it can have no effect and may be overlooked.

(d) The test to adopt in our country (regard being had to our community mores) is that obscenity without a preponderating social purpose of profit cannot have the constitutional protection of free speech,

14. (1868) L.R.3 Q.B.363, 371.

> and obscenity lies in treating sex in a manner appealing to the carnal side of human nature, or having that tendency.

It follows from the above propositions that it is the effect upon the average man and not the intention of the author that is a relevant consideration. The criterion is what will excite the passions of an average man in India.

Every community has its moral values shaped over centuries and influenced by various factors. It is thus futile to lament that while "Lady Chatterley's Lover" is banned in India it is freely available elsewhere. While there is a pull in the direction of liberalizing the law to end the divergence between what is considered obscene in this country and in countries such as America and England, there is also a pull in the direction of stiffening the law to bring to book some obscene publications in respect of which the administration feels helpless. The matter was studied by a Select Committee, and a bill was introduced and carried through in the form of the Amending Act of 1969.

The definition of obscenity in the Amending Act, an amalgam of *Hicklin's* test and its application in *Ranjit* is merely a reiteration of what the courts have already pronounced and acted on. This led a critic to observe: "The amendment does not make the definition of obscenity any more precise than the judicial statements of it. The definition provided in the amended section can almost bring anything under its blanket cover which deals with sex frankly and unconventionally."[15] This, however, is not borne out by the case of *Chandrakant*[16] where, applying the criteria of *Ranjit*, the court found that the story entitled 'Shama' read as a whole did not ponder to the prurient interest. Both in *Ranjit* and in *Chandrakant* the Supreme Court has emphasized that 'treating with sex and nudity in art and literature cannot be regarded as evidence of obscenity . . . It is not necessary that the angels and saints of Michaelangel should be made to wear breoches before they can be viewed."

The advocates of tightening the law should be pleased that the amended law provides for deterrent punishment—from just

15. Garg, Ramesh D., "Many Facets of Obscenity", Vols. II & III All. L.R., p. 9.
16. A.I.R. 1970 S.C. 1390.

3 months to 2 years, and in the event of subsequent conviction up to 5 years. The Supreme Court has held that probation is not permissible in the case of purveyors of pornography treated such offence at par with food adultrators.[17]

The plea of public good has always been available to defendants in cases of obscenity. In *Ranjit*, the court had pointed out that after the constitutional guarantee it is a question of balancing the interests in each case. In the new Act this is now incorporated in the exception. Certainty is not feasible in such a changing and abstract concept as that of obscenity. Ultimately, the court is the arbiter in such cases; and the courts were not found wanting in playing their role. In 1965, out of 42 prosecutions on the charge of obscenity 28 were convicted, and in 1966, 17 out of 28.

We may now study another law for dealing with the problem of obscenity. The Young Persons (Harmful Publications) Act, 1956, was intended to prevent the dissemination of publications harmful to young persons. The statement of objects reads: "Pictorial and other publications containing stories of the glorification of crime, violence and vice, known as 'horror comics', are being circulated in India in large quantities. The dissemination of such stories is likely to encourage anti-social tendencies among children and exert a harmful influence on young persons. So far as the import into India of pictorial publications is concerned the Government of India have imposed a ban under the Sea Customs Act. The object of this Act is to prohibit the production in India of such literature or of any variant and its circulation within India."[18]

The Act is drawn on the lines of the English law, namely, the Children and Young Persons (Harmful Publications) Act, 1955. Young person means a person under the age of twenty years. Harmful publication is one which consists of stories portraying mainly the commission of offences, or acts of violence or cruelty, or incidents of a repulsive or horrible nature in such a way that, taken as a whole, it would tend to corrupt a young person into whose hands it might fall. Any person who sells, lets to hire, distributes, publicly exhibits any

17. See *Uttam Singh* v. *The State*, A.I.R. 1974 S.C. 1230.
18. Gazette of India, Ext., Part II, Section 2. No. 36, dated September 15, 1955.

harmful publication, or prints, makes, produces or has any such work in his possession for the said purposes, is punishable with imprisonment upto six months, or with fine, or with both. The court may order the destruction of all the copies of the harmful publication in respect of which the conviction took place. After consultation with its principal law officer, the State Government may order forfeiture of any harmful publication. Besides, any police officer, or any officer so empowered, may seize any such publication; and if it is held to be harmful, the magistrate or the court at whose instance the warrent for search and seizure was issued, may cause the impugned material to be destroyed. Though the offences under the Act are made cognizable, the law seems to have remained almost a dead letter.[19] It is one thing to adopt the English law but another to implement it. The police in India has its hands full with other crimes. The establishment of special anti-obscenity police force to deal with crimes against decency and morality would be ideal.

There are provisions in the Code of Criminal Procedure, 1973, for the issue, by specific magistracy, of warrants for search and seizure of obscene objects.[20] The State Government is empowered to declare obscene publications to be forfeited and to issue search warrants for the same.[21] Moreover, on conviction for an offence under Section 292 or Section 293 I.P.C., the court may order the destruction of all the copies in respect of which the conviction was had.[22]

For the purposes of 'the maintenance of standards of decency and morality', the Central Government is empowered by the Customs Act, 1962, to prohibit either absolutely, or subject to such conditions (to be fulfilled before or after clearance) as may be notified, the import or export of goods of any

19. In *Narayan* v. *State of Kerala*, 1970 K.L.T. 605, the court held that Proprietor and Manager of a printing press do not fall within the purview of Section 3 of the Act as the person who does printing is really the person at whose request and for whom the printing is made. In view of *Ranjit* that such offences are cases of strict liability, it is not clear why the matter was not taken to the Supreme Court.
20. Section 94.
21. Sections 95, 96.
22. Section 455.

specified description. Thus the entry of obscene matter can easily be banned in the interests of public decency and morality. Smuggling in obscene matter as of everything else, must be prevented.

We may also refer to the Indian Post Office Act, 1898. It is an offence to transmit by post any indecent or obscene article. Similarly, any words, marks, or designs of an indecent or obscene character on any postal article or on the cover thereof, are prohibited. A vendor of patent medicines was convicted under Sections 20 and 61 of the Act for sending post-cards on which was printed an obscene advertisement.[23] Such an advertisement can also be now dealt with under the Drug and Magic Remedies (Objectionable Advertisements) Act, 1954.[24]

CINEMA AND CENSORSHIP

The first Indian film, produced in 1912, had a religious theme. Even the films imported from abroad mostly for the entertainment of the elite were without any overtones of criticism. But the necessity for some kind of censorship arose when a few films originally meant for the entertainment of armed forces during World War I found their way to the important city cinemas. The impact of the war was giving rise to a new morality. It was to deal with this situation that the Cinematograph Act, 1918 was passed. It made licensing of cinema houses but also certification of films for public exhibition obligatory. The Act specified no guidelines. The Bombay Board of Film Censors formulated certain general principles very much on the lines of the British rules of censorship. Nothing was to be approved that was calculated to demoralise an audience or any section of it. Films that extenuated crime or exhibited its *modus operandi*, or undermined the teachings of morality—for example, by bringing into contempt the institution of marriage or suggesting abnormal sexual relations—were classed as objectionable. Among the objectionable film-subjects were: excessively passionate love scenes; indelicate sexual situations; men and women in bed together; 'first night' scenes; scenes laid in brothels: prostitution and procuration; illicit sexual

23 *Sarat* v. *K.E.*, 32 Cal. 247.

24. See *Hamdard Dawakhana* v. *Union of India*, A.I.R. 1960 S.C. 554. For consequent amendments, see Act 42 of 1963.

sexual relationships; nude figures; unnecessary exhibition of feminine underclothing; bathing scenes passing the limits of propriety; indecent dancing etc. With four Boards acting in different parts of the country despite the guidelines there was want of uniformity in their decisions. Some central control seemed to be indicated. The great bulk of films imported into India were 'of the cheap and vulgar American type'; the indigenous industry also produced many films in imitation of the American films. In 1927 an Enquiry Committee examined the prevailing position and recommended the setting up of a Central Board of Censors, and the association of trade and other interests with the viewing of films in an advisory capacity. The report of the committee was shelved

After independence, the Governments of Bombay and Madras framed a Production Code 'with a view to ensuring that the crimes plays its proper role in the building of healthy national life'. The Code cut no ice with the film industry. In 1949, two Cinematograph (Amendment) Acts were passed. The first introduced a two-fold classification of films—films approved for universal exhibition to be certified 'U', and films restricted to adults to be certified 'A'. The second amendment provided for a Central Board of Film Censors. Censorship of films was included in the Union List. Then, a comprehensive legislation, The Cinematograph Act, 1952, was enacted, which repealed the legislation of 1918. In 1958, the Cinematograph (Censorship) Rules were framed under the Act; and directives were issued in the form of 'The General Principles and the Application of General Principles' to provide guidelines to the censors. Drawn mainly on the lines of those issued by the Bombay Board, they contain detailed instructions regarding what types of films or sequences in films must be considered objectionable.

The precensorship of films was challenged for the first time but upheld in the case of *K.A. Abbas.*[25] The court recognised that the treatment of promotion pictures must be different from that of other forms of art and expression. For one thing, the motion picture is able to stir up motions more deeply than any other product of art. For another, the effect of films on children and adolescents is very great since their immaturity makes them prone to suspend their disbelief, and since they are apt to

25. A.I.R. 1971 S.C. 481.

emulate or imitate what they have seen. Thus the classification of films into two categories, 'U' and 'A', was held a reasonable classification and censorship of films, including prior restraint was upheld in the interests of society under Article 19(2) of the Constitution. The Government, however, assured the court that legislation would soon follow to provide for appeals to an independent tribunal and for a time-limit for all actions under the Act.

Earlier to *Abbas* case, the Government of India had set up, in 1968, an Enquiry Committee on Film Censorship under the chairmanship of Mr. G.D. Khosla. The Committee submitted its report in July 1959. In pursuance of the assurance given to the court and of the report of the Khosla Committee, the Cinematograph (Amendment) Act, 1974 was passed. It provides for Appellate Tribunals. The rules framed by the Central Government were to provide for the time-limit within which any action may be taken under the Act. In this way the procedural deficiencies noted in *Abbas* have been rectified. The Act further brings within its scope censorship of films to be exported. The whole machinery of censorship has been oriented to meet the constitutional demands of substantive and procedural reasonableness.[26]

CONCLUSIONS AND SUGGESTIONS

Community mores generally reflect the social, economic and political realities. Moral standards, of course, do vary from society to society. Yet every community punishes obscenity that offends the normal sense of shame. Our Constitution provides for the protection of the interests of decency and morality. A number of legislative measures seek to give effect to this.

And yet pornography has not been laid low. Pornographic literature also muds on the pavements of Delhi, Bombay, Calcutta, Madras and other growing towns. What is not permissible on the Indian screen, can be seen on the front page of a weekly.[27] To push up circulation, the Editor's page must give

26. For detailed discussion of the reasonableness of restrictions, see Bedi, A.S., Freedom of Expression and Security, Ch. 15.
27. See The Illustrated Weekly of India, May 18, 1975.

the anatomy of a woman[28] (and that, too, in the International Women's Year), and articles like 'Man Marries Man', a homosexuality tale[29] from Canada, must be carried between the covers. Referring to the staging of Punjabi plays like the 'Halwa Suji Da, Chaska Duji Da' and Hindi plays like 'Jawani Ki Tarang Boodhon Pe Rang' in the metropolis, a critic observes: "It is shocking that the otherwise sticky Delhi Administration does nothing to prevent the performance of such plays and the number of groups taking to this commercially lucrative type is increasing almost weekly . . ."[30] It is no different in other important towns of India despite the existence of legal machinery to fight the evil. Under the Dramatic Performances Act, 1876,[31] the state government is empowered to prohibit the performance of any play, pantomime or other drama performed or about to be performed in a public place, which in its opinion is 'likely to deprave and corrupt persons present at the performance'.

Has the content of Indian films improved? Can't it, in view of the fact, emphasized by the Khosla Committee, that film industry is a money-making and commercial undertaking, and that film-makers find it profitable to produce films that appeal to low taste? The Committee had recommended that the State construct a large number of small cinema houses not controlled by commercial distributors. Small-budget films of good quality could be shown in those cinema houses. Perhaps the time has come to ask why the film industry be entirely left at the mercy of private sector, which tends to sacrifice social responsibility to profit motive. Even the role of the Board of Censors is at present a negative one. It can only sanction cuts and deletions. It cannot lay down any positive philosophy for the film-maker whose eyes are always on the box-office.

Films are a very powerful medium of instruction as well as entertainment. The present day films are a cheap escape from the realities of life; they create fantastic illusions about life. A person living in such phantasy is bound to lose all sense of

28. *Ibid*, p. 27.
29. The Illustrated Weekly of India, May 4, 1975, p. 39.
30. Kavita Nagpal, "Vulgar Theatre New Menace to Arts," Hindustan Times, May 30, 1975, p. 3, cols. 5-6.
31. See also The Madras Dramatic Performance Act, 1954—extended to Union Territory of Delhi (Section 2 of Act No. 34 of 1963).

values and the true perspective on life.

The Khosla Committee had censured the import of films in these words:

> With regard to the import of the main body of feature films, we suggest a complete change of attitude which is at present commerce and politics-oriented, to an attitude which should be conditioned by considerations of cultural, aesthetic and artistic values only. We have to conserve our foreign exchange . . . If (foreign films) are not more than cheap and erotic entertainment, they should be banned on the ground that we have enough of these commodities manufactured in our own country . . . We are convinced that it was a complete waste of foreign exchange to import the whole series of 'Night Life' films . . . We strongly suggest that these (trade) agreements must not on any account be renewed.[32]

Yet the Selection Committee of the Fifth International Film Festival, which had none other than Mr. Khosla as Chairman, sanctioned the exhibition of films like "Siddharta Godfather", a "Clockwork Orange", "Amarcord" and others all of which had the maximum of sex and violence. Soon one may be sure, there would be Indian versions of "Godfather" and others. Our profession and practice are at variance. So it should cause no surprise that after a lapse of four years the Government has ratified a new four-year film agreement for the import of American films. The least the Government can do is to ensure through its guidelines for censorship that 'Pretty poison' does not further contaminate our public—at the cost, too, of precious foreign exchange.

The import of films with cheap and erotic entertainment highlights our double standards in censorship. The censor makes certain allowance for the divergence of social standards and customs; and the justification advanced for the censor's leniency towards foreign films is that 'there are 6,000 theatres in India out of which only about 80 theatres show foreign films' and that 'the audience generally consists of sophisticated persons sufficiently educated'.

We have shown that the juristic framework for protection

32. Report of the Enquiry Committee on Film Censorship, p. 133.

of public morals is well knit with a number of legislative measures. What is lacking is the will to implement them. We have suggested the establishment of special anti-obscenity police force to deal with crimes against decency and morality. In the meantime, to counter the lackadaisical enforcement of the laws, let 'We the People' organize public morality councils. There is a real danger that national standards and values might be corroded past repairs if we do not wake up betimes and act.

B.C. Ghosal

CHAPTER XI

Health Legislation in India

The public health system in India is attracting the attention of many countries of the world, largely owing to the fact that in a brief period of 27 years since Independence the State has built up a powerful system of medical and health services for the whole population of such a vast country. At the time of Independence, India was far behind the western countries in regard both to medical and health personnel and pharmaceutical industry. It occupied a very low place in regard to the level of its people's health. It now has a powerful material and technological base as well as an advanced system of public health service. Judged by the rate of general mortality, the number of doctors, the number of hospitals relative to the population, the size of health personnel, and the spread of prophylactic service, India has outstripped many of the developing countries.

Health legislation falls under the category of social legislation, as essential perhaps as security laws for any society. Health laws, however, merely working tools with which health administration, not only protects the community from health hazards, but also implements schemes for improving the general health of the people and their physical well-being. It would indeed be ideal to have a comprehensive Central public health Act for the entire country but with provision for such variations as may be demanded by the varying conditions in different States. Such an Act would, again ideally, cover not only the fields of sanitation and control of communicable diseases but also medical and nursing care through hospitals and clinics and laboratory services as well as preventive and promotive programmes for nutrition, maternal and child care, school health, family planning etc. What one actually have, however, piecemeal enactments, often overlapping with one another, passed from time to time either by States or the Centre in response to immediate needs. A comprehensive health legislation would doubtless provide the necessary backing for health services conforming to modern standards made possible by the advancement of science.

MODEL PUBLIC HEALTH COMMITTEE

On the recommendation of the Central Council of Health the Government of India constituted the Model Public Health Committee in 1958 to bring together the existing laws, whether passed by the Centre or States. The Committee was also asked to draft a model comprehensive public health Act, taking into account recent advances in techniques and administration of public health and the need for environmental hygiene. The Committee submitted a draft, which was circulated to all State governments. The whole question was carefully considered in the light of the opinions expressed by the latter, and it was decided to drop the proposal for a Central legislation on public health, the State governments being asked to adopt such of the provisions of the model public health bill as they considered useful in their local conditions.

The Committee's draft is a long document, containing 57 chapters, and cannot be reproduced here, but it would be useful to review the salient features of the draft model public health Act.

Part I—Organisation and Administrative Provisions: This part of the Act provides for the creation of a social machinery for a reasonable standard of health-care of the people. Statutory obligation for the creation of such an organisation rests with the State Governments and local authorities to ensure the fulfilment of the following objectives:

(i) To provide legal status and standards to the medical relief measures and to integrate them with preventive care at all levels.

(ii) To provide for sanitation and other environmental health services through local authorities with financial assistance from State Governments which are empowered to supervise, supplement or take over certain essential institutions or programmes or works if any local authority fails to run them.

(iii) To define State health services, including the Directorate of Health Services and divisions and bureaus. A noteworthy feature of the recommendations is the creation of a division of public health engineering with chapters at district and sub-divisional levels.

(iv) To form cadres of medical officers and public health engineers with prescribed qualifications and to lend their services to local authorities.

(v) To empower the director of health services to deal with emergencies to supervise and control the work of local authorities or other institutions concerned with health programmes.

(vi) To provide minimum funds to local authorities for public health work.

Part II—Medical relief and public health measures: This part deals with—

(i) effective control of communicable deseases;

(ii) powers of health officers;

(iii) standards for hospitals including free beds, and rules for the management of medical institutions;

(iv) compulsory vaccination, revaccination and epidemic regulations;

(v) control of certain non-communicable but widespread nutritional and other diseases such as epidemic leprosy, beri-beri etc.

(vi) assistance to local authorities during emergencies;

(vii) organisation of school health, and nutrition programmes;

(viii) domiciliary nursing and midwifery and family planning programmes;

(ix) institutions for the care of indigent or handicapped children;

(x) licensing for the control of nursing homes and sanitoria and their standards;

(xi) organizing of additional services such as ophthalmic, mental health, dental care, ambulance and laboratory.

Part III—Sanitation: This part deals with environmental sanitation services in a comprehensive manner; it provides for:

(i) procedure for instituting and financing water supply, drainage, housing, collection and disposal of community wastes, and improvement of slum and basti areas;

(ii) control of vectors, places of pilgrimage, holiday camps, paths, playgrounds and other spaces, fairs and festivals, burial and burning grounds, lodging houses, eating houses, and markets;

(iii) control of production and supply of food-stuffs, drugs etc.;

(iv) control of slaughter houses, factories, offensive trades and nuisances;

(v) registration of births and deaths;

(vi) application of the methods of disinfection and disinfestation;

(vii) town and village planning.

Part IV—General provisions: This part contains general provisions, specially those related to financial matters. It gives powers to state government and local authorities to raise public loans and borrow from the Central and State governments for health projects.

There is an annexure attached to the draft Act giving an outline of standards and other particulars for incorporation in the rules and the bye-laws which may be framed by the state governments or local authorities. It gives the latest technical information relating to the minimum standards of harmful living, water supply, sanitation, certain licensable trades, schools etc. to help the government in framing rules and bye-laws.

CONSIDERATION OF SOME EXISTING CENTRAL LEGISLATION

As mentioned earlier, there is a mass of enactments, some by the Centre and some by States. It has not possible in a brief paper like this to discuss the enactments of State governments. The Central Acts can be classified into the following five categories, only some of which will be discussed:

A. Constitution of India, and B. Public Health Acts:

(1) Indian Penal Code 1860 (certain sections only);
(2) The Vaccination Act, 1880;
(3) Epidemic Diseases Act (No. III), 1897;
(4) Prevention of Food Adulteration Act, 1954;
(5) Registration of Births and Deaths Act, 1969 (The Birth and Death Registration Act, 1873);
(6) Medical Termination of Pregnancy Act, 1971;
(7) Indian Steam Vessels Act, 1971;
(8) Maternity Benefit Act, 1961 (certain clauses of Criminal Procedure Code. The Quarantine Act, The Municipal Corporation Acts, Indian Drugs Act, 1949, The Indian Railways Act).

C. Health and Social Security Acts

(1) The Workmen's Compensation Act, 1923;
(2) The Payment of Wages Act, 1936;
(3) The Minimum Wages Act, 1948;
(4) The Factories Act, 1948;
(5) The Employees' State Insurance Act, 1948;
(6) The Employees' Provident Fund Act, 1952;
(7) Industrial Disputes Act, 1947;
(8) Plantation Labour Act, 1951;
(9) Hindu Adoptions and Maintenance Act, 1955;
(10) Hindu Marriage Act, 1955;
(11) Hindu Succession Act, 1956;
(12) Suppression of Immoral Traffic in Women and Girls Act, 1956;
(13) Hindu Minority and Guardianship Act, 1956;
(14) Women's and Children's Institutions (Licensing) Act, 1956;
(15) Orphanages and other Charitable Homes (Supervision and Control) Act, 1960.

D. Acts related to medical profession, medical education etc.

(1) The Medical Act, 1886;
(2) Dentist Act, 1948;
(3) Indian Nursing Council Act, 1947;
(4) Indian Medical Council Act, 1956.

E. Others

The Indian Red Cross Society Act, 1920.

INDIAN PENAL CODE, 1860

Certain sections of Code provide for the control of public nuisances, negligent acts likely to spread infection of diseases dangerous to life, disobedience of quarantine rules, adulteration of food or drink intended for sale, adulteration of drugs, sale of adulterated drugs, misbranding of drugs, fouling of public springs or reservoirs in catchment and other areas, making atmosphere noxious to health, sale of noxious food and drink, rash driving on roads, rash navigation of vessels or bad navigation practices, negligence in respect of poisonous substances and combustive materials; negligence in respect of explosives (Clauses 256 to 292).

This Act, one of the earliest in India, provides for inoculation and vaccination. Parents or guardians are required to take boys between the ages of six months and 14 years, and girls between the ages of six months and eight years, residing in any local area for a period of one month during the vaccination season to voccinators or to send for vaccinators. There are provisions, too, for inspection of vaccinations, procedure for certification etc. If the child is unfit for vaccination, there is provision for the postponement of vaccination.

EPIDEMIC DISEASES ACT, 1897

This Act is meant to prevent the spread of dangerous epidemic diseases. Whenever the authorities consider the ordinary provisions of law for the time being in force to be inadequate for the purpose, they may take or empower any person to take measures or prescribe temporary regulations to be observed by the public for preventing the outbreak or spread of epidemic diseases. The Act applies to urban and rural areas, to sea or airports (including the inspection of ships or vessels), to railways etc.

THE PREVENTION OF FOOD ADULTERATION ACT

A comprehensive Act, it provides for the prohibition of manufacture, sale etc. of adulterated and misbranded foods. It also prohibits import of such food or food articles. The Act is applicable not only to manufacture and sale, but also to storage, distribution and handling of adulterated or misbranded foodstuff. The responsibility for such food rests on the analysis of organization of public analysis, and whose finding can be appealed against to the Central Food Laboratory. The Act defines the powers of the Central and State governments to appoint food inspectors and the powers of food inspectors. The procedure for taking food samples and have them analysed are also laid down in the Act.

REGISTRATION OF BIRTHS AND DEATHS ACT, 1969

This Act provides for the machinery for registration of births and deaths. It consists of the chief registrar, the registration divisions, and the district registrar. The head of the house or household, or the nearest relative of such a head, or the oldest adult male person in the house, is required by this Act as the case may be have to notify births and deaths either orally or in writing within three days of the event. If birth or death takes place in institutions such as hospitals, health centres, maternity homes etc., the medical officer-in-charge or any person authorised in his behalf has to notify the appropriate authority of these events. The Act places certain responsibilities on the mid-wife or any other medical health staff present at the time of birth or death. There are provisions for delayed registration, registration of the name of child, issue of certificate, maintenance of proper records, with special provisions for the registration of births and deaths of citizens outside India.

LEGAL TERMINATION OF PREGNANCY ACT, 1971

This most recent public health Act provides for termination of pregnancy by a registered medical practitioner if there is a risk to the physical or mental health of a pregnant woman, or if there is substantial risk that if a child were born it would suffer from physical or mental abnormality and would be seriously handicapped. Grave injury to mental health through pregnancies caused by rape has been accepted. Similarly, pregnancy occurring because of the failure of any contraceptive devise or method used by any married couple with the purpose of limiting the number of children is presumed to constitute grave injury to the mental health of the woman. Pregnancies can be terminated only in hospitals established or maintained by government or in places approved by the government for the purpose.

MATERNITY BENEFIT ACT, 1961

Intended to regulate the employment of women in certain establishments for certain periods before and after child birth and to provide for maternity and certain other benefits, the Act prohibits the employment of women during six weeks immediately following the day of delivery or miscarriage, and provides safeguards to the health of a pregnant woman against arduous work over a specified period. Women workers under this Act are entitled to maternity benefit at the rate of average daily wage for the period of her actual absence, not exceeding six weeks, preceding and following the delivery.

WORKMEN COMPENSATION ACT, 1923

This Act tries to protect workers' health in the growing complexity of industrial processes. It seeks to reduce accidents and, where they do take place, to mitigate their effects by suitable medical treatment. It also provides for cheaper and quicker disposal of disputes and payment of compensation through special tribunals.

Under the Act the employer is liable to compensate for (1) personal injury or injuries, and (2) occupational disease or diseases. The amount of compensation for temporary and permanent disablement, whether partial or total, and for the contingency of death are specified.

Enforcement of the Act, however, is not free from flaws. The economic power of employers, and the protracted procedure for deciding disputes go against workers. Nor is it easy to determine whether injury was caused or occupational disease contracted during the course of employment.

It was to overcome these difficulties that special social security legislation, such as the Employees State Insurance Act, 1948, and the Factories Act, 1948, has been passed.

THE PAYMENT OF WAGES ACT, 1936

This Act ensures the payment of workers' wages in a particular form and at regular intervals without any unauthorised deductions.

MINIMUM WAGES ACT, 1948

This Act has been passed in pursuance of the Directive Principles of State Policy in Article 43 of the Constitution. In order to protect labourers against exploitation, it imposes restrictions on what is called the freedom of contract. This law protects (1) the basic rate of wages, (2) the cost of living allowance and (3) the cash value of concessions, if any, to workers. The Act specifies the hours of a normal working day and provides for payment for overtime work.

FACTORIES ACT, 1948

This legislation attempts to prevent, protect and promote the health and welfare of workers. Observance of industrial hygiene has been made obligatory under the Act for all factories as defined in the Act. There are four clauses on:

(a) *Health*—which provides for regular cleaning and sweeping, washing and disinfection, proper drainage, disposal of waste and effluents, proper ventilation and temperature, control of dust and fumes, prescribed standards for artificial humidification of specific industrial processes, checking of overcrowding, proper lighting, supply of safe drinking water, latrines and urinals, spittoons etc.

(b) *Safety*—which ensures the safety of workers while they are at work. It lays down regulations for the fencing of machinery and moving parts, avoidance of the employment of young persons on dangerous machines, the type of machinery on which women and children may not work, special safeguards against self-acting machines, casing of machinery etc.

(c) *Welfare*—which provide for washing facility for either sex, storing and drying of clothes, facilities for first aid, canteens, shelters, rest rooms, lunch rooms and sitting facilities, creches for children of women workers and whole-time welfare officers.

(d) *Working Hours*—which specify the number of working hours in a week, maximum hours of working in a day, intervals for rest, extra wages for over-time, restrictions on double employment, overlapping shifts, and restrictions on employment of women on night shifts. Employment of children under 14 years of age is prohibited, and the length of working day for children is specified and the period between which they should not be employed is laid down, also, before employment their fitness has to be certified.

Leave with wages—which provide for annual leave with wages at the rate of one day for 20 days of work for adults and one day for 15 days of work for children, with a minimum of 10 and 14 days respectively in a year.

Notifiable occupational diseases—which give a list of 17 occupational diseases, such as lead, phosphorus, mercury, manganese, arsenic, carbon bisulphide, nitrous fumes, chrome, anthrax, silicosis, halogens, radium or other radio-active substances, X-rays, primary epitheliomatous cancer of the skin, toxic enaemia and toxic jaundices due to poisonous substances.

EMPLOYEES STATE INSURANCE ACT, 1948

This act was framed on the basis of Prof. B.P. Adarkar's report on health insurance scheme for industrial workers. It is a measure of social security for those working in factories using power, and in non-seasonal factories (excluding mines, railway running sheds, and defence installations) in which 20 or more persons are working with remuneration not exceeding Rs. 500 per month. The Act contains an enabling provision for extending its scope to any other establishment or class of establishment, industrial, commercial, agriculture or others.

STATUTORY BENEFITS

For cash benefits in the event of sickness, maternity, disablement and death due to employment injury, a period of 39 weeks of insurance cover is essential. Benefits include,

(a) sickness benefit,
(b) maternity benefit,
(c) disablement benefit,
(d) dependent's benefit (in the event of death),
(e) medical benefit.

Medical care is available immediately on entry into the schemes of insurance. There is a free insurance period ranging from 13 weeks to 9 months after an insured worker ceases to be an employee.

Other benefits which accrue from the very moment of a person's entry into insurable employment is employment injury benefit consisting of,

(i) temporary disablement benefit,
(ii) permanent disablement benefit,
(iii) and dependents' benefit.

Sickness benefit and maternity benefit are subject to fulfilment of certain contributory conditions.

ENHANCED BENEFITS

(1) Extended sickness benefits to insured persons suffering from tuberculosis, mental and malignant diseases, and fractures etc. are available 365 days of the year.
(2) Supplementary benefits such as artificial limbs, dentures, spectacles etc., all free of cost.
(3) Medical care to families within certain scales by state governments.
(4) Doubling the rate of maternity benefit.
(5) Free remittance of cash benefits, without money order fee.

All employees of factories or establishments to which this Act applies contribute towards the insurance fund. Contributions come from both the employer and the employee as per schedule given in the Act.

THE EMPLOYEES' PROVIDENT FUNDS ACT, 1952

Under this Act, both the employer and the employee contribute towards employees' provident fund scheme.

The employer contributes $6\frac{1}{4}\%$ of the basic wage of an employee whose contribution is equal to that of the employer. An employee, however, can contribute upto $8\frac{1}{3}\%$ of his basic wage.

It is actually a provision for old age as the worker gets a lump sum together with such interest as may have accrued on the deposit. However this measure too has been found inadequate and a 'pension scheme' for the benefit of industrial workers is under consideration.

UNEMPLOYMENT BENEFIT

It is a very complex problem. Existing social insurance in India makes no provision for involuntary unemployment. Compensation upto 45 days, and under certain conditions for extra days in a year, at the rate of 50 per cent of worker's wages including allowances is provided for under Industrial Disputes Act, 1947. This is merely a paltry relief; it is neither public assistance nor social insurance.

G.B. Krishna Rao

CHAPTER XII

Urban Land (Ceiling & Regulations) Act, 1976 and its Implications for Urban Development

Socialization of urban lands was declared to be the Government's objective in the Five-Year Plans and in policy statements, but the precise meaning of 'socialization of urban land' was never clearly spelled out. In 1967, the Congress passed a resolution at Delhi which said, *inter alia*, "The pattern of conspicuous consumption and wasteful display which increasingly characterise some of the urban areas are all out of place in a socialistic society. There is thus compelling need to impose limitations on urban property. Concrete steps should therefore be taken for placing restrictions on individual holdings of urban land for preventing racketeering in land in urban areas". The 1971 Election Manifesto of Congress stated: "Limitations must be placed on urban property. Measures will be taken to curb anti-social recketeering in the purchase and sale of land".

The 25th Amendment to the Constitution (1971) paved the way for the Urban Land Ceiling and Regulation Act, 1976 (hereafter called ULC&R Act). Since, however, the problem of taking over, managing and disposing of surplus urban properties were considered colossal, the ULC&R Act imposed a ceiling not on urban property but only on private holdings of vacant lands.

CONCEPT OF URBAN LAND REFORMS

It would be appropriate to refer here briefly to the concept of urban land reform, since the Ceiling Act (the ULC&R Act) is essentially a step in the direction of urban land reforms, even though this may not have been explicitly recognized by the law-makers. Urban land reform is a corollary of agrarian land reform. Agrarian land reform alleviates the hardships of those who depend on farming, but they do not help migrants from the rural to the urban areas. To solve the problems arising from this mass exodus, resort has to be had not only to urban planning but also to urban land reforms.

Urban land reform entails bringing about radical changes in urban economic institutions—such as urban land ownership, holdings and tenancy—regulation of land values, property taxation, availability of pre-emption right and improvements in land acquisition and disposal process, all of which is necessary for assuring the availability of land in adequate quantity at reasonable prices and at the right time to public authorities and individuals.

The importance of urban land reforms has been realized particularly in Latin American countries, and some of them have made considerable progress in this regard. To cite an illustration, Cuba has set up a National Urban Reform Council at the apex of different provincial councils; the Law 218 of 1959 lays down the procedure for compulsory sale of all vacant urban lots; the Law 691 of 1959 lays down that the price of no vacant urban lots can be higher than $4 a sq. mt.; any citizen can enforce the sale of a vacant lot by proving his intent to construct a house, or a factory, or an office building within 18 months. The Urban Reform Law 1960 defined the criteria for indemnifying owners of rented housing that became the property of tenants: the sale price is related to the age of housing and the rent being paid, and the compensation is not to exceed $600 a month. Slums and lodging houses were expropriated without compensation. The law prohibited the exchange or sale of any real property without the permission of Urban Reform Council.*

* Maruja Acosta and Jorge E. Hardoy, "Urbanisation Policies in Revolutionary Cuba", Latin American Urban Research, Vol. 2, 1972.

URBAN CRISIS AND LAND SPECULATION

During a rapid pace of urbanization and industrialization, our towns and cities have been growing at a phenomenal rate in a rather haphazard manner in recent decades. The urban areas are thus beset with baffling problems such as housing shortage and sprawling slums, traffic congestion during peak hours, gross inadequacy of essential services like water supply, sewerage, schools, hospitals, parks and play grounds. To make the situation worse, land values in our cities have skyrocketed in recent times. For instance, land values in Bara Bazaar, Dalhousie Square and Chowringhee in Calcutta are in the range of Rs. 1 to Rs. 1.5 lakhs per cottah, and the land at Nariman point in Bombay was sold recently for Rs. 3,000 to Rs. 5,000 per sq. yd. The spiralling land values are unrelated to any perceivable economic factor and can only be attributed to speculation in land. Land speculators have been cornering large chunks of lands at low prices and selling them as developed plots at exorbitant prices. Substandard and unregulated land colonization and construction of luxury mansions has occurred on an extensive scale, often through the investment of black money.

In point of fact, however, the initial stimulus for the urban land reform came from those who were adversely affected by land reform legislation; they envied the owners of urban properties. That may be why the concept of a ceiling on agricultural land was transferred to the urban scene without giving thought whether socialization of all vacant urban land was not a better remedy than a ceiling limit.

INDIAN CONSTITUTION AND THE URBAN CEILING ACT

If the ULC&R Act was passed by the Parliament in spite of the fact that 'land' is mentioned in the State List in Schedule VII to the Constitution, it was because the legislatures of 11 States requested the Parliament to enact this law in the manner specified in Article 252. It is claimed that the Act is a step towards implementing one of the Directive Principles of State Policy: making ownership of resources subservient to common good and preventing concentration of wealth (Article 39(k) and (e)). It is doubly protected from judicial scrutiny. Article 31(c), which was inserted in the Constitution by the 25th Amendment, bars judicial interference in laws enacted for securing the principles specified in Articles 39(b) and (c) on the ground of such laws being violative of Articles 14 (equality before law), 19 and 31. Parliament has put the Act in the Ninth Schedule to the Constitution so that it cannot be challenged in courts.

BROAD OBJECTIVES OF THE ACT

The Statement of Objects and Reasons attached to the Bill as introduced in the Lok Sabha reads as follows:

"A bill to provide for the imposition of a ceiling on vacant land in the urban agglomerations, for the acquisition of such land in excess of the ceiling limit, to regulate the construction of buildings on such land and for matters connected therewith with a view to preventing the concentration of urban land in the hands of a few persons and speculation and profiteering thereon and with a view to bringing about an equitable distribution of land in urban agglomeration to subserve the common good."

BASIC CONCEPTS AND RESTRICTIONS UNDER THE ACT

The Act was initially applied to 11 States: Andhra Pradesh, Gujarat, Haryana, Himachal Pradesh, Karnataka, Maharashtra, Orissa, Punjab, Tripura, Uttar Pradesh and West Bengal and all Union Territories, and it has been subsequently adopted by Assam, Bihar, Manipur, Meghalaya and Rajasthan.

The ULC&R Act is made applicable to 73 towns and cities (out of 142 class I cities of 1971 census) classified into four categories A, B, C and D with a graded ceiling on vacant land in urban agglomerations varying from 500 to 2000 square metres depending on the category of the city. The ceiling limit is applicable to the peripheral areas of agglomeration ranging in width from 1 kilometre to 8 kilometres (the latter being for category 'A' cities).

The concept of 'vacant land', which is of crucial importance to the understanding of the scope of applicability of the ceiling limit, has been defined by stating what it is not rather than what it is. It means all land in an urban agglomeration excluding: (1) agricultural land (unless shown for non-agricultural use in the Master Plan); (2) land on which construction of buildings is not permitted as per regulations; (3) land occupied by the buildings, as per sanctioned plans (i.e. land on which authorised constructions are located would also be vacant land); (4) land appurtenant to the building; (5) land normally used for keeping cattle other than for the purpose of dairy-farming or breeding live-stock. "Land appurtenant' means such land as is required to be kept open as per regulations (subject to a maximum of 500 square metres) and another 500 square metres of land contiguous to it.

Any person, family, company, firm, association, private trust, Hindu undivided family or housing group owning vacant land in excess of ceiling limit is affected by the ULC&R Act.

The Act also imposes a ceiling on the plinth area of all future dwelling units varying from 300 square metres in the categories of A and B towns to 500 square metres in C and D.

Returns on excess lands should be filed by specified date; notices are then served by the competent authority and objections considered. The government acquires vacant lands upon publication of the final notification by the competent authority.

Taking advantage of the 25th Amendment, the Act does not take the 'market value' as the basis of compensation for the surplus land acquired. Compensation on the other hand is 8½ times the net average annual income actually derived from where there is no such income, the compensation is to be at a rate exceeding Rs. 10 per square metre for categories A and B and Rs. 5 for categories C and D cities, the upper limit being Rs. 2 lakhs. The Government may divide the urban area concerned into zones, having regard to factors such as location, general use of land and utility of land for urban development and fix different rates for different zones. Only 25% of the compensation upto a maximum of Rs. 25,000 is payable in cash and the rest in negotiable bonds, carrying 5% interest, and redeemable after 20 years. The States are empowered, with the previous approval of the Central Government, to extend the Act to other towns with population of over 1 lakh.

The concept of preemption rights, in vogue in France and some Far Eastern countries, has been introduced by the Act for the first time in this country with regard to certain categories of transfer of property. A person cannot transfer any vacant land, within the ceiling limit, to another person without first giving notice to the competent authority and, if the proposed transfer is a sale, the authority has the option to purchase the land, not at the price agreed upon, but calculated according to the Act. In case of a transfer of land with building (s) by sale, mortgage or lease (for over 10 years), the transferor should not only give notice to the authority but also obtain his permission to effect the transfer, and the authority has the pre-emption right to purchase the property at a price agreed upon between the State and the applicant or in accordance with the ULC&R Act. In either case, the right must be exercised within 60 days. No land transaction can be registered unless above conditions have been complied with. The Central Government has given an assurance that the pre-emption right would be exercised only in public interest, e.g. building a government office, public institution, or providing play-grounds, to a school or house-sites to the poor, or widening of a road.

EXEMPTION AND NON-APPLICABILITY OF THE ACT

The following cases are exempted from the operation of ceiling limit on vacant land (Section 19): vacant lands held by the Central and State Governments or by authorities and corporations established under an Act or by public sector undertakings, military, naval and air force; lands held by land mortgage banks, housing co-operative societies; lands held by educational, cultural, technical and scientific institutions or by government approved clubs.

The State Government has discretionary powers to grant exemption to any person if it considered it expedient in public interest, having regard to the location of such land, the purpose for which it is being or proposed to be used and other relevant factors and also in cases where enforcement of the ceiling limit would cause undue hardship.

The State Government can also declare that the ceiling limit will not apply to approved schemes undertaken by individuals for construction of dwellings for the weaker sections of the community (plinth area of each unit not to exceed 80 sq. metres).

Where any plot becomes vacant due to demolition of a building by the owner or due to its destruction from natural causes, the State Government may if the plot is to be redeveloped according to a master plan, permit the owner to retain the excess land, if any, over the ceiling limit.

The Union Ministry of Works and Housing has issued a series of guidelines with regard to the operational aspects of the Act on certain matters such as procedures for sanctioning building construction plans by local bodies on plots within and in excess of the ceiling limit, grant of exemption to industrial plots, and criteria for selecting additional towns for extending the Act.

OVER-RIDING EFFECTS OF THE ACT

The Act will prevail if its provisions relating to maximum size of plot and plinth area conflict with the corresponding standards contained in building rules or zoning laws or statutory scheme bylaws or any municipal act (Section 42).

EMERGING ISSUES FOR URBAN DEVELOPMENT

An attempt will now be made to identify and discuss briefly the various issues which have emerged following the enactment of ULC&R Act and the implications of the Act for urban development.

EXTENT OF VACANT AND AGRICULTURAL LANDS IN URBAN AREAS

A serious impediment in the application of the ULC&R Act will be the lack of any systematic documentation of urban land holdings comparable to the old revenue records which proved useful in imposing ceilings on agricultural holdings.

A study of the following figures gives an indication of the extent of vacant lands in our cities. The figures reveal that a considerable proportion of the total urban land is used for agriculture and hence cannot be treated as 'vacant land' for the purposes of the Act unless otherwise shown in the master plan.

Agricultural Lands and Vacant Lands in Selected Indian Cities*

Name of city	Nature of use	Area within Municipal Area	Percentage of Municipal Area	Area in Planning Area	% of total Planning Area
1. Vishakhapatnam	(a) Agriculture	69	0.60	—	—
	(b) Vacant land	4,929	42	—	—
2. Bhopal	(a) Agriculture	3,323 h.a.	—	3,323	38.4
	(b) Vacant land	565 h.a.	—	1,100	12.8
3. Indore	(a) Agriculture	6,282	45.6	6,282	43.8
	(b) Vacant land	1,400	10.1	1,400	9.8
4. Bhubaneshwar	Agriculture	—	—	1,470	14.27
5. Hyderabad	Agriculture	—	17.84	—	—
6. Vijayawada	Agriculture	2,393	32.0	825.64	11.00
7. Calicut	Agriculture and other uses	5,640	27.54	4,049	22.89
8. Siliguri	Agriculture and vacant land	—	—	14,906	68
9. Allahabad	(a) Good agriculture	—	—	1,40,696	48.56
	(b) Bad agriculture	—	—	16,000	5.53
	(c) Barren land	—	—	8,000	2.76
	(d) Orchards	—	—	10,700	3.70
	(e) Low-lying and water-logged area	—	—	32,200	11.12

(*Source*: Recent Official Master Plan Reports for Selected cities).

* Areas are given in acres unless otherwise specified.

A sample survey of land holdings in the suburbs of Bombay (Borivli area), Sholapur and Pandharpur reveals that the proportion of large holdings (i.e. exceeding 1 acre in size each) in the areas studied constituted over 75% of all the holdings. This means that considerable excess land will be available from our urban areas on the enforcement of the Ceiling Act, though some of it might be exempted for being in agricultural use.

A recent estimate based on a sample survey revealed that 6700 hectares of excess land would be available for Bangalore city. Another survey indicated that 3,183 lakh square metres of excess land will be available from the urban agglomeration in Rajasthan.

Strict enforcement of the Ceiling Act on the extensive palace compounds of former princes in Mysore, Indore, Bhopal, Gwalior, Jaipur and other cities ought to yield considerable excess land. Many of these extend over 15 to 20 acres of which only 1% to 5% is covered.

The statements filed before competent authorities by parties having excess land before the last date gives an idea of the number of holdings in excess of the ceiling limit, e.g. Hyderabad—13,529; Lucknow—16,067; Calcutta—20,714; Greater Bombay—10,000.

SUBSTANDARD COLONIZATION BY SPECULATORS

The assumption underlying land subdivision control is that the colonizer should not only designate land for streets, parks and other community facilities in conformity with the approved layout plan, but also bear the responsibility for laying the streets and developing community facilities. The local body should be responsible only for their maintenance. The municipal law often requires that the streets should be 'levelled, paved, metalled, flagged, channelled, sewered, drained and lighted' to the satisfaction of the municipal council.

However, landlords sell developed or undeveloped plots without fulfilling their legal obligations. The registration department is not required to verify if a layout plan was approved by the local body before registering a sale transaction. The purchasers of plots later exert political pressure on the municipal officials for taking over such substandard unauthorised streets and declare them as public streets. This is, generally, the woeful tale of development of unauthorized and sub-standard colonies in the suburbs of our cities. There are exceptions, to be sure, and there are some well-developed colonies.

The Urban Land Ceiling Act will doubtless put an end to the rapacious speculation of the colonisers. But the question is whether the urban development authorities or the like will be able to fill the vacuum created by the exit of private estate developers. If they fail to do so, there will be utter urban chaos with slums proliferating and squatting occurring on a large scale. For all their drawbacks, the private colonisers operated quickly and efficiently and kept the private estate market elastic enough to respond to the public demand for housing. It is an open question whether official land development and disposal authorities can succeed in doing this to the same extent.

SELECTION OF URBAN AGGLOMERATION AND THEIR GROUPING

The cities have been grouped under categories A, B, C, and D mainly on a consideration of their population size as shown below:—

Category A—Delhi, Bombay, Calcutta and Madras
,, B—Cities with population exceeding 1 million
,, C—Cities with population in range 3 lakhs to 1 million.
,, D—Cities with population in range 2 to 3 lakhs.

Bombay is an island with no space to expand, and there are swampy low-lying lands on either side of Calcutta Connurbation. Both these metropolitan areas have developed with considerable compactness, density and congestion. On the other hand, Madras and Delhi have a vast hinterland into which they could expand; several areas in these cities have a garden-city character. Thus the wisdom of applying the same restrictions with regard to vacant land size and plinth area for the four metropolitan areas in category A is questionable. In fact, there may be need for varying these standards as between the core, suburban and fringe areas of the same metropolis.

The peripheral area of an urban agglomeration in a State may sometimes fall within the boundary of another State, e.g. peripheral area of Delhi agglomeration falling in Haryana. In such cases, the agglomeration shall include only as much of the peripheral area as is within the boundaries of the State wherein it is located.

SHAPE OF EXCESS LANDS

Since the owner has the option of deciding upon the shape and size of the plot to be retained by him within the ceiling limit, excess lands will be available to the government in discontinuous and varying shapes. It may have been more desirable to provide for allotment of alternative plots within ceiling limits at a suitable place to these owners rather than allow them to retain such plots on their own lands.

So as to obtain an extensive continuous lands of regular shape for undertaking large-scale development, the government may have to acquire vacant lands retained by the owners, as also agricultural lands under the Land Acquisition Act, 1894, besides getting the excess lands under the Ceiling Act. The planners will also have to use their ingenuity for suggesting proper uses (such as shops, parking areas, spaces, etc.) for the small truncated marginal lands that may be obtained as excess lands from plots, which are a little larger than the ceiling limit. It might be a better idea not to take excess lands (which do not exceed about 100 sq. mts.) in cases of marginal plots.

The Union Minister for Works & Housing stated recently that only viable land would be acquired, but the ULC & R Act does not leave any scope for discretion with the competent authority, who will be obliged to initiate acquisition proceeding in all cases of excess lands.

MASTER PLAN IN RELATION TO THE ACT

Master plans have been prepared in recent decades for most towns and cities in the country, but in Punjab, Haryana and West Bengal, the master plans do not yet have a legal sanction. Section 2(h) merely stipulates that the master plan should have been prepared in pursuance of law or an order of the government. Calcutta, the largest metropolis in India, does not have a master plan in the sense defined in the Act but has a Basic

Development Plan which provides for the development of infrastructure and civic services. A special requirement of this section is that the master plan should indicate the stages by which the development is to be carried out. Most of the existing master plans are deficient in this regard and it is imperative for the state town-planning departments to take immediate steps to make good this omission immediately.

Lands on which construction of buildings is not permissible in the Master Plan are excluded from the operation of the Act. Hence the public authorities will not be able to procure vacant lands reserved for parks and playgrounds in the Master Plan.

AGRICULTURAL LAND AND THE CEILING ACT

Agricultural lands are excluded from the ceiling limit subject to following conditions: (1) not being used for raising grass, dairy farming, poultry farming and breeding of live-stock, (2) entered in revenue records as being used for agriculture, (3) not specified in the master plan for non-agricultural use.

It is inevitable that cities will encroach upon adjoining agricultural lands in the course of their expansion. Whenever there is a chance between agricultural land and non-agricultural land, there is no question that the former ought to be left untouched. But in most cases there is no such choice, and agricultural areas cannot be insured against expanding towns. It was thus not prudent to exempt agricultural lands from the operation of the Ceiling Act. Increased food production is no doubt important—even imperative—but this ought to be secured through other methods—such as consolidation of holdings, better-agricultural techniques, increased inputs etc.

In certain States, notably Punjab and Andhra Pradesh, there are pressures by the farmers' lobbies for the revision of master plans so that bonafide agricultural lands are not adversely affected by the Act. In fact, the Punjab government has sometimes ordered the revision of master plans in response to such pressures. This is rather an unfortunate trend, for it militates against one of the basic objectives of the Act, viz. to secure all suitable vacant lands under public ownership in the interest of public good.

On the fringes of our cities, there are generally several villages inhabited mainly by farmers with small holdings. Since compensation for lands acquired for urban expansion would be merely nominal, the Act would cause great hardship to the owners. Displaced from their normal occupation, these agriculturists would be forced to swarm into the cities in search of jobs. In Kerala, where large compounds of houses are used for farming, a rigorous application of the Act can result in the lowering of agricultural production.

INDUSTRY AND THE CEILING LIMIT

The ULC & R Act has created uncertainties in the minds of industrialists about expansion, modernization and diversification of existing factory sites. But, according to the guidelines issued by the Central Government, land required for expansion of industry within the next 5 years, and vacant lands upto 1/2 acre should be exempted, specially since there are safeguards against transfer of vacant land. The Act also requires expansion to be completed within a specified period.

EXEMPTION IN CASES OF HARDSHIP

The State Governments have discretionary powers to grant exemption from the operation of ceiling limit on considerations of 'public interest' and 'undue hardship'. These expressions are vague and the Central Government would be well advised to issue some general guidelines in this regard.

A genuine case of hardship that deserves a grant of exemption is that of middle-class retired officials who may have invested all their savings, provident fund and borrowed money on building a house on a plot exceeding the ceiling limit in the suburbs of a large city. It must, however, be realised that, in the metropolis today, man can no longer be permitted the luxury of living in a bungalow with a large compound.

IMPACT OF THE ACT ON THE ESTATE MARKET

Since the enactment of the ceiling law, there has been, generally, a sharp decline in prices of vacant lands in urban agglomerations. This is due to a variety of reasons. Firstly, the compensation payable under the Act for excess land bears no relationship to land value. Then, the Act has generated a sense of insecurity resulting in a tendency for potential buyers to adopt an attitude of 'wait-and-see'. Land transactions have, generally, come to a standstill. Several landlords have, in anticipation of the legislation, disposed of plots. For instance, there were 21,495 land transactions registered in Ahmedabad during 1975 as against 15,638 in 1974. There is no doubt that quite a few of those were 'benami' transactions.

Side by side with this, however, an increase in the value and rental of existing large bungalows and spacious flats was noticeable. This may be attributed to the fact that because of the restrictions imposed by the Act such buildings will be in short supply. There have also been reports of a phenomenal increase in the value of such plots as are within the ceiling limit. This is understandable.

Building activity in the private sector is reported to have slowed down considerably in the urban areas covered by the Act. This may create serious unemployment problem, at least in the short run, for those who depend on this activity, such as contractors, architects, engineers, skilled and unskilled workers, employees of building material industry and furniture-makers. There has, however, been a slight improvement in the situation after the issue of the guidelines by the Central Government regarding the grant of building permits. In the long run, though i.e. after the development authorities have developed the excess land and launched public housing projects or have disposed of the developed lands, construction activity will not only be renewed with added vigour but expand considerably.

IMPACT ON DENSITY AND BUILDING HEIGHT

The Act imposes restrictions on the size of plot and plinth area but does not impose any restriction on the total number of dwelling units that may be constructed on a floor or in the building, or on the vertical height of the building. It may, therefore, be expected that the development of suburban areas of larger cities will take place at higher densities than before. As a result, the garden-city character of suburbs will have ended. Also, an increase in the heights of new buildings could be expected. But because of the ceiling, the increase in height may not be considerable. There might be fewer skyscrapers in private housing in our metropolitan areas, implying a lack of optimum use of land.

BULK ACQUISITION OF LAND AND NEW VISTAS

Most master plans for towns and cities have remained unimplemented so far because of paucity of funds for acquiring land on the scale required for development. This reason will no longer hold since extensive agricultural lands on the periphery of cities can now be acquired for a moderate price regardless of what it is in the open market. For large-scale corporate development, the government may have to compulsorily acquire vacant land (under the Land Acquisition Act) in addition to taking possession of excess land under the Ceiling Act.

Massive public ownership of urban vacant land opens up new vistas in urban development. In a sense, an urban revolution is under way in India now; it could well be a model for other developing countries. Planners can now prepare imaginative plans for development of housing colonies, shopping centres, industrial estates, recreation centres, and even new towns. The spactacular results of this are visible in Delhi.

One must, however, enter the caveat that a policy of bulk acquisition of land can also worsen an urban situation, e.g. by causing inflation of land values, growth of slums and squatter colonies (as has indeed happened in Delhi). In Delhi, the preliminary notification under Section 4(1) of the Land Acquisition Act in respect of vacant lands was issued as far back as 1957 when the prices of lands were very low (i.e. less than about Rs. 10 per sq. yd.) Delhi Administration had taken possession of 36,000 acres of land by Jan. 1975; of these, 25,000 acres have passed into the hands of Delhi Development Authority, which developed 14,094 developed plots by the end of 1976. Of these plots, 23%, 23% and 12% were given to high, middle and low-income groups respectively.* The low-income group, which constitutes the bulk of Delhi's population, received a very small share. At the same time, there has been a phenomenal increase in land values at times, exceeding Rs. 500 per square metre. It is therefore not surprising that there were about 1,50,000 families squatting in Delhi in 1975. The D.D.A. has made a huge profit of Rs. 12.23 crores out of sales of plots to the high-income group during the last 14 years.

* Howland Mary: 'Delhi's large scale Land Acquisition, Development and Disposal Policy: An Appraisal'. *Urban and Rural Planning Thought Journal*, January 1975, New Delhi.

It is high time the town-planning departments and the urban development authorities prepared detailed plans for utilising lands acquired. These should allocate lands to the public or private sector for developing them. The plans should also identify areas in which the pre-emption right over transfer of property may be exercised by the government. Priority should be given to urban development authorities, municipal bodies and housing boards in the matter of allocation of land among public agencies. The long-term objective should be to have a separate urban land bank in every agglomeration.

THE HOUSING ASPECT

The housing backlog in our urban areas is enormous—at a rough estimate about 20 million. Priority therefore should be given to using the vacant land acquired under the Ceiling Act for housing. Special attention must be paid to constructing dwelling units for the economically weaker sections.

Vacant land used by private individuals for housing the weaker sections are exemped from the ceiling limit to the extent of 80 square metres per unit. This limit appears rather high. Section 21 of the Act should be so amended as to exempt owners of vacant lands who intend to sell plots to persons of weaker sections who want to build their own houses.

A spurt in the construction of houses for lower income groups may be expected in both public and private sectors in near future. But there is danger of too many houses. There are instances of too many houses having been built for lower income groups. Several houses remaining unsold due to lack of purchasing power with them e.g. several unsold tenements. For example at Ahmedabad several tenements built by the Housing Board remain unsold. A careful assessment of demand, therefore, must be made, keeping in view the requirement as much as the purchasing power of the group for which tenements are built.

Housing for the weaker sections of society on strips of land obtained from large vacant plots in existing posh colonies may create heterogeneous communities, causing many sociological problems. On the other hand, housing them in separate colonies amounts to creating ghattoo. A balance could be struck by having a mixture of adjacent income groups in some of the new colonies.

Vacant lands for group housing schemes, sanctioned by authorities before the passing of the Act, are exempted from the ceiling limit, but no period has been specified for completion of the group housing. A spurt in co-operative housing activity may be expected in the urban agglomerations since registered co-operative societies are exempted from the Act. Care, however, must be taken to ensure that they are kept free from malpractices that have been noted recently.

To turn over all surplus land to public sector agencies, thus keeping private capital out of housing projects, may slow down building activity and speedy provision of much-needed housing in towns. It may, therefore, be advisable to allot some blocks of lands to private individuals and firms ready to invest on estate development on such conditions as may be specified.

FUNDS FOR LAND DEVELOPMENT

The urban development authorities and the housing boards should be geared to fill the vacuum created by the exit of private colonisers and estate developers. They should be enabled to form a revolving fund with subsidies from State and Central governments. The D.D.A. could play the dynamic role that it did in the development of lands in Delhi only because the Central Government had given it initially a revolving fund of Rs. 5.0 crores and subsequently another Rs. 12.31 crores to meet the cost of acquisition and development. A major part of the funds allocated for housing and urban development by the HUDCO and other financing agencies should be given to the development authorities operating in the urban agglomerations.

ORGANIZATIONAL ASPECTS

A serious shortcoming in the ULC&R Act is that it does not specify the type of organization needed to implement the Act. The need for an appropriate organizational structure at the central, state and local levels for ensuring affective implementation of the Act cannot be over-emphasized. In most of the States, officials belonging to the administrative cadres in the revenue department have been declared as competent authorities. There is a high level Central Co-ordination Committee to review periodically the progress made in the implementations of the Act and to suggest measures for monitoring the progress. Likwise, high-level co-ordination committees were appointed in most of the States where the Act is in operation.

Committees consisting of local officials have been set up by several States to make recommendations for the exercise of preemption right and for the utilisation of excess lands. In some States, exemptions are granted by either the Cabinet (e.g. U.P.) or the concerned Minister (e.g. Rajasthan). It is too much to expect a Minister or Cabinet to examine the merits of every application for exemption and they should only formulate the policy, leaving the implementation to local committees. Rajasthan State has taken a lead in setting up a separate directorate for dealing with urban ceiling matters.

The Act may encourage corruption at all levels of administration connected with the enforcement of the Act. This may range from getting the revenue records or the master plan changed so as to show agricultural use for a particular piece of land to enable the owner to seek exemption from the ceiling limit, or to prevent the exercise of pre-emption right.

SUPPLEMENTARY MEASURES

The Central Government has recommended to the States following legislative measures: (1) tax on vacant land; (2) tax on built-up plots in excess of ceiling; (3) tax on built-up areas in excess of maximum plinth areas; (4) a development charge when land is developed; (5) a charge for change in land use; (6) restrictions on transfer of agricultural land within urban agglomerations; (7) change in municipal building by-laws to make them conform to ULC&R Act. The States have, however, been rather tardy in taking action. Only West Bengal and Tamilnadu have enacted the urban land tax acts.

CONCLUSIONS

The ULC&R Act has met with vehement criticism from several quarters. Some critics consider it ill-conceived, ambiguous and obscure in details. Some go so far as to advocate withdrawal or suspension of the Act. The *Hindu*, in its editorial dated 15th December, 1976, summed up the public reaction to the Act thus: "This hastily enacted legislation bristles with anomalies, seeks to impose irksome restrictions on the ownership and transfer of property, fixes an unimaginative arbitrary ceiling, all clothed in intricate official jargon and confusing and contradictory provisions that have provoked wide controversy. Lawyers and jurists who have sought to interpret the key sections find themselves as much at sea as the lay citizen. Official clarifications offer little help and less solaces. The elaborate complicated form that has to be filled by the helpless urban property owners is the last straw to break his back." However, those at the helm of affairs, particularly at the Central Government level, are maintaining, with considerable skill, a delicate balance between making adjustments to take care of practical difficulties and hardships arising from the operational aspects of the Act while at the same time not sacrificing the basic objectives and spirit of the Act.

The Urban Ceiling Act appears to have been inspired more by political ideology than by an earnest desire to promote orderly urban development. The Act could nevertheless be made a useful tool for attaining goals of urban development with some modifications. The objectives of the Act, it has been pointed out, can be attained in a less drastic manner by adjusting the wealth tax and imposing a graded tax on large urban holdings.

Socialization (i.e. taking under public ownership) of all vacant lands outside the built-up areas in towns and cities on payment of equitable compensation might be a better alternative to the cumbersome Urban Land Ceiling Act.

V.A. Seyid Muhammad

CHAPTER XIII

Wakf Law and Administration of Wakfs in India

ORIGIN OF WAKF

The origin of wakf may be traced to the direct prescriptions of the Prophet. "The validity of wakfs", says the *Ghait ul-Bayan*, "is founded on the rule laid down by the Prophet himself under the following circumstances, and handed down in succession by Ibn 'Auf, Nafe and Ibn Omar as stated in the Jam'aa ut-Tirmizi. Omar had acquired a piece of land in the canton of Khaibar, and proceeded to the Prophet and sought his counsel, to make the most pious use of it, whereupon the Prophet declared, 'tie up the property (Asl or corpus) and devote the usufruct to human beings, and it is not to be sold or made the subject of gift or inheritance; devote its produce to your children, your kindred, and the poor in the way of God." Accordingly, Omar dedicated the property in question, and the wakf continued in existence for several centuries until the land turned barren.

The author of the Fath ul-Kadir, a work of great authority among Sunnis, states that the law of wakf has its origin with the Prophet himself who, besides having prescribed the above rule to Omar, is reported to have declared that all human actions end with the life of the individual, except such benefactions as are perpetual in their character; and that, in accordance with these principles, trusts or dedications were frequent in the lifetime of the Prophet and in the early centuries.

of Islam. The author gives examples of such wakfs, some of which were in existence at the time when he was writing his work, e.g., the wakf by the Prophet himself of a piece of land which he had acquired in the canton of Khaibar for the support of travellers; the wakf of Omar of the land called Sammagh in the same canton for his children, kindred, and the poor; of Zubair ibn Awwam for his daughter; of Akram in favour of his son; of Abu Bakr in favour of his children; of S'aad ibn Abi Wakkas of his lands in Medina and Egypt for his children "which still exists"; and of Osman of his lands called Baruah, "which still continues".

Says Ameer Ali, "The doctrine of wakf is thus interwoven with the entire religious life and social economy of the Mussulmans."[1]

WAKF IN INDIA

Husain and Rashid[2] find the earliest descriptions of wakfs in India in a rare book, *Insha-i-Mahru*, by Aynul Mulk Multani. According to Multani, Muizuddin Sam Ghaor dedicated two villages in favour of Jama Masjid of Multan, and handed its administration to the Shaikhul Islam, that is, the highest ecclesiastical officer of the empire.

(1) **Under the Sultanate**: Under the Sultanate, many more wakfs were created. Ibn Battuta, who himself was appointed a Mutawalli of the wakf in favour of a tomb, has given a detailed and interesting description of wakf. Shams-i-Siraj Afif gives the following useful information:

> It is a custom among kings, while they are on the throne, to appropriate villages and lands to religious men in order to provide means for the maintenance and repair of their [sic] tombs. But these endowments (wakfs) had been destroyed, and the grantees being divested of them, were reduced to distress . . . Sultan Alauddin carefully repaired all the tombs and restored the lands and villages after bringing into cultivation such as had been laid waste.

(2) **Under the Mughals**: Even after the ouster of the Delhi

1. Syed Ameer Ali; *Mahammedan Law*, pp. 192-193.
2. S.A. Husain and B.K. Rashid: Wakf Law and Administration in India, 1973 edition, p. 14.

Sultans by the Mughals in A.D. 1526, the traditions laid down by the former were continued, and a large number of wakfs were created during the Mughal period.

A very elaborate and centralized machinery for the administration of wakfs was created, with the Mutawalli, who looked after individual wakfs put under his care, at the base, and the Sultan at the upper of the administrative pyramid. Akbar placed some checks on Sadr-us-Sudur (the chief acclesiastical officer, who recommended grants and stipends) and thus mitigated the defects inherent in over-centralisation.[3]

(3) **Under the British**: When the East India Company was appointed the Diwan of the Subah of Bengal in 1765 by a Royal Firman, it decided to leave the personal laws of Hindus and Muslims alone. Section 27 of the Regulation of 1772 states: "in all suits regarding inheritance, succession, marriage, castes and other religious usages or institutions, the laws of the Quran with respect of Mohammedans and those of the Shastras with respect of Gentoos (Hindus) shall be invariably adhered to".

In keeping with this policy, which continued up to 1810, the administration of wakf was allowed to remain as under the Mughals. But later, when it was found that many of the wakfs were mismanaged and administered contrary to the objects of the relevant wakfs, the government made certain provisions to control the administration of the existing wakfs. Regulation XIX of 1810 of Bengal Code, and Regulation VI of 1817 of the Madras Code sought to do that. Realising that the personal laws of Hindus and Muslims contained elaborate and detailed rules for religious endowments, the Government of India decided to divest itself of all direct concern with the management of these central religious endowments.

(*i*) *Endowment Act, 1863*. Accordingly, the Religious Endowment Act of 1863 was passed. Under this Act the properties and management of endowments, till then under the Board of Revenue or local agents, were transferred to trustees or managers. The Act was, however, applicable only to public religious endowments and not to private institutions. There were special provisions relating to the management of mosques, temples or other religious establishments.

3. Hussain and Rashid, *op. cit.*

(ii) Qazis Act, 1864, and Charitable Act, 1890: In 1864, the Qazis Act was passed which practically abolished the institution of Muhammadan Law Officers. In 1890, came the Charitable Endowment Act, which left it to the trustees and administrators of the endowments to apply for vesting and settling of schemes.

(iii) Wakf Validating Act, 1913: Following the decision of the Privy Council in 1894, in the case of *Abul Fata Muhammad* v. *Russomoy* (22 IA 76), declaring *wakf-al-aulad* to be an invalid wakf, there was considerable agitation and resentment among the Muslims, and the Mussalman Wakf Validating Act 1913, was passed to restore the validity of such endowments. But, as observed by Tayyibji,[4] it is not a general law of wakfs, but only an enactment to validate what is known in Mohammadan Law as *Wakf-al-aulad,* and thus the Act takes the law back to the ancient and original text.

(iv) Civil Procedure Code: It is necessary in connection with the Wakf Law in India to make a mention of Section 92 of the Civil Procedure Code (Act 5 of 1908). It empowers the Advocate-General to institute a suit against trusts of a charitable or religious nature. The court may give a decree removing the trustee, appointing a new trustee, or vesting property in a trustee, directing examination of accounts, authorising lease, sale, mortgage or exchange of trust property, and formulating a scheme for the administration of the trust. After a series of conflicting decisions, it is now settled that in acting under Section 92 the Advocate-General does not act judiciously but only in an administrative capacity, and that his decisions are not amenable to the writ of certiorari. It is also settled that the Advocate-General does not act as the representative of, or as the law officer on behalf of the State but discharges a specific statutory duty.

(v) Mussalman Wakf Act, 1923: The Mussalman Wakf Act, 1923, made it obligatory for mutawallis of every wakf except *wakf-al-aulad* to submit regular statements of accounts to the notified authority, as also to have the accounts audited. A penalty up to Rs. 500 was provided for untrue or false statements.

Since the Mussalman Wakf Validating Act, 1913 was not retrospective and hence did not apply to wakfs created before

4. Muhsin Tayyibji: Muslim Law, 4th edition, pp. 555-556.

its enactment, a short Act, The Mussalman Wakf Validating Act, 1930, was passed making the 1913 Act applicable to wakfs created before its commencement.

(4) In Independent India

(*i*) *Wakf Act, 1954*: In 1954, the comprehensive Wakf Act, 1954, was put on the statute book. The Act provides for: the constitution of non-official boards both at the Centre and in the States; imposition of strict and precise obligations on Mutawallis and making violations of these obligations penal offences; conferring authority on the Central Government to lay down policies to be adopted by the State boards, and providing for the proper and effective administration of wakfs in the country. The Act extends to the whole of India except the State of Jammu and Kashmir. The Gentral Government has issued a notification to make the Act applicable in all the States except Bihar, Uttar Pradesh and Bengal, which have their own Wakf Acts.

Some of the important provisions of the Wakf Act, 1954, are summarized below:

Under Section 4, each State Government is empowered to appoint a State Commissioner of Wakf whose duty is to make a preliminary survey of wakfs and submit a report to the State Government. The State Government forwards a copy of the report to the State Wakf Board, which then publishes a list of existing wakfs in the official gazette.

Section 6 provides that if a question arises as to whether a particular property is wakf property or not or whether a wakf is a Shia wakf or a Sunni wakf, the Board or the *Mutawalli* of the wakf or any other interested person may take the matter to a civil court of competent jurisdiction whose decision shall be final.

Section 8A provides for the appointment of a Central Wakf Council with the Union Minister in charge of wakfs as chairman, and members not exceeding twenty in number. Every State Board is to pay from its wakf fund a contribution of 1% of the net annual income to the Central Wakf Council. Section 8A (1) makes it clear that the main function of the Central Wakf Council is to advise on matters concerning the working of State boards and the administration of wakfs.

Chapter III deals with the constitution, establishment, power and functions of the State board, which is a body corporate consisting of 11 members with a chairman elected by the members. The members are to be appointed from among the members of State legislature, persons having good knowledge of Muslim law, persons of administrative and financial knowledge and experience, and Mutawallis of wakfs in the State. All the members must be Muslims. Section 25 requires all past, present and future wakfs to be registered with the State Wakf Board which shall maintain a register of all wakfs.

Chapter V deals with the powers and duties of Mutawallis. Under Section 41, the failure of the *Mutawalli* to apply for registration, to furnish statements or particulars of accounts, to deliver possession of any wakf property if ordered by the board or the court, or to carry out the directions of the board or to discharge his duties etc. is punishable with fine which may extend to Rs. 1000. The Board has power to remove the *mutawalli* if he has been convicted of an offence under Section 41, or of criminal breach of trust, or of any other offence involving moral turpitude, or of misappropriation of wakf properties. Under Section 46, the *mutawalli* of every wakf shall pay annually to the board a contribution not exceeding 6% of the annual income of the concerned wakf property.

Section 55 empowers the board to institute a suit without recourse to the procedure under Section 92 of the Civil Procedure Code. Under Section 62, the Central Government is empowered to issue such directions as it may think fit on questions of policies to be followed by State boards and the State board shall be guided by such directions. Section 63 empowers State Government to issue certain types of directions to the board. It the State government is of opinion that the State board fails or is unable to perform its duties, it may supersede the Board for a specified period (Section 64). By Section 69, the Bengal Charitable Endowments, Public Buildings and Escheats Regulation, 1810, the Religious Endowments Act, 1863, the Charitable Endowments Act, 1890, the Charitable and Religious Trusts Act, 1920, the Mussalman Wakf Act, 1923, are made inapplicable to any wakf to which the Wakf 1954 Act applies. It is also provided in that section that if immediately before the commencement of the 1954 Act there is in force any law which corresponds to this Act, such corresponding law stands repealed.

(*ii*) *Public Wakfs (Extension of Limitation) Act, 1959*: Following the partition of the country in 1947, large numbers of Muslims migrated to Pakistan from East Punjab, Rajasthan, Delhi and some other territories adjoining the newly created State of Pakistan. Thousands of wakf properties were left behind many of which were taken over by the Custodian of Evacuee Property and many were illegally occupied. Because it took some time for the 1954 Act to be implemented effectively and because of various other reasons the possession of many of the wakf properties illegally occupied had become adverse. To remedy this situation the Public Wakfs (Extension of Limitation) Act, 1959, was passed. Section 3 of this Act extended the limitation for filing suits in respect of public wakfs dispossessed at any time between 14 August, 1947 and 7 May, 1954, upto 15th day of August, 1967. This date was extended from time to time.

OPERATION OF WAKF LAWS IN INDIA

We may now examine the problems and difficulties which arise in the application and operation of the wakf laws in this country. This will be done after stating some of the basic principles of wakf.

(1) **Definition of Wakf**: The term 'wakf' literally means "I have bound up or detained", but technically it denotes permanent dedication of property either in express terms or by implication for any charitable or religious object or to secure any benefit to human beings.[5]

According to Abu Yusuf, wakf is the detention of a thing in the ownership of Almighty God in such a manner that its profits may be applied for the benefit of human beings. Dedication, once made, is absolute so that the thing dedicated can neither be sold, nor given nor inherited. Imam Mohammad, the fellow desciple of Abu Yusuf, agrees with him on this point, but thinks that the right of wakif does not cease in the property until he has appointed a mutawalli or curator and delivered it in his hands.[6] It is universally accepted among Muslim jurists

5. Ameer Ali, Mohammadan Law, 4th edition, Vol. I, p. 194.
6. *Ibid*, pp. 195-196.

that the act of dedication extinguishes absolutely and for ever all the rights of the donor and transfers those rights to the juristic ownership of the Almighty for the benefit of his creatures.

(2) **Delivery of Possession** : Under the Hanafi law, it is not necessary that there should be actual delivery of possession to complete a *wakf.* A mere declaration by the *wakif* is sufficient to turn the property into a wakf, and the *wakif* from then on would remain a mere trustee. The question whether making over possession to a mutawalli was necessary to constitute a valid wakf came up for consideration before the High Court of Calcutta in *Doedem Jan Bibi* v. *Abdoollah Barber*, and the court held that it was not.[7]

Tayyibji points out the difficulties in accepting *in toto* either of the two extreme positions and therefore recommends the following *via media*: Dedication by way of wakf is completed when the *wakif* makes a declaration in good faith with the intention of divesting himself of the ownership of the property he intends to dedicate. Where a mutawalli is nominated, the intention is formalized by delivery of the property to him. But the fact that no person is nominated as mutawalli does not necessarily negative such intention, although failure to deliver possession, if not satisfactorily explained, may indicate the absence of intention.[8]

(3) **Wakf by non-Muslims** : Section 3(1) of the Wakf Act, 1954, defines "wakf" as the permanent dedication by a person professing Islam of any movable or immovable property for any purpose recognised by the Muslim law as pious, religious or charitable and includes a wakf by user and a *wakf-al-aulad.* According to this definition, dedication by a non-Muslim is altogether excluded. But under the law of Islam non-Muslims also may be *wakif* provided the purposes are recognised by Muslim Law as pious, charitable or religious.[9] Referring to the various authorities, Ameer Ali also comes to the same conclusion.[10] Without accepting this position, the government modified the stand of the Act through an amendment (Act 34 of 1964) which states that notwith standing anything contained in this

7. *Ibid*, pp. 237-241.
8. Tayyibji, Muslim Law, 4th ed., pp. 515-518.
9. *Ibid.*, p. 570.
10. See Ameer Ali, *op. cit.*, p. 203.

Act, where any movable or immovable property has been given or donated by any person not professing Islam for the support of a wakf being a mosque, idgah, imambara, dargah, khankah or a maqbara, a Muslim graveyard, a choultry or a musafar-khana, then such property shall be deemed to be a wakf.

(4) **Objects of Wakf** : The objects of wakf should be those that are recognised by Muslim Law as charitable or religious or pious. Under Hanafi Law, the ultimate end of wakf is the benefit of the poor. The Wakf Act, 1913 recognises *wakf-al-aulad* too. The expression charity is used by Muslim jurists in the broadest sense.

(5) **Who can be a wakif**? Any person who is of a sound mind is competent to become a *wakif*. On this point all the authorities, including Fatawa Alamgiri, are of the same opinion. According to Raddul Muhtar, an imbecile can make a valid wakf, but Abu Yusuf holds that such a wakf will take effect only on its being sanctioned by the judge.

(6) **Dedication and Intention** : The dedication should be permanent, that is to say, the intention to constitute wakf in perpetuity should be clear. There is a difference of opinion among Muslim jurists on whether the intention should be explicit or implied. However, it is well settled that though it is not necessary for dedication to be in perpetuity, the intention to dedicate property should be explicit. But a valid wakf can be created even through implied intention.[11] It is also well settled that one may dedicate movable as well as immovable properties. Under the impact of modern commercial transactions, it is accepted that not only money, but, as in Egypt, shares, stocks and bonds can also be dedicated.

(7) **User** : It is well accepted that dedication can be inferred from long use. If a piece of land, for example, has been used from time immemorial for a religious purpose, the land is wakf although there may be no evidence of an express dedication.[12] Similarly, if a mosque has been used for a long time by public for daily prayers, it becomes wakf.[13]

(8) **Wakif's own benefit** : Under the Hanafi law, the wakif

11. Ameer Ali, *op. cit.*, pp. 228-240.
12. *Mazhar Hussain* v. *Aditya Ram* 1948(1) MLJ. 3, p. 259.
13. *Miru* v. *Ram Gopal* 156 IC 942. See also *Abdul Rahim* v. *Fakir Mohammad*, A.I.R. 1946 Nag. 580.

may provide for his maintenance in a wakf property. He may, if he so wishes, reserve the whole income to himself for his life-time. He may provide for the repayment of his debt out of the income of wakf property. But according to Shia law, a wakf is not valid unless the wakif divests himself of the ownership of the property in question. A settler cannot reserve a life-interest in any part of the income from such property.

(9) **Revocation**: Abu Hanifa holds that wakf is revocable unless there is a decree of the court confirming it. Abu Yusuf and Imam Mohd. are opposed to this view. Fatawas do not support Hanifa's view.[14] It is well settled now that a non-testamentary wakf is irrevocable under the Muhammadan Law because, although a voluntary transaction, it brings *iwas* to the wakif in the form of approach to God.[15] A testamentary wakf, on the other hand, being no more than a bequest for a religious or charitable purpose, may be revoked like any other bequest. A wakf created during Marz-ul-maut (mortal illness) stands on the same footing. If at the time of creating a non-testamentary wakf, the wakif reserves to himself the power of revoking the wakf, the wakf is invalid.[16]

(10) **Mutawalli**: Section 3(f) of the Wakf Act, 1954, defines a *Mutawalli* as "any person appointed either in deed or instrument by which a wakf has been created to be the Mutawalli of wakf."

What was once a controversial question, viz., whether a female can be appointed as a *mutawalli*, has now been settled. In *Doedem Jan Bibee* v. *Abdoollah Barber* it has been stated as follows:

"It is equally clear and without dispute that a female may be appointed as *Mutawalli.* It is hardly necessary to cite authorities for this proposition. Mr. Macnaghten's book, p. 343, points out the distinction between the *Guddy Nasheen* (or superior of an endowment) and the *Mutawalli*, and adds that the office of trustee, i.e. *Mutawalli*, may be held by a woman, and the duties may be discharged by proxy."

In *Mussumaut Hyatee Khanum* v. *Mussumaut Koolsoom*

14. Baillie, pp. 549-550.
15. Tayyabji, p. 527
16. *Fatmabibi* v. *Advocate-General of Bombay*, (1882) I.L.R. 6 Bombay 42 at 51.

Khanum it is stated that it is legal for a female to be a trustee according to all the authorities of the law.[17]

It is well settled that alienation of wakf property is permissible on grounds of necessity. Consequently, the *Mutawalli* can lease out or mortgage or pledge wakf property.[18]

(11) **Doctrine of Cypres:** It is relevant to examine whether the well accepted doctrine of Cypres is applicable to Muslim wakfs. Abu Yusuf is of the opinion that on a dedication of wakf being complete, even the illegality of its object does not make it void but that the property must be applied to other valid objects of wakf. Tayyabji gives the following quotation from A. Rahim's *Mohammadan Jurisprudence*:

> If, however, the specified objects be limited or happy to fail, but a general charitable intention (Section 474 (6)) is to be inferred from the words of the grant, the wakf will be good, and the income or profit will be devoted for the benefit of the poor, and in some cases to objects as near to the objects which failed, as possible. This rule is analogous to the doctrine of Cypres of the English law.[19]

Ameer Ali agrees with the above position when he states: "More vagueness or uncertainty will not lead to the failure of a wakf, for in such a case the law does itself supply the defect by declaring that the trust should be in favour of such objects as approach nearest in character to the intended object of the wakf; or, even when that is not expressed, be applied to the support of the poor and needy. In the absence of explicit directions on the part of the wakif, the judge has the power of framing a scheme by himself or in consultation with the beneficiaries, for the administration of the wakf which has been occasionally endeavoured to be applied to wakfs is not applicable to trusts or consecrations under the Mahomedan Law. For the Cypres doctrine is carried to the utmost limit in the Moslem system, and the failure of the original purpose does not in any case cause the failure of the wakf."[20]

(12) **Trust, gift and wakf:** Before concluding, it is necessary to point out the difference between trust and wakf. Even

17. Ameer Ali, *op. cit.*, pp. 230-240.
18. *Ibid.*, p. 255.
19. Tayyabji, *op. cit.*, p. 562.
20. Ameer Ali, *op. cit.*, p. 414.

though these two have very many features in common, wakf requires a religious or charitable motive whereas a trust may be made for any lawful object. The author of a trust may be a beneficiary under it but, except under the Hanafi law, the wakif may not reserve to himself any such benefit.

The *mutawalli* of a wakf has much more limited and restricted powers than a trustee under the Indian Trust Act. The position of the *mutawalli* is analogous to that of receivers and managers appointed over property in England, who, by virtue of their appointment, have no estate in the property which they are called upon to manage.[21]

Similarly, there is difference between wakf and gift. Under Sunni law, when a gift is made, the donee, who is a human being, takes an absolute interest in the subject of the grant, whereas in a wakf, since the donee is the Almighty God, the property is kept in the custody of the Almighty for the benefit of mankind; and therefore, even if the original purpose stated in the constitution of the wakf fails, the benefit is applied to other purposes of a like nature. The beneficiaries have no right in the property; they are only entitled to the benefit of the trust to the extent specified in the wakf.[22]

AN APPRAISAL OF THE OPERATION OF WAKF LAW

A survey of the actual operation of the Wakf Act, 1954, and the Wakf law in India as revealed from the various reports available gives rise to mixed feelings. While many commendable things have been done, many remain undone, and some of the hopes and aspirations and objects remain still to be fulfilled. There are a number of problems for which solutions have to be found.

The value of the wakf property so far surveyed comes to about Rs. 800 million.[23] But the latest report available shows that the value of registered wakfs properties is only to the tune of 340 million.[24] It is thus clear that property worth less than half the total value has been recovered. The financial

21. Tayyibji, *op. cit.*, pp. 497-498.
22. Ameer Ali, *op. cit.*, pp. 346-347.
23. Concept and purpose of Central Wakf Act, Ministry of Petroleum and Chemicals, Govt. of India, Feb. 1965, p. 5.
24. Review of Wakf Administration, 1972-73, Wakf Section, Ministry of Law & Justice, Govt. of India, p. 38.

position of the Wakf Boards seems to be far from satisfactory. In 1969-70, the total arrears due from the State Wakf Boards was to the tune of Rs. 1,26,000.[25] In 1972-73 the arrears remained at a higher figure, namely Rs. 1,58,000.[26] In 1967-68, the total income of State Wakf Boards amounted to Rs. 31,72,000, out of which a sum of Rs. 11,25,000 was spent on salaries and allowances, i.e. any expenditure of more than one-third of the total income on establishment alone. This is a very high proportion.

An encouraging feature is that while on 31-3-70 the number of wakf properties registered with wakf boards was only 16,964, three years later on 31-3-73, the number had risen to 58,033 that is to say, three and a half times.

It was found that in certain cases accounts were not properly maintained and important and reliable documents were not well cared for. It was also found that in disregard of statutory provisions, wakfs under the management of mutawallis had given *waris*; even the boards had diverted income of properties directly under their management to general expenditure of the boards. Directions were given to rectify these irregularities.[27]

Quite a large number of wakf properties, such as buildings and lands, were under the occupation of various State governments and local bodies, and the efforts of State boards through administrative channels to have them restored have not been very successful. Understandably, wakf boards are reluctant to initiate legal proceedings against Governments even in respect of cases coming within the purview of the Public Wakf (Extension of Limitation) Act, 1959.[28] The Review of Wakf Administration, 1969-70 shows that 30,850 items of wakf properties are under adverse possession and 20,555 cases regarding wakf properties are pending in various States.

Wakf property has not been property surveyed in many States. To rectify this situation a registration drive is being organized together with an intensive effort to collect arrears. State governments and wakf boards have been urged to tighten

25. Review of 1969-70, p. 16.
26. Review of 1972-73, p. 40
27. Review of 1969-70, pp. 64-65.
28. Review of Wakf Administration, 1969-70, p. 68.

collection measures and explore all other possible sources of augmenting the wakf boards' income. Laxity of control led to many defaults in the submission of budgets statutorily required.[29]

In order to meet the chronic financial difficulties of the wakf boards, many avenues have been explored. One of the suggestions is to develop wakf properties in urban areas. The sub-committee that was set up to look into this has decided to request the Life Insurance Corporation for loan for the purpose. No further information in this regard is available.

The lacunae and deficiencies of the Wakf Act discovered in the course of working of the wakf administration have been substantially remedied by the Wakf Amendment Act, 1964.

The Central Wakf Council as well as the state boards are rendering a valuable service by awarding scholarships to deserving students for higher studies abroad as well as in this country. Certain facilities for training bright students for the central administrative examinations have been provided. The question of providing a combined curriculum of secular and religious education is being experienced by a committee. Certain Acts, whether of the Centre or States, impinge on the Wakf Act. Some of the obvious examples are Land Reforms Laws, Rent Control Act, Income Tax Act. In 1971, Wakf Inquiry Committee of three members of Parliament was set up to enquire into some serious problems faced by the wakf administration. The committee submitted an interim report in 1973 which, *inter alia*, states, "On a scrutiny of the information furnished by the State Boards we were struck by the failure on the part of almost all the State Wakf Boards in carrying out or being unable to carry out statutory duties and obligations . . . This failure has . . . in our opinion thrown the entire system of Wakf Administration under the Act of 1954 into a melting pot.[30]

The committee also recommended emergency legislation to save wakf properties turnover into jeopardy by the decisions of certain High Courts. For example, the Rajasthan High Court by holding, in *Radhakrishnan* v. *Rajasthan Wakf Board*

29. Concept and Purpose of the Central Wakf Act, Government of India, Feb. 1955, pp. 5-6.
30. Wakf Inquiry Committee—Interim Report, 1973, Ministry of Law & Justice, p. (iv).

in Writ Petition No. 74 of 1965, that the list of wakf properties published by the board under sub-section (2) of Section 5 of the Central Wakf Act could not be final and conclusive as contemplated in sub-section (4) of Section 6 against third parties who are not persons interested within the meaning of clause (h) of Section 3 of the Act, virtually nullified the entire survey of wakf properties undertaken at enormous expense by the States. The Mysore and Andhra Pradesh High Courts have also given similar judgements. If other courts were to accept this interpretation, the working of the Wakf Administration would become almost impossible. These decisions affect also Sections 5, 6, and 27 of the Act. Hence the Committee's recommendation for appropriate amendments to the Central Wakf Act.[31]

Again the judgement of the Punjab High Court in the *Punjab Wakf Board, Ambala Cantt*. v. *Punjab Garhi Brahmi* (reported in A.I.R. 1969 Punjab) has made a serious inroad into the well established principle of wakf by user in Muhammadan law, viz., that once a wakf is established by user, the discontinuance of the user for some time does not change the character of the wakf, because the wakf is created in perpetuity and the non-user does not destroy the character of the wakf. The committee has therefore recommended that an explanation may be added to sub-clause (1) of Clause 1 of Section 3 of the Wakf Act, 1954 retrospectively as under:

> A wakf by user shall not cease to be wakf by reason only of the user having ceased irrespective of the period of such dis-user.

In conclusion, it may be said that the Wakf Act with the subsequent amendments, and the administrative machinery created by that Act have advanced the cause of wakfs to a considerable extent. The number of wakfs involved, the value of the wakf properties, the vast potential income therefrom, and the social and economic problems facing the Muslim community have transformed the institution of wakf from a strictly religious plane to one of great social significance. The successful mobilization of the resources of the wakf and their channelization into socially useful and purposeful avenues will render great service to the Muslim community and to the country as a whole.

31. Wakf Enquiry Committee Interim Report, 1973, pp. 1 to 6.

S.N. Dubey

CHAPTER XIV

Social Welfare and Panchayati Raj Institutions

Article 40 of the Constitution under the chapter 'Directive Principles of State Policy' (Part IV) lays down that "the State shall take steps to organize village panchayats and endow them with such power and authority as may be necessary to enable them to function as units of self-government". In pursuance of this directive, efforts have been made to revitalize these units of self-government. Measures have been taken to delegate, develop and decentralize power and authority to the village panchayat. The Community Development Projects and the National Extension Service were the earliest efforts, after independence, to prepare people to share power in the organization and management of their affairs. Though an official machinery was created to guide and assist the planning and implementation of the community development programme, the main responsibility for improving the socio-economic conditions in the village was left to the people themselves. People's participation in the planning and the execution of the programme was considered a vital aspect of community development. With this end in view advisory boards and committees consisting of non-officials at the district and at the block levels respectively were set up (Government of India, 1952).

The programme, however, had only limited success. The Block Advisory Committees lacked the capacity, vitality and power to represent people's points of view. They were often unrepresentative of some important sections of the local populace. The district boards lacked both experience and resources to take up massive developmental work (Maheshwari 1963:8). The village panchayats were ineffective in mobilizing the masses in support of the programme. Implementation of the programme through *ad hoc* bodies, like *Vikas Mandals*, was also attempted, but popular participation enlisted through them remained inadequate.

It was, therefore, felt that representative and democratic institutions were needed to evoke local interest and energize local initiative in the field of development. The Second Five Year Plan emphasized the need for creating, within the district, a well organized democratic structure of administration in which the village panchayats would be organically linked with popular organizations at the higher levels. In such a structure, the functions of the popular body were to include the entire general administration and development of the area. A Study Team on Community Projects and National Extension Services, under the chairmanship of late Balwantrai Mehta, was appointed in 1957 by the Government of India to study the extent of participation of the people in the programme and to suggest an institutional framework which would link the local level institutions to the institutions at the block, district, and state levels. The team felt that it was not practical to link the village panchayat directly to the existing bodies (*ad hoc* bodies, district boards, etc.). It therefore suggested a three-tier institutional structure, to be statutorily created, that would provide for meaningful and effective participation of the people and that would take charge of developmental work in several areas. These institutions are: the *Panchayat* at the village level, the *Panchayat Samiti* at the block level, and the *Zilla Parishad* at the district level (Committee on Plan Projects, 1957: 5-13).

THE RATIONALE FOR PANCHAYATI RAJ

Three basic reasons can be identified for the creation of panchayati raj institutions:

(1) **To make community development programmes relevant to the needs and problems of the people**: One of the criticisms of the community development programmes was that a large number of programmes was organized in rural areas without

due regard to the needs, interests and the life-style of the rural population. Because the programmes were generally inappropriate, fragmented and unsuitable, they failed to make any lasting and positive impact on rural poverty, and a majority of the villagers continued to live in an atmosphere of apathy (Poston, 1962). If the rural population was to be involved in the programmes, they had to be free from biases stemming from considerations of careerism and public relation needs of government departments and their personnel. It was argued that the villagers themselves could define their own needs. The study team consequently observed that "so long as we do not discover or create a representative and democratic institution which will supply the local interest, supervision and care, necessary to ensure that expenditure of money upon local projects conforms with the needs and wishes of the locality, invest it with adequate power and assign to it appropriate finances, we will never be able to evoke local interest and excite local initiative in the field of development" (Committee on Plan Projects, 1957: 5).

(2) **Transfer decision-making authority to villagers**: Another rationale of panchayati raj is to transfer decision-making authority regarding development matters to villagers and their elected representatives. The Second Five Year Plan stressed the need for a well organized democratic structure of administration within the district—the village panchayats organically linked with the popularly elected district boards which would be charged with the entire general administration and development of the area, including administration of justice and certain functions pertaining to revenue administration. But district boards were neither fitted by tradition nor endowed with resources to take on such a responsibility. Moreover, their very size necessitated the delegation of authority and discretion to their own officers, which meant replacing state officers drawn from larger cadres by officers of limited experience in restricted fields. Since a district consisted of hundreds of village panchayats, its direct link with each was far from easy. The block advisory committees, generally appointed to reflect people's perspective in the community development programme, did not have enough power and authority to take decisions on matters of development. The district planning committees were

also powerless and ineffective. The Study Team, therefore, recommended a single elective and statutory representative body, called the panchayat samiti, to take charge of all aspects of development work in the block area. It was to be clothed with authority and given adequate resources to discharge these functions (Committee on Plan Projects, 1957: 67). Thus panchayati raj institutions were designed to create a power base for the people in rural areas by giving them control over programmes, funds, jobs, information, and by granting them legal, constitutional and official status.

(3) **Value of participatory democracy**: Panchayati raj is considered the foundation of participatory democracy in India. Jayaprakash Narayan, one of the wellk-nown commentators on Indian democracy, observed: "It is a matter of great satisfaction that in our country a beginning has already been made in laying the foundation of participatory democracy in the shape of panchayati raj or what was called at first 'democratic decentralization" (Narayan, 1970: 75). S.K. Dey pointed out that in panchayati raj system the people of India would govern themselves through their representatives in institutions from the panchayat to the Parliament and thus democracy would travel from Lok Sabha to Gram Sabha. Panchayati raj thus reflects the concept of interconnected democracy from the Gram Sabha to the Lok Sabha (Dey, 1961: 4-16).

ORGANIZATIONAL PATTERN OF PANCHAYATI RAJ

As has been noted earlier, the Study Team recommended a three-tier organizational structure for the Panchayati raj: the village panchayat with elected representatives of the adult population at the grass-roots level; the panchayat samiti consisting of the sarpanches of panchayats in the block area at the intermediate level; and the zilla parishad with chairmen of panchayat samitis as *ex-officio* members at the district or apex level. This kind of democratic decentralization was first adopted by Rajasthan in October 1959, followed by Andhra Pradesh in November, 1959. The State of Maharashtra adopted it on 1 May, 1962. By now, most of the states in the country have adopted panchayati raj.

An examination of the organizational structure of the panchayati raj institutions in various states reveals that, though the ideals and basic objectives of the institutions are similar in all states, their powers, mode of representation, and the nature of interrelationship among them are not uniform (Maheshwari, 1963: 25; Dayal, 1970: 37-39; Narayan, 1970: 106-112; Jathar, 1964:58-102; Government of Maharashtra, 1961).

In some States the unit is the district, while in some others it is the block or tehsil. There are variations also in the mode of representation: direct election in some States and indirect election or a combination of both in others. For example, the State of Rajasthan, which adopted the panchayati raj pattern suggested by the Study Team *in toto,* made the panchayat samiti the most powerful body, responsible for the planning and the execution of all development programmes, with the zilla parishad as only a supervisory and coordinating body. A special feature of the system in Rajasthan is that the zilla parishad cannot modify the budget proposals of the panchayat samitis, though it can suggest modifications. The Panchayat samiti consists of directly elected sarpanches of village panchayats in the area and the representatives of Scheduled Castes, Tribes, and Cooperatives (Dayal, 1970: 37-44; Jathar, 1964: 87-90). The State of Andhra Pradesh has given planning and executive powers to both panchayat samiti and zilla parishad. Development programmes, including maintenance of minor irrigation, welfare of Backward Classes, have been transferred to the Samiti and the Parishad. The Parishad has supervisory powers in certain areas, while in others it has executive powers. The mode of representation is similar to that in the State of Rajasthan. The pattern in Maharashtra is different from the pattern in Andhra Pradesh and Rajasthan. The Zilla Parishad here is the most powerful body. Its main functions are planning and execution of all development programmes; primary, basic and secondary education; distribution of fertilizers, agricultural implements, and improved seeds, etc. The mode of representation is also different. The Panchayat Samiti in Maharashtra consists of (i) about four elected councillors of the Zilla Parishad, (ii) eight panches and sarpanches elected by Panchayat members from each electoral division in the block, (iii) two members co-opted as 'associate members' representing the purchase and sale union and a co-operative society in the block, and (iv) one or two scheduled caste or scheduled tribe members and a woman member if they are not already represented in the panchayat samiti. The zilla parishad is composed of (1) directly elected members (not less than 40 and not more than 60, (2) chairmen of the Panchayat samitis in the district as *ex-officio* members, (3) scheduled caste and scheduled tribe members according to the reservation made by the Government on the basis of population, (4) chairmen of five federal cooperative bodies co-opted as 'associate members', and (5) two women, co-opted members, if the directly elected members do not include a woman or women (Government of Maharashtra, 1971: 14-20).

THE CONCEPT OF SOCIAL WELFARE

The First Five Year Plan made a distinction between social services and social welfare services. While social services constitute an investment for the betterment of human resources in general, social welfare services are designed to enable the under-privileged or handicapped sections of the community to rise as close to general level of the community as possible. Social welfare services, primarily rehabilitative in their approach today, will not be able to attain their objective unless they are accompanied by preventive and constructive measures. One has therefore to take a long term view of welfare needs which emerge as a result of rapid socio-economic development. On such a view the welfare of the following broad groups need to be paid special attention: (a) Socially under-privileged groups such as scheduled castes, orphans, widows, unmarried mothers, women in danger of moral degradation, aged and infirm; (b) women and children; (c) socially maladjusted groups such as beggars, prostitutes, delinquents, persons discharged from correctional and non-correctional institutions; (d) physically and mentally handicapped persons; (e) economically under-privileged such as destitutes, unemployed, scheduled tribes, etc. (Committee on Plan Projects, 1959: 19-20).

In other words, one may define social welfare services as these are intended to cater to the needs of persons and groups who, by reason of some handicap (social, economic, or physical), are traditionally denied or are incapable of taking advantage of the amenities and services provided by the community. Welfare service is thus the field of service for those who need special care (Dubey, 1971: 20-35).

After independence, the government directly shouldered the responsibility for the development of welfare services in the country. State governments established Directorates of Social Welfare, and the Central Government sought to develop and promote voluntary organizations as major instruments for implementing social welfare programmes. But it was found that voluntary organizations were ill-equipped for this purpose; their efforts were generally sporadic and un-coordinated, and they suffered from paucity of resources. The Central Social Welfare Board was therefore set up in August. 1953, with an allocation of Rs. 4 crores in the First Five Year Plan to provide technical assistance and give grants-in-aid to enable voluntary social welfare organizations to strengthen, improve and extend their activities, especially pilot projects. The Board was composed predominantly of non-officials who had actual experience of field work in this area. Within a year the Central Social Welfare Board created an organizational machinery right from the centre to the district and village levels for the execution of social welfare programmes. It also requested the State governments to constitute similar advisory boards to coordinate the welfare activities in the State.

SOCIAL WELFARE PROGRAMMES UNDER PANCHAYATI RAJ INSTITUTIONS

The introduction of panchayati raj has added a new dimension to the programme of social welfare, for it is a system not merely of civic administration of interlinked statutory organizations for promoting development and welfare of the entire rural population. It is intended to make the government more responsive to the needs and wishes of the local people. It is, thus, a very important instrument of social welfare (Nanavatty, 1961-62: 5). In many States, most of the schemes relating to social welfare and welfare of scheduled tribes and scheduled castes have been transferred to the panchayati raj institutions. For example, in the State of Maharashtra, the following welfare activities have been transferred to the panchayat samitis and zilla parishads under the Maharashtra Zilla Parishads and the Panchayat Act, 1961:

(1) Educational development of the backward classes including grant of scholarships, freeships, examination

fees, and establishment of hostels and schools.

(2) Economic development of the backward classes through financial assistance—loans and subsidies to individual cultivators for purchasing agricultural inputs; financial assistance to individual artisans; supply of spinning wheels to *Vimukta Jatis*; development of communication in backward areas; subsidies for co-operative stores and multi-purpose co-operative societies; establishment of handicraft centres; and development of cattle-breeding and poultry farms.

(3) Removal of untouchability through celebration of Harijan weeks; *zunka-bhakar* programme; encouragement of marriage between caste Hindus and Harijans; awarding prizes to villages which do outstanding work in the removal of untouchability.

(4) Welfare of women and children through establishment and maintenance of *Balwadis*.

(5) Provision of houses for the backward classes.

(6) Provision of drinking water wells.

(7) Training of backward classes through organization of training camps and technical centres and training in improved methods of carrying out hereditary occupations.

Similarly, in Rajasthan, under *the Rajasthan Panchayat Samiti and the Zilla Parishad Act, 1959*, the Panchayat samitis are charged with the maintenance of government aided hostels for scheduled tribes and other backward classes; and the development of voluntary organizations and coordination among their activities; the propagation of temperance; and removal of untouchability.

In the State of Gujarat, the panchayat, at the village level, is responsible for carrying out the directives or orders of the State government or any other competent authority in regard to the amelioration of the condition of the scheduled castes and scheduled tribes, and other backward classes, and in particular in regard to the removal of untouchability. The *taluka panchayat*, at the taluka level, is responsibile for (i) providing houses in rural areas; (ii) campaigning against alcohol and drug addiction; (iii) implementing schemes for women's and children's welfare; (iv) maintaining women's and children's welfare centres, educational centres, craft centres; and (v) establishing beggars' homes. The district panchayat, at the district level, is responsible for (i) providing necessary assistance and encouragement to the work of institutions of social welfare; (ii) conducting necessary social welfare activities in the district; (iii) arranging fairs and festivals other than those arranged by the State Government.

In Andhra Pradesh, under the provision the following welfare programmes, previously administered by departmental officers, have been transferred to the panchayati raj institutions under Andhra Pradesh Panchayat Samiti and the Zilla Parishad Act, 1959:

(1) Implementation of rural housing schemes.
(2) Implementation of the programme of eradicating untouchability.
(3) Implementation of programme relating to women and children in rural and tribal areas.
(4) Maintenance of diseased beggars' homes and control of vagrancy.
(5) Promotion of the voluntary social welfare organizations and coordination of their activities.

In the State of Karnataka, under the Mysore Village Panchayat and Local Board Act, 1959, the Taluka Development Boards are responsible for:

(1) Educational programmes such as (i) maintenance of the backward classes hostels, (ii) maintenance of ashram schools, (iii) women welfare-cum-nursery schools, (iv) distribution of books, clothes, etc. to children of nomadic and semi-nomadic tribes, (v) construction of school buildings, (vi) maintenance of tailoring centres.
(2) Economic upliftment programmes such as (i) loan/subsidy for purchase of bullocks and agricultural implements, (ii) loan subsidy for land development, irrigation, etc. (iii) loan subsidy for upkeep of milch cattle, poultry, etc. (iv) establishment and promotion of co-operative institutions.
(3) Health, housing and other schemes such as (i) distribution of nutritive foods, (ii) digging of drinking water wells, (iii) running of mobile dispensaries, (iv) forming of individual and co-operative housing schemes, (v)

providing house sites, (vi) providing legal aid, (vii) removal of untouchability, (viii) running community halls, etc.

In the State of Tamil Nadu, responsibility for the following welfare programmes have been transferred to the Taluka Development Boards:

(1) Providing midday meals to the children of primary schools.
(2) Managing social education programmes including (i) organization of young farmers', clubs, (ii) forming *mathar sangram* (women's associations), (iii) organizing farmers' forum, (iv) running community recreation centres, (v) holding gram sahayaks', training camps, (vi) setting up adult literacy schools, (vii) organizing social education centres, (viii) organizing village libraries, (ix) arranging production and display of community posters, information charts, wall newspapers, etc. (x) holding talks, lectures, etc., (xi) arranging community entertainment, (xii) running children's parks, (viii) handling women's and children's welfare programmes, etc.

In the Punjab, under the Panchayat Samiti and Zilla Parishad Act, 1961, panchayat samitis have been assigned the task of (1) establishing information, community and recreational centres; (2) forming youth organizations, Mahila Mandals, farmers' clubs, villagers' clubs, etc., (3) establishing and popularizing libraries, (4) promoting physical culture through encouragement of games and sports, etc.

IMPLEMENTATION OF SOCIAL WELFARE PROGRAMMES UNDER PANCHAYATI RAJ INSTITUTIONS

The organizational links responsible for the implementation of social welfare schemes are zilla parishads (at the district level) and panchayat samitis (at the block level). They have each a social welfare committee, which is responsible for the implementation of social welfare schemes. The exact pattern, however, differs from State to State. In Andhra Pradesh, the Standing Committee on Social Welfare in each zilla parishad and panchayat samiti consists of nine members, with the chairman of the zilla parishad and the District Collector as *ex-officio* members. The remaining seven are elected by the members of the zilla parishad from among themselves. Five of the seven elected members have to be from among the scheduled castes and scheduled tribes if there are as many or more on the zilla parishad itself, or from among the registered voters of Scheduled Castes and Scheduled Tribes in the district if there aren't (Ganeshchandra, 1973: 45-46). This is to ensure maximum representation of disadvantaged sections of the population in accordance with the Andhra Pradesh Panchayat Samiti and Zilla Parishad Act, 1959. Each panchayat samiti is required to review once every three months the progress made in the implementation of social welfare schemes. Similarly, the zilla parishad is required to watch and review, also at least once in three months, the special measures taken for the benefit of the under-privileged.

In Karnataka, there is a separate functional sub-committee in each Taluka samiti to look after the welfare of the weaker sections of society. The committee consists of seven non-officials and officials such as the Block Development Officer, Social Welfare Inspector, etc., with the president of the Taluka Development Board as the *ex-officio* chairman. The main functions of the committee are to discuss various issues relating to the implementation of Backward Classes' Welfare schemes in the taluka, and to decide which scheme to implement where, whom to give loan and/or subsidy, etc. It is the responsibility of the committee to prepare a plan of action for various schemes financed out of the Board's budget.

In Maharashtra, each zilla parishad had a Social Welfare Subject Matter Committee presided over by a councillor belonging either to scheduled caste or to a scheduled tribe. It consists of ten members, five belonging to scheduled castes and scheduled tribes, three to socially and educationally backward classes besides, two women co-opted by the zilla parishad. The social welfare officer is the secretary to the committee.

DIFFICULTIES IN THE IMPLEMENTATION OF SOCIAL WELFARE PROGRAMMES UNDER PANCHAYATI RAJ

Nanavatty (1961-62: 16) notes the following difficulties in the way of implementation of social welfare programmes by the panchayati raj institutions: (1) lack of available data on the needs of the rural population, (2) lack of financial resources required to carry through welfare programmes, (3) inexperience in organizing welfare services, (4) lack of trained workers, paid or voluntary, (5) lack of proper leadership both in statutory and in voluntary organizations, (6) domination of vested interests in the panchayati raj institutions, (7) protrusion of village feuds and group rivalries, and (8) lack of confidence on the part of weaker sections in the capacity of the panchayati raj institutions and their leaders to promote their welfare.

In addition to these, one may identify the following other main difficulties:

(1) A very small portion, if any, of the zilla parishad's budget is allocated to social welfare schemes and to schemes for the welfare of backward classes. The special schemes for backward classes, sponsored by the Government of India, have been designed to supplement the benefits they may derive from general developmental programmes. However, experience shows that panchayati raj institutions instead of allocating funds from the general developmental budget to the welfare of backward classes, tend to replace general developmental programmes by special schemes for which funds are made available by the Central Government. For example, in the State of Maharashtra, certain districts have spent practically nothing from their general grants on the development of backward classes. Some zilla parishads have not provided any fund whatsoever from their own resources, and some others only nominal amounts (Govt. of Maharashtra, 1971: 141).

(2) Since no proportional representation of the backward classes in panchayati raj institutions has been specifically provided for in the panchayati raj acts of the various States, those who get elected to the panchayati raj institutions generally belong to the upper economic strata. Even in villages predominantly inhabited by the scheduled castes or scheduled tribes, money-lenders or caste Hindus manipulate to occupy positions of leadership. In isolated tribal areas, where in the past, the money-lenders wielded only economic powers, they have been enabled by the panchayati raj to grab political power. Consequently, the representation of backward classes in the panchayati raj institutions is very inadequate. A study conducted by the Commissioner for Scheduled Castes and Scheduled Tribes indicated that out of 2,648 elected members in

panchayat samitis in Orissa, only 148 or 6 per cent of the total were tribals, though they constituted 20 per cent of the population in the state. Further, out of 307 chairmen of panchayat samitis, only 9, or 3 per cent of the total, were tribals. Among vice-chairmen, only 19, or 6 per cent of the total, were tribals (Shrikant, 1961: 143). Another study conducted by the Commissioner for Scheduled Castes and Scheduled Tribes (1964-65) on the working of the panchayati raj institutions in relation to weaker sections in Gujarat State indicated that out of 6,863 sarpanches only 35, or .05 per cent of the total, belonged to scheduled castes. In taluka panchayat samitis, the representation of scheduled castes was much less compared to their population in the State. In the district panchayats, it was merely 3 per cent. The position in village panchayats was no different in the districts of Baroda, Broach, Surat and Bulsar. The representation of tribals in taluka and district panchayats was also very much below their proportion to the population.

(3) Co-option as a mode of involving the members of backward classes and vulnerable groups, provided for in most panchayati raj acts, has serious limitations. First of all, the dominant leadership does not take into account the proportion of backward classes to population. For example, although in Uttar Pradesh, there is a provision in the act to co-opt three to ten scheduled caste members to the zilla parishads if no such member has been elected, their representation is very inadequate. In Saharanpur district, although the scheduled castes constitute about one-third of the total rural population, only five scheduled caste members have been co-opted to the zilla parishad, which has a total membership of 107. Likewise, in Hamirpur district, where the population of scheduled castes is one-fourth of the total rural population, only one scheduled caste member has been co-opted to the zilla parishad having a total of 53 members. In Pratapgarh district, where one-fifth of the population belongs to scheduled castes, only 4 scheduled caste members have been co-opted to the zilla parishad which has 103 members (Moorthy, 1969: 88-105). Secondly, even when persons from backward classes are co-opted they are generally drawn from the relatively well-off sections of these classes. Such co-opted members can hardly be expected to have the right perspective on the appropriate-

ness and the purposes of the programmes or much enthusiasm for protecting the interests of their weaker brethren.

Shrikant (1961:141) points out that the resources earmarked for particular schemes meant for backward classes are diverted by panchayati raj institutions to other general schemes without authority. In some cases, subsidies meant for scheduled tribes are given to caste Hindus. When the co-opted representatives of backward classes come from the really disadvantaged section of the community, they do not possess functional skills such as reading, writing and speaking required for effective participation in a formal organization. As Verba points out, there are four main prerequisites for effective participation in formal organizations: (1) Resources, both material and social, besides information about situations, issues, communication channels and rules of participation as well as skill in written and oral expression; (2) motivation to participate; (3) structural conduciveness, by which is meant the availability of formal participatory structures, the presence of regularized procedure, and (4) cultural conduciveness to support general norms of democracy (1967: 53-78). Backward classes are disadvantaged group in respect of all these.

It is, therefore, important to consider the following steps to rectify the situation in order to ensure effective implementation of social welfare programmes.

(1) Panchayati raj acts should be amended to provide proportional representation to backward classes in panchayati raj institutions.

(2) The Sarpanch, who holds a key position in executing schemes for scheduled tribes and scheduled castes, should preferably be elected directly by the people. This will make him more responsive to the interests of backward classes at least where they form a significant part of the electorate.

(3) Statutory provisions should be made in panchayati raj acts requiring each zilla parishad to allocate funds from the general funds to the welfare of backward classes in proportion to their population in the district.

(4) Voluntary agencies should organize a campaign to educate backward classes about their rights and privileges. The idea that panchayat elections should be free from politics seems naive and unrealistic in the modern world. What is

needed is that backward classes should be given the necessary skills to compete with others in the political field.

(5) There should be a separate committee at the zilla parishad level to deal with the subject of social welfare.

(6) Social welfare should be treated as a technical department, and the officer-in-charge should be accorded the status of a head of department like other technical officers.

(7) The officer-in-charge of social welfare programmes at the zilla parishad level should be provided a vehicle so that he can move about and supervise welfare programmes in the district.

(8) At the national and state levels it has been agreed that the government will assume the responsibility of promoting facilities of education, health and sanitation in cooperation with voluntary organizations and will promote social welfare services by providing grants-in-aid to them. The same approach should be adopted in the development of welfare programmes at the village and block levels. The panchayat and panchayat samiti should recognize the voluntary organizations and entrust them with the responsibility of promoting social welfare services.

S.P. Joshi

CHAPTER XV

Social Security Legislation in India

Independent India, wedded as she is to the goal of economic growth coupled with social justice, has made steady progress in social security measurses. This progress is particularly remarkable in respect of industrial labour, which, although numerically small, is considered to be the backbone of the nation. The Constitution of India provides that the State shall, within the limits of its economic capacity and development, make effective provision for securing the right to work and to education, and for public assistance in the case of unemployment, old age, sickness, disablement and other cases of undeserved want. Some of the measures statutorily enforced during the last few years have added a new dimension to social security—such as the Family Pension-cum-Life Assurance Scheme of 1971 for the members of the Employees' Provident Fund Scheme; the Payment of Gratuity Act, 1972, applicable to employees drawing upto Rs. 1000 per month in every factory, mine, port, oil-field, plantation and shops/establishments employing ten or more persons; the Kerala Agricultural Workers' Act, 1974, which provides for Provident Fund Scheme for agricultural workers; and the amendment to the Industrial Disputes Act made in 1976 to restrict for the first time the right of employers in factories employing 300 or more workers to lay off or retrench labour.

It has often been stated that India is too poor and too undeveloped to have the luxury of social security. In a B.B.C.

broadcast many years ago, Sir William Beveridge, the champion of social security in the U.K. was put this very question. "Well" said Beveridge, "I am often asked whether Britain can afford the Beveridge plan and my reply is . . . It is like asking if a housewife can afford to buy bread for her family before she buys a radio. Of course, she can and she should." Beveridge proceeded to say that "in a sense, the poorer you are the more you need it (social security)—by maintaining your health it will help you to increase productivity."[1]

THE CONCEPT OF SOCIAL SECURITY

Social security in its broadest sense connotes those governmental measures which are intended to mitigate the rigours of want. It embodies the endeavour of the community as a whole to afford relief in certain well-defined contingencies with which an individual cannot adequately cope up—such as sickness, unemployment, old age or death. This is the definition implicit in the Social Security (Minimum Standards) Convention, 1952, adopted by the International Labour Conference in that year.[2] The extent of social security available in a society is a measure of the progress it has made towards the ideal of welfare state.

Social security measures fall under two main heads: social insurance and social assistance. The field of the former is the class of persons well organized and relatively better off, such as wage earners. It is based on compulsory mutual aid and entails contributions by those covered. The field of social assistance, on the other hand, is the class of persons too poor to contribute and too scattered. Its beneficiaries are non-contributors. It is a recognition of the unilateral obligation of the community towards its dependent groups.

EVOLUTION OF SOCIAL SECURITY IN INDIA

With the gradual break-up of the joint family system—the ancient institution of social security in India—and with the onward march of industrialization and urbanization and the consequent emergence of money economy, the need for new mechanisms became urgent.

1. Adarkar, B.P.: *Social Insurance in India*, 1973, Shroff Memorial Trust, Bombay, p. 6.
2. *Social Security*, 1958, International Labour Organization, p. 11.

Social security in India was given a start by Workmen's Compensation Act passed in the year 1923. It was based on the pattern of the U.K. It provided financial protection in the event of injury or death due to an accident arising out of and in the course of employment. A further step was taken by passing of the Maternity Benefit Acts by various State governments which provided enabling for cash benefits in the event of confinement. Maharashtra, then the Presidency of Bombay, passed the first Maternity Benefit Act in 1929. The responsibility for workmen's compensation and maternity benefits was put on employers. The formation of the International Labour Organization in 1919, with which India was associated right from the beginning, further helped the cause of social security. In 1927 it adopted the Convention regarding health insurance for workers in industry, commerce and agriculture. The question of having a health insurance scheme in India came up for consideration in 1929 but was rejected on financial, administrative and other grounds. The Royal Commission on Labour, in its report in 1931, recommended that a tentative scheme be tried as an experimental basis for single establishment. The response of provincial governments was, however, lukewarm. Several labour enquiry committees meanwhile also recommended introduction of health insurance for workers. The mention of social security in the Atlantic Charter of 1941 gave a fillip to the concept of social insurance in India. In 1943, Prof. B.P. Adarkar was appointed by the Central Government a Special Officer to frame a scheme. He submitted his Report on Health Insurance in 1944, for which Sardar Patel called him "Chhota Beveridge". Two ILO experts (Mr. Stack and Mr. Rao) gave their comments on the Report. Subsequently, the Report of the Labour Investigation Committee (under Shri D.V. Rege) and the Report of the Health Survey and Development Committee (known as the Bhore Committee) was also available. It may also be mentioned that the Preparatory Asian Regional Conference of the ILO meeting in 1974 at New Delhi adopted a resolution stressing the urgent task of establishing security services as an essential condition of building up a genuine democratic society. Earlier, in 1946, the Government introduced the Workmen's State Insurance Bill which was put on the statute book as the Employees State Insurance Act in 1948.

Of the three distinct phases that Prof. B.P. Adarkar has mentioned, the first phase, viz. initial planning, corresponds to the period 1942-48; the second viz. structural foundation, occurred during 1948-52 and comprised the ESI Act of 1948, the Coal Mines Provident Fund Scheme of 1948, the Fund Scheme of 1948, and the Employees Provident Fund Act, 1952; the third stage, viz. expansion, began in 1952 and is still continuing.

INVESTIGATIONS

During this period there have been some periodical investigations. The first investigation (1957-58) was by a Study Group under the chairmanship of Shri V.K.R. Menon to find out how the various schemes of social security and other benefits could be combined in a comprehensive social security system. The main recommendations of the Group were: the unification of the ESI and EPF schemes under a single organization by converting Provident Funds into a Statutory Pension Scheme, the adoption of a single contribution for cash benefits in respect of sickness, maternity and employment injury, old age, invalidity and survivorship pension-cum-gratuity payments. The Group's emphasis was on integration rather than extension.

The second principal investigation (1963-66) was done by a tripartite ESI Review Committee under the chairmanship of Shri C.R. Pattabhi Raman. It made 176 recommendations, most of which have been since implemented.

The third major investigating body which was asked to report, *inter alia*, on the working and reorganization of social security schemes in India was the National Commission on Labour (1969) under the chairmanship of Dr. P.B. Gajendragadkar. The Commission reviewed the progress in the enforcement of the ESI Review Committee's recommendations. It further made a general statement that "an ideal arrangement will be to gradually work towards a comprehensive social security plan by pooling all the social security collection in a single fund which different agencies can draw upon for disbursing various benefits according to needs".[3]

As a step towards the merger of the ESI and EPF schemes, the ESI Corporation presented an "Operation Plan" in 1968-69. A working group was set up in 1969 to study all aspects of the

3. Report of the National Commission on Labour, 1964, p. 178.

proposal of integration including its feasibility and its advantages and disadvantages. The report seems to be under consideration.

In 1972, a committee, called the Committee on Perspective Planning was set up by the WSI. The Committee's report submitted in the same year has been published. It has made several far-reaching recommendations (which we shall discuss later).

The ESI Amendment Act, 1975, has already incorporated some of the suggestions. A high-powered committee is already engaged in an in-depth study of the various suggestions.

LABOUR LAWS REGARDING SOCIAL SECURITY

About one-third of the labour laws in India are in respect of social security. A list of these laws is given in Appendix I. We discuss here only the Employees State Insurance Act, 1948.

THE EMPLOYEES STATE INSURANCE ACT, 1948

Starting with about 1.20 lakh insured persons in Delhi and Kanpur on February 24, 1952, the total coverage of employees under the Employees State Insurance Scheme as on 31st December, 1974, stood at about 43.13 lakhs. The total number of beneficiaries as far as medical benefit was about 184.48 lakhs inclusive of insured persons.[4]

The coverage as on 31-3-75 was as follows:[5]

1. Centres	365
2. Employees	43,85,000
3. Insured persons	47,75,000
4. Family units	47,54,150
5. Insured women	3,46,550
6. Total beneficiaries	1,84,66,950

It is clear from the above that the ESI scheme has made steady progress. The Act covers all power-using non-seasonal factories wherein 20 or more persons are employed or were employed for wages in any of the preceding 12 months, excluding mines and railway running sheds. The Act extends to the whole of India. All

4. Report of the Labour Ministry, 1974-75, Vol. I., p. 51.
5. *Source*: ESI Annual Report, 1974-75, p.(vi).

employees, i.e. direct employees, contractor employees, permanent, temporary, casual, whether manual, clerical, supervisory or otherwise, including those connected with the administration of the factory or establishments or any part, department, or branch thereof, or with the purchase of raw materials, or for the distribution or sale of the products, and whose monthly remuneration (excluding remuneration for overtime work) does not exceed Rs. 1000 p m. The wage limit was first increased from Rs. 400 to Rs. 500 p.m. in 1966 and then to Rs. 1000 p.m. on 30-11-75. This benefited about six to seven lakh additional industrial workers. The Act is proposed to be extended, under Section 1(5), to new classes of establishments, namely small power-using factories employing 10 to 19 persons and non-power using factories employing 20 or more persons, and also to shops, hotels and restaurants, cinemas and theatres, road-motor transport establishments and newspaper establishments employing 20 or more persons. It already covers all or some of the above-mentioned classes of establishments in Andhra Pradesh, Assam, Bihar, Haryana, Kerala, Punjab, West Bengal and the Union Territory of Delhi, benefiting about 1.7 lakh employees. In other States, an estimated three lakh employees will be covered by the end of 1975-76.

CONTRIBUTIONS:

Consequent upon the raising of the wage limit to Rs. 1000 p.m. in 1975, the Table in the First Schedule specifying the rates of weekly contribution of employees and employers and corresponding daily standard benefit rates have been revised as shown in a Table on page 228.

It will be observed that under the revised table, employee's contribution is not payable by employees whose average daily wage is below Rs. 2 in 1966, the exemption unit was raised from Re. 1 per day to below Rs. 1.50 per day.

Working of Employee's State Insurance Act

(a) No. of factories and employees covered

	1962	1967	1972	1973	1974
1. No. of centres	132	273	318	339	350
2. No. of factories covered	14,391	17,797	23,496	25,108	26,005
3. No. of employees in factories covered ('000)	1,865	3,212	3,976	4,150	4,303
4. No. of Insecured persons ('000)	2,164	3,545	4,344	4,525	4,750
5. No. of Family (insured persons) units ('000)	1,515	3,289	4,295	4,516	4,741
6. No. of Beneficiaries covered ('000)	6,528	13,017	16,715	17,532	18,404

Source: ESIC—Pocket Book of Labour Statistics 1975, page 92.

(b) Number of factories and employees covered under the E.S.I. Act during 1974-75 Statewise

State	Implemented Area		Non-implemented area		All areas	
	No. of factories	No. of employees as on 31-3-75	No. of factories	No. of employees as on 31-3-75	No. of factories	No. of employees as on 31-3-75
Andhra Pradesh	1,034	1,50,300	34	16,000	1,068	1,66,300
Assam	193	18,400	41	7,400	234	25,800
Bihar	591	79,600	226	1,31,000	817	2,10,600
Chandigarh	91	7,220	—	—	91	7,200
Delhi	1,872	1,35,000	—	—	1,872	1,35,000
Gujarat	1,829	4,21,000	405	81,300	2,234	5,02,300
Haryana	933	1,22,700	54	5,700	987	1,28,600
Himachal Pradesh	—	—	12	1,600	12	1,600
Karnatak	1,236	2,24,500	75	22,100	1,311	2,46,600
Kerala & Mahe	1,179	1,85,900	30	4,200	1,209	1,90,100
Madhya Pradesh	586	1,20,300	19	70,700	605	1,91,000
Maharashtra	6,250	10,32,600	417	65,300	6,667	10,97,900
Orissa	146	51,500	122	61,200	268	1,12,700
Pondicherry	37	13,500	—	—	37	13,500
Punjab	1,478	10,900	33	3,500	1,511	1,12,500
Rajasthan	487	85,700	30	5,200	517	90,900
Tamil Nadu	2,659	3,60,500	148	34,200	2,807	3,94,700
Uttar Pradesh	1,459	4,17,300	41	37,500	1,500	4,54,800
West Bengal	3,594	8,50,000	103	1,17,900	3,697	9,67,900
All India (1975)	25,659	43,085,000	1,790	6,65,000	27,444	50,50,000
All India (1974)	24,289	4,303,000	1,716	6,37,000	26,005	49,40,000

Source: ESIC—Annual Report, 1974-75, page 49.

(c) Number of centres, employees, insured persons, family (insured persons) units and beneficiaries covered on 31-3-75 Statewise

State	No. of Centres	No. of Employees	No. of Insured persons	No. of Family (Insured persons) units	No. of Beneficiaries
Andhra Pradesh	42	1,50,300	1,60,000	1,58,200	6,15,600
Assam	10	18,400	21,000	20,100	78,900
Bihar	19	79,600	85,000	85,000	3,29,800
Chandigarh	1	7,200	9,000	9,000	34,900
Delhi	1	1,35,000	1,56,000	1,56,000	6,05,800
Gujarat	14	4,21,000	5,09,000	5,09,000	19,74,950
Haryana	17	1,22,700	1,44,000	1,42,250	5,53,700
Karnatak	28	2,24,500	2,45,000	2,42,800	9,44,250
Kerala & Mahe	52	1,85,900	1,97,000	1,97,000	7,64,350
Madhya Pradesh	20	12,03,000	1,27,000	1,27,000	4,92,750
Maharashtra	22	10,32,600	10,95,000	10,95,000	42,48,650
Orissa	13	51,500	54,500	54,500	2,11,450
Pondecherry	1	13,500	14,500	14,500	56,250
Punjab	21	1,09,000	1,35,000	1,35,000	5,23,800
Rajasthan	18	85,700	91,000	89,850	3,49,750
Tamil Nadu	42	3,60,500	3,82,000	3,73,600	19,57,950
Uttar Pradesh	39	4,17,300	4,50,000	4,45,350	17,32,600
West Bengal	5	8,50,000	9,00,000	9,00,000	34,92,000
All India (1975)	365	43,85,000	47,75,000	47,54,150	1,84,66,950
All India (1974)	350	43,03,000	47,50,000	47,41,050	1,84,04,100

Source: ESI—Annual Report, 1974-75, pages 50-51.

Table

Group of employees whose average daily wages are	Employee's weekly contribution (recoverable from employees)	Employer's weekly contribution	Total weekly contribution (employees & employers contribution)	Corresponding daily standard benefit rate
1. Below Rs. 2	Nil	75 P.	75 P.	100 P.
2. Rs. 2 and above but below Rs. 3	40 P.	80 ,,	120 ,,	130 ,,
3. Rs. 3 and above but below Rs. 4	5) ,,	100 ,,	150 ,,	150 ,,
4. Rs. 4 and above but below Rs. 5	70 ,,	140 ,,	210 ,,	250 ,,
5. Rs. 6 and above but below Rs. 8	95 ,,	190 ,,	285 ,,	350 ,,
6. Rs. 8 and above but below Rs. 12	125 ,,	250 ,,	375 ,,	500 ,,
7. Rs. 12 and above but below Rs. 16	175 ,,	350 ,,	525 ,,	700 ,,
8. Rs. 16 and above but below Rs. 24	275 ,,	550 ,,	825 ,,	1000 ,,
9. Rs. 24 and above	375 ,,	750 ,,	1125 ,,	1500 ,,

BE NEFITS

The main features of the benefits described as 'Panchdeep' are as follows:—

(i) **Sickness benefit**: It consists of periodic cash payments to an insured person in case of sickness, subject to certain conditions. To qualify for this benefit an insured person should have paid his/her contribution at least for 13 weeks in the relevant contribution period (26 weeks). The benefit is payable for a maximum number of 56 days in a continuous period of 365 days. There is a waiting period of 2 days which is waived, if the insured person falls sick again within 15 days of the previous sickness.

Extended sickness benefit: For those in continuous employment for two years and suffering from diseases of prolonged nature such as T.B., leprosy, mental and malignant diseases, extended cash benefit is paid for a period of 309 (365—56) days after they have exhausted the normal period of entitlement to sickness benefit. This is payable at the full rate of sickness benefit.

(ii) **Maternity benefit**: This is also a periodic cash payment in case of confinement, subject to certain qualifying conditions. The maximum duration is 12 weeks. The daily rate of benefit is double the standard sickness benefit rate and is roughly equal to average daily wage of the insured woman. Additional benefit is payable for 6 weeks is case of miscarriage.

(iii) **Disablement benefit**: It is available for disablement caused by employment injury, including occupation disease. Disablement may be temporary or permanent, partial or formal. For temporary disablement, cash benefit is paid for the duration of the disability at the rate of about half the normal wage. Benefit is derived if the incapacity does not exceed 3 days, but if it exceeds 3 days, the benefit is paid for the first day of incapacity. The rate of permanent disablement benefit is in proportion to the extent of less of earning capacity. This is payable for life. The loss is assessed by medical boards.

(iv) **Dependents' benefit**: Dependent(s) of an insured person who dies as a result of employment injury are given periodic payments at specified rates. Funeral benefit not exceeding Rs. 100 is paid towards expenses on the funeral of an insured person.

(v) **Medical benefit**: The benefit of comprehensive treatment of the insured person and of his family where the scheme is extended to the family. Artificial limbs etc. are also provided free of cost when necessary as a result of employment injury.

It is provided either through the service system (i.e. full-time or mobile dispensaries) or the panel system (i.e. medical practitioners on the panel at whose clinic treatment is given).

The sharing of cost of medical care between State governments and the Corporation is as follows:

(1) For areas covering insured persons only—The State government's share is 1/4th.

(2) For areas covering insured persons and their families—the State government's share is 1/8th.

The medical benefit is provided by the respective State governments, except in the Union Territory of Delhi where the ESI has taken over such responsibility since 1-4-1962.

Members of families are being progressively covered for medical care. It begins with 'restricted' medical care of the outdoor general practitioner type in the first instance. It is followed in certain states by "expanded" medical care, i.e. all facilities for hospitalization.

Sickness Benefits under E.S.I. Scheme

	1962	1967	1972	1973	1974
Sickness benefit					
(A) Amount paid (Rs. lakhs)	302.4	706.0	1,369.6	963.8	1187.9
(B) Average daily rate (Rs.)	2.3	3.0	4.3	4.3	4.6
(C) Extended sickness amount paid (Rs. lakhs)	11.4	64.9	104.5	104.1	111.4

Source: ESIC—Pocket Book of Labour Statistics, 1975, p. 94.

Maternity benefits under E.S.I. Scheme

	1962	1967	1972	1973	1974
1. No. of confinements	6,997	14,060	15,107	16,363	17,562
2. Rate of confinement per 100 women employees	6.1	7.0	5.8	5.9	5.9
3. Amount paid as maternity benefit (Rs. '000)	1,871	3,755	6,455	7,102	8,052
4. Average amount paid per confinement (Rs).	267	267	427	434	458

Source: ESIC—Pocket Book of Labour S'atistics, 1975, p. 57.

Disablement and dependents benefits under ESI scheme

	1962	1967	1972	1973	1974
1. Amount of temporary disablement benefit paid (Rs. '000)	3,063	8,043	30,227	20,184	22,948
2: No. of permanent disablement cases admitted	2,630	7,401	10,985	9,458	9,976
3. Capitalized value of PDB claims (Rs. '000)	4,507	12,053	28,890	27,549	30,395
4. No. of death cases admitted	143	262	373	390	527
5. Capitalized value of dependent benefit claims admitted (Rs. '000)	1,249	3,229	6,669	6,205	11,273

Source: ESIC—Pocket Book of Labour Statistics, 1975, page 95.

No. of E.S.I. hospitals and beds available

No. of beds	1962	1967	1972	1973	1974
1. *E.S.I. hospitals*	757	2,478	6,927	7,855	8,904
(A) General	689	2,030	5,734	6,121	6,862
(B) Maternity	22	28	368	368	771
(C) T.B.	46	420	825	1,366	1,271
2. *Annexes*	288	474	426	442	442
(A) General	132	186	144	160	160
(B) Maternity	21	21	—	—	—
(C) T.B.	135	267	282	282	282
3. *Other hospitals*	2,286	3,319	2,904	2,742	2,801
(A) General	1,089	1,587	1,125	1,144	1,183
(B) Maternity	128	191	127	133	189
(C) T.B.	1,069	1,541	1,652	1,465	1,429
Total No. of Beds provided	3,331	6,271	10,257	11,039	12,147

Source: ESIC—Pocket Book of Labour Statistics, 1975, p. 94

ADMINISTRATION

The administration of the scheme is entrusted to the Employees' State Insurance Corporation (ESIC), an autonomous body set up by the Government of India. The Union Minister for Labour and Employment is the chairman. It consists of representatives of the Central and State governments, the Parliament, employers, employees and the medical profession. There is also a standing committee selected by the members of the Corporation and it acts as the executive body. A Medical Benefit Council is set up to advise on the medical aspects. The Chief Executive Officer of the ESIC is the Director General. He is mainly concerned with formation of policy, overall supervision, coordination and liaison with Central/State governments. There are tripartite regional boards presided over by the respective State labour minister. They have to hold quarterly meetings and give suggestions for the smooth functioning of the scheme. Regional offices maintain records in respect of insured persons and administer local offices and inspectors' offices. Claims for insured persons are received and benefits paid at local offices which have been set up generally in labour areas.

15 regional offices, 2 sub-regional offices, 285 local offices, 4 sub-local offices, 77 miniature local offices, 247 pay offices and 121 inspection offices were functioning as on 31-3-75.[6]

PENAL PROVISIONS

Under the ESI (Amendment) Act, 1975, the penal provisions have been amended to provide for imposition of enhanced and more deterrent penalties for defaults in the payment of contributions and non-compliance with the provisions of the Act.

6. VESK Annual Report, 1974-75, p. 6.

S.D. Balsara

CHAPTER XVI

Legal Aspects of Untouchability

One of the earliest legislative attempts to do away with the evil of untouchability was the "Temple Entry Proclamation" issued by the Maharaja of Travancore in 1936. It declared that there should be no restriction on any Hindu, whether by birth or religion, entering or worshipping at any temple controlled by the Maharaja or his government. A little before this pioneering effort, Britain's Prime Minister Ramsay MacDonald had announced his Communal Award. Gandhiji's resolve to eradicate untouchability in a period of ten years had been made known.

Immediately after independence, there was a crop of legislation in the States for temple entry and for removal of civil disabilities.

A momentous step in this direction was taken when our Constitution was framed in 1950. Untouchability was abolished—if it is possible to abolish a social evil by a legislative fiat—and the practice of untouchability in any form was forbidden. The most significant provision on untouchability is article 17 of the Constitution. It states in unequivocal terms, "Untouchability is abolished and its practice in any form is forbidden." The article further puts teeth into this provision by laying down: "The enforcement of any disability arising out of untouchability shall be an offence punishable in accordance with law."

Thus the article confers and guarantees social justice and dignity of man, the twin privileges which were denied to crores of human beings for centuries. Thus, this article fulfils in law, though unfortunately not at all in fact as yet after 28 years of Independence, the dream of Gandhiji.

The Constitution empowered the State to make reservations regarding appointments or posts in favour of backward classes, to make laws for providing for social welfare and reform and for throwing open of Hindu religious institutions of a public character to all classes and sections of Hindus, and to promote educational and economic interests of the Scheduled Castes. The Constitution also provided for reservation of seats for the Scheduled Castes in Lok Sabha and legislative assemblies of States, for appointment of a Special Officer for the Scheduled Castes and of Commissions to investigate the condition of backward classes.

Finally, the Untouchability Offences Act, 1955, was passed by Parliament to punish the evil practices of imposing any religious, social or economic disabilities on "untouchabilities".

WHAT IS UNTOUCHABILITY

Article 17 of our Constitution does not define the word "untouchability", nor does the Untouchability Offenders Act, 1955, which was passed to give effect to the penal provisions of article 17. The Oxford English Dictionary defines an "Untouchable" as a non-caste Hindu whom the caste man may not touch. In the Untouchability Offences Act, an attempt was made to define an untouchable but was given up. The courts also fight shy of defining the term. The Mysore High Court states that the word "Untouchability" in the Untouchability Offences Act can only refer to those regarded as untouchables in the course of historical development.[1] A literal construction of the term would include persons who are treated as untouchables for various reasons, e.g. because they are suffering from some contagious disease or because of social boycott resulting from caste or other disputes. The imposition of untouchability in such circumstances has no relation to the causes which relegated certain classes of people beyond the pale of the caste system. Such relegation is based on birth in certain cases. So untouchability is not to be understood in the literal sense. It means the practice as it has developed historically in this country. This practice is a matter of common knowledge and can be taken judicial notice of. In short, the

1. *Devarajiah* v. *B. Padmanna*, A.I.R. 1958 Mys. 84.

Parliament and the courts consider that it is not easy to define an untouchable, but you know who is meant.

THE UNTOUCHABILITY OFFENCES ACT, 1955

A. **Applicability**: The Act has been made applicable to all religions and religious denominations; it is not confined to Hindus. The underlying idea of the Act is that whatever is open to the public or to Hindus generally should be equally open to everybody including members of the Scheduled Castes.

B. **Religious Disability** (Section 3): Every "Untouchable" is free to enter any place of public worship which is open to other persons professing the same religion or belonging to the same religious denomination or any section thereof as himself. He may worship, offer prayers and perform any religious services therein. He may also bathe in and use the water of any separate tank, well, spring or water course used by other persons belonging the same religion.

It must be understood, however, that there are important limitations on the exercise of the right of religious worship. They are:

(i) The object of Section 3 is not to create any new rights in favour of untouchables, but it is intended only to put them on par with other caste Hindus.

(ii) Therefore, where a temple is a pure denominational temple confined to Jains alone and the non-Jain caste-Hindus could not enter the temple as of right, an untouchable, who, though a Hindu but not a Jain, could not insist upon entering the temple.[2]

(iii) The section preserves the distinction not only between such places as belong to different religions, but even between such places as belong to different denominations or sections in the same religion. The Kerala High Court has held that where only members of the Gowda Saraswath Brahmin community who wear the sacred thread have entered the "Nalambalam", no offence is committed by preventing persons belonging to a different community or denomination from entering the "Nalambalan".[3]

2. *State* v. *Puranchand*, A.I.R. 1958 Madhya Pradesh 352.
3. *State of Kerala* v. *Venkateswara Prabhu*, A.I.R. 1961 Kerala 55.

Some States have laid down that every place of public worship which is open to Hindus generally, or to any section or class thereof, shall be open to all sections and classes of Hindus, e.g. the Bombay Hindu Places of Public Worship (Entry Authorisation) Act, 1956 (applicable to Maharashtra and Gujarat); the U.P. Temple Entry (Declaration of Right) Act, 1956; and the Kerala Hindu Places of Public Worship (Authorisation of Entry) Act, 1968. Thus some States have thrown open Hindu temple to all sections and classes of Hindus. The Elayaperumal Committee on Untouchability has rightly suggested that other States should enact necessary laws to the effect that the Scheduled Castes may enter and worship in all Hindu temples.

The temple must be public. In the Nathdwara temple case, the Supreme Court observed that a private temple may attract a large number of devotees and the mere fact that large numbers are allowed to worship in the temple would not necessarily make the private temple a public one. Thus an orthodox owner or *poojari* who, as a matter of fact, permits all persons professing Hindu religion to offer prayers would be able to deny the privilege of worship to members of the Scheduled Castes. The Elayaperumal Committee therefore recommends that the test of a place of public worship should not be ownership of the place, but whether in actual practice persons professing the Hindu religion are generally allowed.

C. **Social and Economic Disabilities** (Sections 4, 5, 6 & 7): Every "Untouchable" now has the right

(i) to enter shops, public restaurants, hotels and places of public entertainment and to use all articles kept in any hotel, dharamshala, sarai or musafirkhana;

(ii) to practise any profession or to carry on any occupation, trade or business;

(iii) to use any river, stream, spring, well, tank cistern, water-tap or other watering place or any bathing ghat, burial or cremation ground, any sanitary convenience, any road passage or other place of public resort;

(iv) to enter any place used for a charitable or public purpose maintained wholly or partly out of State funds or dedicated to the use of general public or to the use of persons professing the same religion or belonging to the same religious denomination;

(v) to enjoy the benefit of any charitable trust created for the benefit of the general public or persons professing the same religion or belonging to the same religious denomination;

(vi) to use any public conveyance;

(vii) to construct, acquire, or occupy residential premises in any locality whatsoever;

(viii) to use any dharamshala, sarai, or musafirkhana which is open to the general public or to persons professing the same religion or belonging to the same religious denomination;

(ix) to use any jewellery and finery; and

(x) to observe any social or religious custom, ceremony and to take part in any religious procession (Section 4).

Similarly, every hospital, dispensary, educational institution, or hospital, established or maintained for the use of the public or any section thereof shall be open to every untouchable and he is entitled to equal treatment after admission thereto (Section 5). It is interesting to note here that the courts have rejected the "separate but equal treatment" theory. The Kerala High Court punished the head-master of a girls high school for segregating Harijan students into separate section under the pretext of giving them better coaching and raising their standard of education.[4]

Again, no person can refuse to sell any good or render any service to an "untouchable" at the same time and place and on the same terms and conditions at or on which such goods are sold or services are rendered to other persons in the ordinary course of business (Section 6).

No person can in any way prevent any person from exercising any right accruing to him by reason of the abolition of untouchability under Article 17 of the Constitution or boycott or excommunicate him. No person can incite or encourage any person or public to practise "Untouchability" in any form or boycott or excommunicate any person for refusing to practise untouchability (Section 7).

It is difficult to understand why in almost all cases the

4. *Ramachandran Pillai* v. *State of Kerala*, (1964) 11 KLR 226.

courts fight shy of imposing a sentence of imprisonment, though the Act provides for imprisonment. In one instance, in U.P., certainly not an isolated instance, the Panchayat members maltreated a Harijan for giving water to a high caste Thakur at the latter's request. They terrorised the Harijan and wrongfully confined him so that in future he might not commit such a "crime". The Allahabad High Court, after stating that a serious view should be taken of a violation of Untouchability Offences Act, confirmed the lower court's sentence of fine of Rs. 150 only.[5] It appears imperative to write into the statute a minimum term of imprisonment for the commission of the offence of untouchability even for the first time. It may be argued that severe punishment may lead to the disturbance of peace and harmony of rural life and that therefore a change of heart should be attempted. But the lenient attitude of the courts seems only to perpetuate the practice. If any real change of heart is brought about, the Act itself provides for compounding of the offence. In another case[6] on the accused pleading that the Scheduled Caste complainant had profaned him by touching his utensils and thus prevented her from taking water from a public water tank, the High Court reduced the paltry fine of Rs. 20 to Rs. 10. If there are strong age-long anti-social prejudices only find encouragement in lenient sentence.

The Elayaperumal Committee on Untouchability observes:

> During the tour in various States, the Committee came to know that the powerful weapon of social and economic boycott is very often used against a member of the Scheduled Caste by the caste Hindus, whenever the former attempts to free himself from the bondage of age-old traditions of performing certain menial jobs . . .
>
> What the Committee has observed during the course of its tours is that forced labour is still being practised in disguise. No doubt, forced labour is a penal offence but if a Scheduled Caste person refuses to perform some menial jobs, he may not be compelled but he may be socially and economically boycotted and refused to be given any employment on frivolous grounds. The Committee feels that

5. *Bisheshwar Prasad* v. *State of U.P.*, 1967 Cri. L.J. 1102.
6. *Bihari Lal* . *State*, A.I.R. All. 130.

its proposal to set up boards at Taluka level may provide the means to combat the problem.

D. **Penal Provisions:** The following penalties have been provided in the Act for the offence of untouchability in one form or another:

(i) Sections 3, 4, 5, 6 and 7 lay down that whosoever practises "untouchability" shall be punished with imprisonment which may extend to 6 months or with fine which may extend to Rs. 500 or with both.

(ii) When a person is punished for refusing to sell goods or to render services, the court may also cancel or suspend the licence of the offender in respect of his profession, trade, calling or employment (Section 8).

(iii) The Government may suspend, or resume the grant of land made by it to a place of public worship, if its manager or trustee is convicted of an offence under the Act (Section 9).

(iv) Abetment (by instigation, intentional aid, or conspiracy) of any offence under the Act is punishable just as the act (Section 10).

(v) On subsequent conviction for an offence or for abetment by one who has already been convicted under the Act, the offender is punishable with both imprisonment *and* fine (Section 11), whereas in the first instance the punishment is imprisonment *or* fine or both.

E. **Presumption by court that the act complained of was committed on the ground of untouchability**: Normally it is a principle of criminal jurisprudence that the accused is believed innocent until proved guilty and the burden of providing the guilt is on the prosecution; the onus of providing his innocence does not lie on the accused. However, the Untouchability Offences Act shifts the burden of proof of innocence on the accused.

Section 12 provides that where any act constituting an offence under this Act is committed in relation to a member of a Scheduled Caste, the court shall presume, unless the contrary is proved, that such an act was committed on the ground of "untouchability". In other words, when the victim is a member of a scheduled caste, the commission of a forbidden act shall be *prima facie* presumed to have been committed of the ground of untouchability.

The Supreme Court, in a case of presumption of guilt under the Prevention of Corruption Act, has ruled that where the burden of an issue lies upon the accused, he is not required to prove his case beyond reasonable doubt. The onus on the accused may be compared to the onus on a party in a civil proceeding, in which the court adopts the test of probabilities. So also in a criminal proceeding the court must hold that the plea made by the accused is proved if a preponderance of probability is established by the evidence led by him.

F. **Some miscellaneous provisions**. (*i*) *Limitation of jurisdiction of civil courts*: No civil court may entertain or continue any suit or proceeding if the claim involved is in any way contrary to the provisions of the Act, nor may it pass or execute any order or decree when to do so would, in any way, be contrary to the provisions of the Act; nor may any court recognize any custom or usage imposing any disability on any person on the ground of "untouchability" (Section 13).

Further, the Act overrides other laws. Section 16 renders null and void any provisions in any other law which are repugnant to the provisions of the Act. Thus, in *Souriyar* v. *N.S. Pillai* (AIR 1973 Madras 24) the Madras High Court disallowed a suit by caste Hindus for a declaration that they were exclusively entitled to use the suit property for burial and cremation and for a permanent injunction restraining others from using that property.[7] The court refused to recognize a custom sanctioning the exclusive use of this land by the caste Hindus.

(*ii*) *Offences by a company* (Section 14). Where an offence is committed by a company, firm or association of individuals, every person who is in charge of and is responsible for the conduct of its business and every director or officer who may have permitted or consented to the offence is liable, unless the accused proves that the offence was committed without his knowledge or in spite of his due diligence to prevent the commission of the offence.

G **Implementation of the Act**: It is unfortunate that the enthusiasm shown in putting social welfare laws on the statute

7. *Sourivar* v. *N.S. Pillai* A.I.R. 1973 Mad. 24

book is conspicuously lacking in enforcing them. We think that once a law is passed, the problem has been solved. It is no exaggeration to say that compared to the spread of the evil of untouchability, the Untouchability Offences Act is the most poorly administered law. The Elayaperumal Committee report graphically points out the poor implementation of the law:

(i) "The guardian of the law who are expected to take cognizance of the offences under the Act were mostly ignorant of it" (Page 43).

(ii) "Copies of the Act were not even available at many of the district offices and that many Government officials had no knowledge of the provisions of the Act" (Page 43).

(iii) "The sentinels (small committees at State and District level) recommended by the Joint Committee of both Houses of Parliament which were absolutely essential to gauge the working of the Act were not created by the various Governments and thus, watch was not kept on the working of the Act, which was very essential for the removal of social disabilities" (Page 43).

(iv) "Some cases are deliberately delayed in order to subject the Scheduled Caste people to various hardships, so that they may be tired out as a result of procrastination and may not be left with any energy and resources to contest the cases" (Page 51). For example, in a case in Maharashtra, the trial dragged on for two years and then the case was dismissed because the complainant was absent . . . A unique feature of the case was that during all the hearings the accused was never present in the court.

(v) "In a case of Untouchability Offences Act, 1955, the Scheduled Caste people will not get protection from the police and the Magistrate. The police and the Magistrate naturally love their class more" (Page 52). The result is that the accused escape with a light fine. Imprisonment is rare and that also only seven days' simple imprisonment.

(vi) "We have to welcome the Gujarat Government for taking a radical step by issuing special instructions to all the village panchayats to throw open the public wells and water-tanks, and if it is not done, Government will be constrained to stop their developmental and other grants" (Page 41).

Dr. P.T. Borale, in his excellent thesis "Segregation and Desegregation in India", complains that there is no right to economic independence and abolition of the ghetto system which is at the root of the system of untouchability. According to him, the present legislation, therefore, "is absolutely inadequate and is also not covering the real spirit of the Constitution."

If the Act is to be successfully implemented, an entirely separate machiney for its implementation is necessary. There must be a separate wing of the police only to unearth causes of violation of the Act. There must be separate courts for trying offences under the Act. There must be an administrative wing for making people aware of the provisions of the Act.

When the Untouchability Offences Bill was introduced in Parliament, it was both hailed and criticised. It was referred to as "a milestone in the march of the Nation towards a truly welfare State." It was also described as "a calculated eye-wash just to hoodwink the Harijan population." Both were right: if sincere efforts are made to implement the law, it will definitely become a milestone in the march of the nation; in the absence of such efforts, it will remain a calculated eye-wash. While debating the bill, Dr. K.N. Katju said in Parliament that the Bill "does not finish the job". After 20 years, one feels that the job is not even seriously begun.

OTHER PROVISIONS OF THE CONSTITUTION

In addition to Article 17, which abolishes" Untouchability", there are various other articles in our Constitution conferring safeguards to Scheduled Castes and Scheduled Tribes. We may briefly run through them:

(i) **Prohibition of discrimination** (Article 15): No citizen shall be subject to any disability or restriction with regard to access to shops, hotels and places of public entertainment or with regard to the use of wells, tanks, bathing ghats, roads and places of public resort maintained wholly or partly out of State funds or dedicated to the use of the general public.

This provision, intended for the benefit of weaker sections

of society, has sometimes been used to strike down any concession that is given to them. When, for example, Harijans and Muslims in a place in Rajasthan were exempted from paying the cost of stationing an additional police force to guard against the inhabitants of the locality harbouring dacoits, the Supreme Court held that there was discrimination against the members of other communities on the ground of religion or caste.[8]

To overcome such legal hurdles, the Constitution was amended to enable the State to reserve seats for Scheduled Castes and Tribes in public educational institutions and Government services as well as to make such other special provisions as may be necessary for their advancement. Accordingly, an order acquiring land for constructing a colony for Harijans has been upheld under Article 15(4),[9] although previously such an order was held discriminatory and void under Article 15(1) by the Bombay High Court.[10] Further, a provision to be valid under Article 16(4) must be for the advancement of the backward classes and not for abridging their rights. Thus, if a State prescribed a maximum of 15% seats in a teaching institution for the backward classes, and if the students from those classes, by their merit, secured more than 15% seats in the general competition, then the rule of 15% cannot be invoked to reject the students over and above the prescribed percentages, for in that case their fundamental rights of admission into a State-aided educational institution under Article 29(2) would be infringed.

However, the Supreme Court had held that the reservation cannot be so excessive (reservation of 68% of seats in technical institutions for backward classes) as to practically deny a reasonable opportunity for employment to members of other communities.[11]

(ii) **Equality of opportunity in matters of public employment** (Article 16): While Article 16(1) guarantees equality of opportunity to all citizens in matters relating to employment to and office under the State, the State is empowered under Article 16(4) to make any provision for the reservation of

8. *State of Rajasthan* v. *Pratap Singh*, 1961 ISCR 222.
9. *Moosa* v. *Kerala*, A.I.R. 1960 Ker. 355.
10. *Jagwant Kaur* v. *Bombay* A.I.R. 1952 Bombay 461.
11. *Balaji* v. *the State of Mysore*, A.I.R. 1963 SC 649.

appointment or posts in favour of any backward classes of citizens not adequately represented in the services under the State.

Here, again, the Supreme Court has held that while making the reservation for backward classes, the State cannot unreasonably encroach upon the field of equality.[12] And, further that Article 16(4) is only an enabling provision and confers a discretionary power on the State to make reservations in appointments for backward classes, but that it does not confer any right on members of the backward classes, the government being under no constitutional obligation to make reservations for Scheduled Castes and Scheduled Tribes either at the initial stage of recruitment or at the stage of promotion.[13] In another case the Supreme Court declared "the carry forward" rule invalid.[14] This rule provided for the reservation of 17½% posts for Scheduled Castes and Scheduled Tribes, and if, in a particular year, all posts were not filled up for want of suitable candidates, then the shortfall could be made good in the next two years. The Supreme Court emphasized that in the name of advancement of the backward communities, the fundamental rights of other citizens could not be completely ignored. Moreover, it held that the right conferred to members of the Scheduled Castes etc., was limited by Article 335 which required maintenance of efficiency of administration to be taken into consideration when claims of Scheduled Castes, etc., to services and posts were considered.

(iii) **Throwing open of Hindu religious institutions** (Article 25): While the Constitution guarantees the right to freedom of religion, the State is empowered to make laws for providing for social welfare and reform or for throwing open of Hindu religious institutions of a public character to all classes and sections of Hindus (Article 25). Under this article the Supreme Court has upheld the Bombay Hindu Places of Public Worship (Entry Authorisation) Act, 1956.[15] Under the Act, the Harijans have the same right to enter a public temple for "Darshan" of the deity, or to pray in it, or to perform

12. *General Manager* v. *Rangachari* A.I.R. 1962 SC 36.
13. *Rajendra* v. *Union of India*, A.I.R. 1968 SC 507.
14. *Devadesan* v. *Union of India*, A.I.R. SC 179.
15. *Yagnepurushadasji* v. *Muldas*, A.I.R. 1964 SC 1119.

religious service in it as any other Hindu, but it does not give the Harijan the rights of authorized *Poojaries* also. (In many Hindu temples the innermost portion of the temple is reserved for the authorized *poojari* or priest). Article 25(2) must therefore be read in harmony with Article 26 which gives to every religious denomination freedom to manage its religious affairs.

(iv) **Promotion of educational and economic interests** (Article 46): The Directive Principles of State Policy is laid down enshrined in our Constitution enjoins to promote, with special care, the educational and economic interests of the weaker sections of the people, and, in particular, of the Scheduled Castes and Scheduled Tribes, and to protect them from social injustice and all forms of exploitation. It was in accordance with this principle that in a dispute regarding grant of a licence in which the authority favoured a Scheduled Caste member on the ground of his being member of the Scheduled Caste, the order was held valid under Article 46.[16] (*Bhanu Ram* v. *Commer*, *Hills Division*, AIR 1957 Assam 182).

(v) **Reservation of seats for Scheduled Castes** (Articles 340 and 342): Seats are to be reserved for the Scheduled Castes, etc., in Lok Sabha and in Legislative Assemblies of the States. The number of seats reserved depends upon the proportion which the Scheduled Caste population bears to the total population (Articles 340 and 342). Originally, this reservation was to operate only upto 1960; but twice its duration has been extended, each time, for 10 more years that is upto January 1980. Each time it was felt that the handicaps and disabilities under which the Scheduled Castes labours had not yet been removed and that they needed continued reservation to be able to catch up with the rest of the nation. However, there is no separate electorate; elections are held on the basis of a single electoral roll and every voter, whether or not belonging to scheduled castes, is entitled to vote. In a reserved constituency, all the voters elect the Scheduled Caste representative. This is calculated to lead to the gradual integration of Scheduled Castes in the main stream of national life. Further, a member of the Scheduled Caste is not barred from contesting a general seat instead of a reserved seat;[17] the claim for eligibility for the

16. *Bhanu Ram* v. *Commer, Hills Division*, A.I.R. 1957 Assam 182.
17. *V.V. Giri* v. *V.S. Dora*, A.I.R. 1959 SC 1318.

reserved seat does not exclude the claim for general seats.

(vi) **Special Officer for Scheduled Castes** (Article 338): To ensure that the safeguards provided to the Scheduled Castes under the Constitution do not just remain on paper but are implemented effectively, the founding fathers set up a machinery to keep a continuous watch over the working of these safeguards throughout the country and to bring to the notice of the authorities the defects, drawbacks and lapses in the working of these safeguards. Article 338 requires the President to appoint a Special Officer for the Scheduled Castes and Scheduled Tribes. The Special Officer is charged with the duty of investigating all matters relating to the safeguards and report to the President, who causes all such reports to be laid before the Parliament. The office was created in 1950, and the Commissioner for Scheduled Castes and Scheduled Tribes has been functioning since. It is, however, to be regretted that while he is given an independent status, he is not clothed with adequate powers to take action.

(vii) **Commission to investigate the conditions of backward classes:** The President is empowered to appoint a Commission to investigate the condition of socially and educationally backward classes and the difficulties under which they labour and to recommend the steps to be taken by the Union or any State government to improve their condition and to remove their difficulties. The Commission investigates matters referred to it and presents to the President a report setting out the facts as found by it and makes such recommendations as it thinks proper. The President must cause a copy of the report, together with a memorandum explaining the action taken thereon, to be laid before the Parliament (Article 340).

(viii) **What are Scheduled Castes** (Articles 341 and 366(24)): To avoid all disputes as to whether. for the purposes of the Constitution, a caste is a Scheduled Caste or not, Article 341 provides that the President may, with respect to any State (after consultation with the Governor thereof) or Union Territory, specify the castes, races or tribes or parts or groups thereof which shall, for the purposes of the Constitution, be deemed to be Scheduled Castes in relation to that State or Union Territory. As the specification is to be made by each State and Union territory, the schedule may vary from State to State and Union Territory to UnionTerritory. The Scheduled Caste Order, 1950 was promulgated by the President under this Article.

Once the notification is issued by the President, any modification therein, either by way of including or excluding from the list any caste, race or tribe or a part or group thereof, can be made only by Parliament by law. A Presidential notification is thus final unless modified by Parliament. Under this power, Parliament modified the Presidential Order by enacting the Scheduled Castes and Scheduled Tribes Order (Amendment) Act, 1956. The Supreme Court has emphasized the conclusiveness of the Order.[18]

In order to belong to a Scheduled Caste under the Presidential Order, the person must "profess" to be either a Hindu or a Sikh. When a person has made a public declaration of his conversion to Buddhism, he cannot thereafter claim to be a member of a Scheduled Caste on the ground that his conversion to Buddhism was not valid because there was no strict compliance with rituals or because a "Bhikku" was not present for officiating a conversion ceremony.[19] However, a member of the Mahar Caste, despite his conversion to the Mahanubhava Panth, continues to be a member of the Scheduled Caste, because such a conversion imports little beyond an intellectual acceptance of certain ideological tenets and does not alter the convert's caste status.[20] (*Chatturbhuj* v. *Moreshwar*, 1954 SCR 816).

CONCLUSION

Though Gandhiji resolved to abolish untouchability in a period of ten years and though he worked to that more than any single individual, he was prophetic in stating, "Untouchability will not be removed by the force even of Law. It can only be removed when the majority of Hindus realise that it is a crime against God and men are ashamed of it". We have passed many laws, but during the period of twenty years the result has not been at all encouraging. In spite of the laws, "we have not", in the words of Vinobaji, "done much for the

18. *Basavalingappa* v. *Munichinappa*, A.I.R. 1955 SC 1260.
19. *Punjabrao* v. *Meshram*, A.I.R. 1965 SC 1179.
20. *Chaturbhuj* v. *Moreshwar*, 1954 SCR 816.

untouchables". The remedy lies not so much in improving the laws as in changing the attitude of the people. Untouchability, like war, starts in the minds of men, and if we want to eradicate the abnoxious evil, it is the minds of men that will have to be changed.

Table of Cases

Index